THE NEW CAMBRIDGE SHAKESPEARE

GENERAL EDITOR
Philip Brockbank, *Director, The Shakespeare Institute, University of Birmingham*

ASSOCIATE GENERAL EDITORS
Brian Gibbons, *Professor of English Literature, University of Zürich*
Bernard Harris, *Professor of English, University of York*
Robin Hood, *Senior Lecturer in English, University of York*

TWELFTH NIGHT

THE NEW CAMBRIDGE SHAKESPEARE

TWELFTH NIGHT
OR WHAT YOU WILL

Edited by
ELIZABETH STORY DONNO

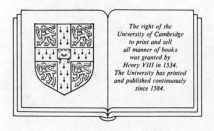

The right of the
University of Cambridge
to print and sell
all manner of books
was granted by
Henry VIII in 1534.
The University has printed
and published continuously
since 1584.

CAMBRIDGE UNIVERSITY PRESS

Cambridge
New York   New Rochelle   Melbourne   Sydney

Published by the Press Syndicate of the University of Cambridge
The Pitt Building, Trumpington Street, Cambridge CB2 1RP
32 East 57th Street, New York, NY 10022, USA
10 Stamford Road, Oakleigh, Melbourne 3166, Australia

First published 1985
Reprinted 1987

Printed in Great Britain by the
University Press, Cambridge

Library of Congress catalogue card number: 84–28482

British Library cataloguing in publication data
Shakespeare, William
[Twelfth night]. Twelfth night or What you
will.—(The new Cambridge Shakespeare)
I. Title   II. Donno, Elizabeth Story
III. Twelfth night or What you will
822.3′3   PR2837
ISBN 0 521 22752 6 hard covers
ISBN 0 521 29633 1 paperback

UP

THE NEW CAMBRIDGE SHAKESPEARE

The *New Cambridge Shakespeare* succeeds *The New Shakespeare* which began publication in 1921 under the general editorship of Sir Arthur Quiller-Couch and John Dover Wilson, and was completed in the 1960s, with the assistance of G. I. Duthie, Alice Walker, Peter Ure and J. C. Maxwell. *The New Shakespeare* itself followed upon *The Cambridge Shakespeare*, 1863–6, edited by W. G. Clark, J. Glover and W. A. Wright.

The New Shakespeare won high esteem both for its scholarship and for its design, but shifts of critical taste and insight, recent Shakespearean research, and a changing sense of what is important in our understanding of the plays, have made it necessary to re-edit and redesign, not merely to revise, the series.

The *New Cambridge Shakespeare* aims to be of value to a new generation of playgoers and readers who wish to enjoy fuller access to Shakespeare's poetic and dramatic art. While offering ample academic guidance, it reflects current critical interests and is more attentive than some earlier editions have been to the realisation of the plays on the stage, and to their social and cultural settings. The text of each play has been freshly edited, with textual data made available to those users who wish to know why and how one published text differs from another. Although modernised, the edition conserves forms that appear to be expressive and characteristically Shakespearean, and it does not attempt to disguise the fact that the plays were written in a language other than that of our own time.

Illustrations are usually integrated into the critical and historical discussion of the play and include some reconstructions of early performances by C. Walter Hodges. Some editors have also made use of the advice and experience of Maurice Daniels, for many years a member of the Royal Shakespeare Company.

Each volume is addressed to the needs and problems of a particular text, and each therefore differs in style and emphasis from others in the series.

PHILIP BROCKBANK
General Editor

CONTENTS

ILLUSTRATIONS

Illustrations 3–11 are reproduced by courtesy of the Henry E. Huntington Library and Art Gallery; illustrations 12–16 by courtesy of Joe Cocks Studio. My gratitude to Dennis Kay (Lincoln College, Oxford) for suggesting no. 6 to me.

PREFACE

The editor of a Shakespeare text who is responsive to traditions must at once acknowledge his indebtedness to other editors, beginning with the earliest and continuing down to the most recent. M. W. Black and M. A. Shaaber in *Shakespeare's Seventeenth-Century Editors* (1937) alerted me to early concern for the text, but I was very impressed by the care and attention that eighteenth-century editors, so frequently ill-treated in accounts of historical scholarship, gave to textual interpretation through their concern with pointing. I hope that the collation in this volume shows, in some measure, my respect for their efforts. Of more or less recent editions, the New Shakespeare volumes, G. L. Kittredge's fully annotated texts of sixteen of Shakespeare's plays and the many fine examples in the Arden series were of great value to me.

Any acknowledgement must extend to many fellow Shakespeareans for contributions either in published form or in conversation, and, for the latter, I am grateful most specifically to Hallett Smith and S. F. Johnson. Philip Brockbank, the General Editor of this series, and Robin Hood, the Associate General Editor most closely concerned with this volume, gave me much good advice and were unfailingly responsive to my queries. The General Editor has contributed the section Recent Years in the pages on theatre history. I also wish to acknowledge aid and assistance from my husband Daniel J. Donno, who invariably reacted sharply to a (non-Shakespearean) hysteron proteron or a Sir Tobyan wayward locution.

The Henry E. Huntington Library, where I did most of my research, afforded me not only its excellent collection of Shakespeare texts but also the help of its genial staff. To this institution I am also grateful for permission to reproduce nine of the illustrations.

E.S.D.

Huntington Library, California

ABBREVIATIONS AND CONVENTIONS

1. Shakespeare's plays

The abbreviated titles of Shakespeare's plays have been modified from those used in the *Harvard Concordance to Shakespeare*. All quotations and line references to plays other than *Twelfth Night*, unless otherwise specified, are to G. Blakemore Evans (ed.), *The Riverside Shakespeare*, 1974, on which the *Concordance* is based.

Ado	*Much Ado about Nothing*
Ant.	*Antony and Cleopatra*
AWW	*All's Well That Ends Well*
AYLI	*As You Like It*
Cor.	*Coriolanus*
Cym.	*Cymbeline*
Err.	*The Comedy of Errors*
Ham.	*Hamlet*
1H4	*The First Part of King Henry the Fourth*
2H4	*The Second Part of King Henry the Fourth*
H5	*King Henry the Fifth*
1H6	*The First Part of King Henry the Sixth*
2H6	*The Second Part of King Henry the Sixth*
3H6	*The Third Part of King Henry the Sixth*
H8	*King Henry the Eighth*
JC	*Julius Caesar*
John	*King John*
LLL	*Love's Labour's Lost*
Lear	*King Lear*
Mac.	*Macbeth*
MM	*Measure for Measure*
MND	*A Midsummer Night's Dream*
MV	*The Merchant of Venice*
Oth.	*Othello*
Per.	*Pericles*
R2	*King Richard the Second*
R3	*King Richard the Third*
Rom.	*Romeo and Juliet*
Shr.	*The Taming of the Shrew*
STM	*Sir Thomas More*
Temp.	*The Tempest*
TGV	*The Two Gentlemen of Verona*
Tim.	*Timon of Athens*
Tit.	*Titus Andronicus*
TN	*Twelfth Night*
TNK	*The Two Noble Kinsmen*

Tro.	*Troilus and Cressida*
Wiv.	*The Merry Wives of Windsor*
WT	*The Winter's Tale*

2. Editions and general references

Abbott	E. A. Abbott, *A Shakespearian Grammar*, 1901, first published 1869 (reference is to numbered paragraphs)
Alexander	*William Shakespeare: The Complete Works*, ed. Peter Alexander, 1951
Ard.	*Twelfth Night*, ed. J. M. Lothian and T. W. Craik, 1975 (Arden Shakespeare)
Cam.	*The Works of William Shakespeare*, ed. W. G. Clark, J. Glover and W. A. Wright, 1863–6 (Cambridge Shakespeare)
Capell	*Mr William Shakespeare his Comedies, Histories, and Tragedies*, ed. Edward Capell, IV [1768]
Collier	*The Works of William Shakespeare*, ed. John Payne Collier, 1842–4
Collier²	*The Plays of Shakespeare*, ed. John Payne Collier, 1853
conj.	conjecture
Dent	R. W. Dent, *Shakespeare's Proverbial Language: An Index*, 1981 (reference is to numbered proverbs)
Douai MS.	Douai MS. 7.87, Douai Public Library (contains transcripts of six plays by Shakespeare, including *Twelfth Night*. See G. Blakemore Evans, 'The Douai Manuscript – six Shakespearean transcripts (1694–95)', *PQ* 41 (1962), 158–72)
Dyce	*The Works of William Shakespeare*, ed. Alexander Dyce, 1857
Dyce²	*The Works of William Shakespeare*, ed. Alexander Dyce, 1891, first published 1864–7
ELH	*ELH: A Journal of English Literary History*
ELN	*English Language Notes*
ES	*English Studies*
F	*Mr William Shakespeares Comedies, Histories, & Tragedies*, 1623 (First Folio)
F2	*Mr William Shakespeares Comedies, Histories, & Tragedies*, 1632 (Second Folio)
F3	*Mr William Shakespeares Comedies, Histories, & Tragedies*, 1664 (Third Folio)
F4	*Mr William Shakespeares Comedies, Histories, & Tragedies*, 1685 (Fourth Folio)
Furness	*Twelfth Night, or What You Will*, ed. Horace Howard Furness, 1901 (New Variorum)
Halliwell	*The Works of William Shakespeare*, ed. James O. Halliwell, 1853–65
Hanmer	*The Works of Shakespear*, ed. Thomas Hanmer, 1743–4
Johnson	*The Plays of William Shakespear*, ed. Samuel Johnson, 1765
Kittredge	*Sixteen Plays of Shakespeare*, ed. George Lyman Kittredge, 1946, first published 1939
Kökeritz	Helge Kökeritz, *Shakespeare's Pronunciation*, 1953
Linthicum	M. Channing Linthicum, *Costume in the Drama of Shakespeare and his Contemporaries*, 1936

Luce	*Twelfth Night: or, What You Will*, ed. Morton Luce, rev. edn 1929, first published 1906 (Arden Shakespeare)
Mahood	*Twelfth Night*, ed. M. M. Mahood, 1968 (New Penguin Shakespeare)
Malone	*The Plays and Poems of William Shakespeare*, ed. Edmond Malone, 1790
MLN	*Modern Language Notes*
MP	*Modern Philology*
Nashe	Thomas Nashe, *Works*, ed. Ronald B. McKerrow, 5 vols., 1904–10, rev. F. P. Wilson, 1958
N&Q	*Notes and Queries*
NS	*Twelfth Night or What You Will*, ed. Arthur Quiller-Couch and John Dover Wilson, 1930, rev. edn 1949 (New Shakespeare)
ODEP	*Oxford Dictionary of English Proverbs*, ed. F. P. Wilson, 1970
OED	*Oxford English Dictionary*
Onions	C. T. Onions, *A Shakespeare Glossary*, 1949, first published 1911
PBSA	*Papers of the Bibliographical Society of America*
Pope	*The Works of Shakespear*, ed. Alexander Pope, 1723–5
PQ	*Philological Quarterly*
Rann	*The Dramatic Works of Shakespeare*, ed. Joseph Rann, 1786–[94]
RES	*Review of English Studies*
Rowe	*The Works of Mr William Shakespear*, ed. Nicholas Rowe, 1709
Rowe³	*The Works of Mr William Shakespear*, ed. Nicholas Rowe, 1714
SB	*Studies in Bibliography*
Schmidt	Alexander Schmidt, *Shakespeare-Lexicon*, 2 vols., 1962, first published 1874
SD	stage direction
Seng	Peter J. Seng, *The Vocal Songs in the Plays of Shakespeare: A Critical History*, 1967
SH	speech heading
Sisson	C. J. Sisson, *New Readings in Shakespeare*, 2 vols., 1956
SQ	*Shakespeare Quarterly*
SR	*A Transcript of the Registers of the Company of Stationers, 1554–1640*, ed. Edward Arber, 5 vols., 1875–94
S.St.	*Shakespeare Studies*
S.Sur.	*Shakespeare Survey*
Staunton	*The Plays of Shakespeare*, ed. Howard Staunton, 1866, first published 1858–60
STC	*A Short-Title Catalogue of Books Printed in England, Scotland, & Ireland, and of English Books Printed Abroad, 1475–1640*, compiled by A. W. Pollard and G. R. Redgrave, 1956, first published 1926; 2nd edn, rev. W. A. Jackson, F. S. Ferguson and Katherine F. Pantzer, 1976–
subst.	substantively
sugg.	suggestion
Theobald	*The Works of Shakespeare*, ed. Lewis Theobald, 1733
Tilley	M. P. Tilley, *A Dictionary of the Proverbs in England in the Sixteenth and Seventeenth Centuries*, 1950 (reference is to numbered proverbs)
TLS	*The Times Literary Supplement*
Tyrwhitt	Thomas Tyrwhitt, *Observations and Conjectures upon Some Passages of Shakespeare*, 1766
Upton	John Upton, *Critical Observations on Shakespeare*, 1746

Var. 1821	*The Plays and Poems of William Shakespeare*, ed. James Boswell, 1821 (3rd Variorum)
Walker, W. S.	W. S. Walker, *A Critical Examination of the Text of Shakespeare*, 3 vols., 1860
Warburton	*The Works of Shakespear*, ed. William Warburton, 1747

All references to the Bible are to the Geneva version, 1560. All references to classical texts are to the Loeb Library editions. Full references to other works cited in the Commentary in abbreviated form may be found in the Reading List at p. 157 below.

INTRODUCTION

Date and title

On 2 February 1602 – Candlemas Day – the barrister John Manningham noted in his diary[1] that the members of the Middle Temple were entertained during their feast with a play called 'Twelve night or what you will', presumably presented by Shakespeare's own company, the Lord Chamberlain's Men (see illustration 1). This is the earliest reference both to the play and to any performance of it, but on the evidence of topical allusions in the text it seems likely that it was written a year or possibly even two years earlier.[2] The date of the performance noted by Manningham does not suggest that the play was considered specifically occasional, and the fact that the text contains no allusions to the actual date of Twelfth Night – that is, to the Feast of the Epiphany celebrated on 6 January[3] – makes it even more likely that its title was originally intended simply to evoke a festive occasion comparable to that celebrating the last of the Christmas holidays when revelry and folly were permitted to turn the real world topsy-turvy under a Lord of Misrule. Both plots of *Twelfth Night* – the romantic fantasies of the young lovers and the saturnalian high jinks of Sir Toby and his crew – give evidence of the illusions, deceptions and misrule that could characterise such an occasion, but these actions are distanced from the real world by being set in the never-never land of Illyria. That the locale conveys a sense of remoteness is signalled immediately when Viola, just rescued from the shipwreck in which her twin brother Sebastian has perhaps drowned, asks of her rescuer: 'And what should I do in Illyria?' (with a stress probably upon 'I').

If the topical dating references suggest either of the years 1600 or 1601 for the composition of *Twelfth Night*, which is the more likely? In 1955 Leslie Hotson argued (in *The First Night of 'Twelfth Night'*) that the play was specially commissioned for a performance on 6 January 1601 when Don Virginio Orsino, the Duke of Bracciano, was to be entertained at court. In the subsequent quarter of a century his argument has been rejected for two reasons: (1) the play with its portrayal of a lovesick Orsino would be an affront both to the queen and to her noble visitor and (2) the time that would have been available for Shakespeare to write the play and for the actors to rehearse it was far too short – only some ten days: news of the duke's visit did not

---

[1] *The Diary of John Manningham of the Middle Temple* (1602–3), ed. Robert Parker Sorlien, 1976, p. 48.

[2] See Commentary at 2.5.149 and 3.4.236 on the Sophy or Shah of Persia; 3.2.20–2 on Barents's voyage; 3.2.62–3 on the new map of the Indies. The snatches in 2.3.86–96 are from a song included in Robert Jones's *First Booke of Songes and Ayres* published sometime within the year 1600.

[3] W. W. Greg ('Two notes', *Elizabethan and Jacobean Studies Presented to Frank Percy Wilson*, 1959, pp. 59–64) corrects *OED* and its identification of Twelfth Night as the night before the twelfth day (i.e. 5 January): 'In the sixteenth and seventeenth centuries at least Twelfth Night was taken to mean Twelfth Day at night (6 January).'

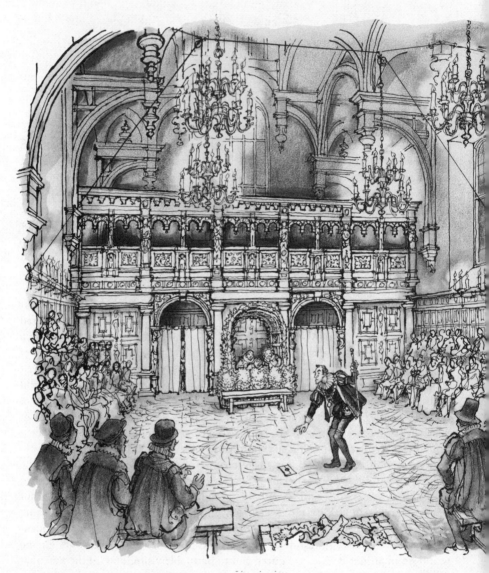

1   *Twelfth Night* as presented in Middle Temple Hall, London, on the night of 2 February 1602, by
C. Walter Hodges
a   Act 2, Scene 5: 'What employment have we here?'

arrive until 26 December. For presentation at court, a badly rehearsed performance
would have been unthinkable.

Since the Orsini family was well known from the twelfth century on, with a
distinguished line of churchmen and other public figures, Shakespeare's use of the
name could have been fortuitous, but the indisputable facts remain: one of the heroes

b Act 3, Scene 4: 'There's no remedy, sir.
He will fight with you for's oath sake.'

of the play that Manningham saw at Candlemas 1602 bears the name Orsino and the
title of the play evokes the festive occasion when Don Virginio Orsino had been a
visitor in London. The simplest way to account for this double coincidence is to
assume that Shakespeare composed the play sometime *after* the visit of the duke in
January 1601, and that the mood he established in the play prompted him to recall
both the name of the visitor and the time of his visit.

Certainly the text provides some clues as to the seasonal setting that Shakespeare
projected for his play. Three scenes are said explicitly to take place in the Countess
Olivia's garden (2.5, 3.1 and 4.3); this suggests not a mid-winter season but either

spring or summer. At the end of 1.1 Orsino dismisses his courtiers by evoking just such a season:

> Away before me to sweet beds of flowers:
> Love-thoughts lie rich when canopied with bowers.

Bits of dialogue provide supporting indications. At 3.4.50, Olivia terms Malvolio's deranged behaviour a 'very midsummer madness'; and at 3.4.120 Fabian describes Sir Andrew's challenge to Cesario as providing 'More matter for a May morning'. More significantly, perhaps, at 1.5.14–15 Maria charges Feste with truancy and threatens him with being turned out of the household; to this he retorts that 'for turning away, let summer bear it out' – that is, let the season make it endurable. While the consistency of the play's seasonal indications and allusions can provide no firm evidence for a time of composition and perhaps a first performance in late spring or early summer (however tempting the inference), it must be taken to confirm, especially in such details as the artistically contrived impression of 'literalness' in Feste's retort, the metaphorical nature of the title *Twelfth Night*.

Shakespeare's alternative title – *What You Will* – is also the title of a comedy by John Marston, which was entered in regular fashion in the Stationers' Register on 6 August 1607 and published in that year by Thomas Thorpe. However, since Marston's play is often thought to reflect something of the 'War of the Theatres', a poetomachia that involved Marston and Ben Jonson in the years 1599 to 1602, its original date of production is frequently assigned to 1601 or 1602, a date which raises the question of the relationship, if any, between the two plays.

Like Shakespeare's, Marston's has been called a 'festive' comedy because of its 'boisterous gaiety' and use of disguise,[1] but, given the admittedly common motifs of mistaken identity and the gulling of a character in both, there is little else to suggest a connection between the two – apart, that is, from what should now be recognised as the catch-phrase 'what you will'. The Induction to Marston's play makes the nature of that phrase clear. When it is asked what kind of a play is to be performed – comedy, tragedy, pastoral, moral, nocturnal or history – the character Philomuse responds:

Faith perfectly neither, but even *what you will*, a slight toy, lightly composed, too swiftly finish'd, ill plotted, worse written, I fear me worse acted, and indeed *what you will*.[2]

To illustrate the proverbial nature of the expression 'what you will', Dent's index of proverbs (w280.5) cites instances (with either 'Anything' or 'What') from 1593 on, including Shakespeare's own use of it in *A Midsummer Night's Dream* (1.2.92), *As You Like It* (2.5.20), *Twelfth Night* itself (1.5.90), and *Othello* (4.1.36). From these early and late examples it is clear that the phrase is equivalent, in Elizabethan idiom, to 'whatever you would'.[3] Taken together, Shakespeare's title and its alternative evoke the mood of twelfth-night holiday: a time for sentiment, frivolity, pranks and misrule – indeed, for whatever you wish.

---

[1] Philip J. Finkelpearl, *John Marston of the Middle Temple*, 1969, p. 165.
[2] John Marston, *What You Will*, ed. M. R. Woodhead, 1980, lines 87–90. For what Barnaby Riche, the translator of the tale that gave Shakespeare his main plot, has to say of its frivolity, see p. 7 below.
[3] The alternative title given in the Douai MS. is 'ou ce que vous voudrez'.

Interestingly, there is another catch-phrase in *Twelfth Night* which has not often been recognised as such, though it is frequent in the canon: 'That's all one.' This appears early on at 1.5.106 in a variant with 'it's' ('it's all one'), and three times more at the very end of the play, where it adds to the air of lightheartedness and inconsequence proper to a comedy whose subtitle is *What You Will*. When Sir Toby enters with his head bleeding, Orsino solicitously enquires of him 'How now, gentleman, how is't with you?', to which Sir Toby tersely replies, 'That's all one' – in effect, 'no matter' (5.1.181). Again, in reminding Malvolio of the reason for his hostility (5.1.351 ff.), Feste pointedly observes that he, too, was one in the interlude – 'one Sir Topas, sir – but that's all one' – an off-hand observation calculated to increase Malvolio's discomfiture. The third instance again involves Feste when, in place of an epilogue, he sings a final song. The last stanza begins portentously, 'A great while ago the world begun', a truism that is undercut in the third line by the phrase 'that's all one' – no matter – and followed by the half-line, 'our play is done', a conclusion serving to signal an end to theatrical illusion. (As Oscar Wilde commented, 'Where there is no illusion, there is no Illyria.'[1]) Shakespeare makes use of the phrase some ten times in the early and middle plays, and there are four instances of it in *The Two Noble Kinsmen* but in scenes generally conceded to Fletcher – itself an indication that the expression was widely current.[2]

Sources

In recording the performance of *Twelfth Night* that he saw in the Middle Temple, John Manningham noted that it was 'much like' the *Comedy of Errors* or Plautus's *Menaechmi* but 'most like' an Italian play called *Inganni*. As he recognised, Shakespeare had turned, in what was perhaps his earliest comedy, to the basic situation of the *Menaechmi* but further complicated the plot by introducing twin servants to twin masters; though it was probably written *c.* 1592 or 1593, we know that it received a performance at Gray's Inn on 28 December 1594, Holy Innocents' Day, where it was described as a play of 'Errors and Confusions'.[3] In likening *Twelfth Night* to the Italian play *Gl' Inganni*, Manningham may have been referring to the play of that title by Nicolò Secchi (1562), in which a woman disguised as a man acts as a surrogate wooer for the man she loves, or to an imitation of it by Curzio Gonzaga (1592), in which the disguised heroine is called 'Cesare'. The earliest of sixteenth-century Italian comedies of mistaken identity and cross-wooing, entitled *Gl' Ingannati*, was performed by the Sienese Academy of the Intronati (the 'Thunderstruck') on Twelfth Night in 1531. Here the disguised heroine is called 'Fabio'.[4]

[1] '*Twelfth Night* at Oxford', *Dramatic Review*, 20 Feb. 1886, reprinted in Wilde's *Reviews* (*Collected Works*, 1908, XIII, 46).

[2] See *TGV* 3.1.265, *Shr.* 3.2.81, *MND* 1.2.49, *AYLI* 3.5.133, *1H4* 4.2.47, *LLL* 5.2.527, and *Wiv.* 1.1.30 (where there is no elision) and *Tro.* 1.2.211 (where 'it's', as in *TN* 1.5.106, is used in place of 'that's'). For the four instances in *TNK*, see 2.3.31, 5.2.16, 5.2.32 and 5.2.85.

[3] E. K. Chambers, *William Shakespeare*, 2 vols., 1930, II, 320.

[4] See Geoffrey Bullough, *Narrative and Dramatic Sources of Shakespeare*, II, 269–372. He includes a translation of almost the whole of *Gl' Ingannati* as a 'probable' source and a scene from the Secchi play

Whether or not Shakespeare had access to these comedies, he could have known the derivative prose tales in either the Italian version of Bandello (*Novelle* (1554), II, 36) or the French of Belleforest (*Histoires Tragiques* (1570), IV, 59), and he most certainly knew the English derivative called 'Apolonius and Silla', which appears as the second 'historie' in Barnaby Riche's *Farewell to Military Profession* (probably based on Belleforest's version). This was first published in 1581, reprinted in 1583, and again in 1594 – an edition newly recorded in *STC* and the one which probably stirred Shakespeare's interest. Riche's dedicatory epistle includes some remarks on dancing that may be echoed by Sir Toby (1.3), and his fifth 'historie', 'Of two Brethren and their wives', may have suggested Malvolio's being incarcerated in a dark room (as well as providing an interesting analogue to Falstaff's punishment in *The Merry Wives of Windsor*).[1]

Manningham refers to one of the heroines of *Twelfth Night* as a 'widow' (probably because Shakespeare's Olivia was dressed in sombre black to accord with her bereavement), and the equivalent heroine in Riche's story is, in fact, a beautiful and wealthy widow, just as the duke who is enamoured of her is noble, worthy and very young. Riche's second heroine, Viola's equivalent, has fallen in love with this young duke, and it is his departure from her homeland that occasions her sea-voyage, in this case to Constantinople, with a faithful servant. *En route* there is a lascivious sea captain (in contrast with Viola's kindly rescuer) and a violent storm which occasions the death of her servant, but she herself is washed ashore along with the captain's chest, which is filled with apparel and coins. Taking the name of her twin brother, she disguises herself as a page and enters the service of the duke where (like Viola) she quickly gains favour and serves as his ambassador of love but becomes herself the object of love. Meanwhile her brother, seeking her, arrives in Constantinople where he encounters the beautiful widow who calls him by name, invites him to supper, and that night offers herself to him. Amazed at her invitation and 'assuryng hym self that she was deceived and did mistake hym, [he] did thinke, notwithstandyng, it had been a poincte of great simplicitie, if he should forsake that whiche Fortune had so favourably proffered unto hym' (*Farewell to Military Profession*, p. 76). So he spends the night and gets her with child. Aware the next morning that she must indeed have mistaken him, and fearful of future evils, he leaves to continue his search for his sister.

From the servants' gossip, the duke learns that his page is likely to fare better than he in the courtship and imprisons him in a dungeon, which prompts the widow to seek out the supposed father of her child, thus further enraging the duke. Of necessity the page reveals her sex; the duke, acknowledging her travail undertaken only for love of him, accepts her as the 'braunche of all vertue and the flowre of curtesie itself'.

as an 'analogue', as well as all of Shakespeare's English source, Barnaby Riche's prose tale, which is discussed below. Kenneth Muir believes that because of its close plot resemblance to *TN*, Manningham was referring to *Gl' Ingannati* (*The Sources of Shakespeare's Plays*, p. 133).

[1] Bullough, *Sources*, II, 276. A facsimile of Riche's full text (Bullough omits 'Of two Brethren') has been edited with useful notes by T. M. Cranfill (1959), and all quotations within the text are from that edition with the punctuation modernised. Bullough also includes brief excerpts from Emanuel Forde's romance *Parismus, the renowmed prince of Bohemia* (1598), but thinks Shakespeare took little from it except hints for the names 'Violetta' and 'Olivia' and 'something of the romantic mood' (*Sources*, II, 277).

News of the sumptuous wedding recalls her twin, who willingly makes amends by marrying the widow, to the 'greate joye and contentation' of all parties.

What Shakespeare has done with this material is to scale down the more scandalous elements, transforming the character of the sea captain, deleting the possibility of a pregnancy, reducing the duke's harsh treatment of the page to Orsino's single line, 'I'll sacrifice the lamb that I do love', and moderating the sexual shock of a woman's infatuation with another woman by carefully ordering the structure of his play; after Olivia's falling in love with Cesario (1.5), the following scene immediately focuses on Sebastian's arrival in Illyria, dressed exactly like Cesario, so that an audience is aware from the outset that there is a real-life male surrogate for her. He also elevates the plot relating to the lovers to a plane of romance and sentiment by dressing it with a lyricism that is quite at odds with Riche's rather arch humour. Still, Riche's attitude toward this material, set forth in an address to his readers, is probably much like that of the dramatist; it is, he says, 'forged onely for delight, neither credible to be beleved, nor hurtfull to be perused' (*Farewell to Military Profession*, p. 19).

Ever the craftsman, Shakespeare also counters the fantasy of the main plot by inventing a sub-plot which presents another aspect of Olivia's household, where the rowdy Sir Toby holds sway and where the 'noble gull-catcher', the 'devil of wit' Maria, hatches the device against Malvolio. In this domain the characters speak a vigorous and colloquial prose though the language is marked by 'sportive' abuse on the part of Sir Toby and Feste, Olivia's 'corrupter of words'. The one exception is Sir Andrew. Styled a 'carpet knight', unused to actual combat, and alarmed at the prospect of a duel, he exhibits a verbal deficiency that contrasts with the exuberance of the others. He is either forced to seek out meanings – 'Accost'...'What's that?', 'What is "*pourquoi*"?', 'Wherefore, sweetheart? What's your metaphor?' – or he is reduced to parroting Sir Toby as he does so notably at the end of Act 2. Such parroting is comically repeated in the following wooing scene where Sir Andrew's two speeches consist of a rapt iteration of Cesario's fine words – 'Odours', 'pregnant' and 'vouchsafed' – 'I'll get 'em all three all ready.' By means of this verbal inadequacy, Shakespeare conveys Sir Andrew's mental inadequacy and unfitness to cope with a region where airy illogic and (short-lived) madness prevail.

Although he invented the diverting minor plot, Shakespeare economised in construction by recalling techniques and incidents which he had used in earlier plays. Mention has been made of the motif of mistaken identity with a double set of twins in *The Comedy of Errors*. In *The Two Gentlemen of Verona* he had used the device of a woman (here Julia) disguised as a male acting as a surrogate wooer for the man she loves (and taking the name of Sebastian). Moreover, while Viola-Cesario recalls Julia-Sebastian, Orsino, according to Harold Jenkins, is the inconstant Proteus transformed.[1] In *The Merchant of Venice* all three women – Portia, Jessica and Nerissa – resort to male disguise for safety's sake (like Rosalind in *As You Like It*, but not Celia); and Antonio's love for Bassanio in that play is recalled, it seems, in Antonio's love for Sebastian in this. The tricking of Beatrice and Benedict in *Much*

[1] See 'Shakespeare's *Twelfth Night*' (Rice Institute Pamphlet), pp. 19–42, for a full account of the similarity of *TN* to *TGV*.

Ado about Nothing by means of trumped-up conversations parallels the tricking of Malvolio by Maria's trumped-up letter. The infatuation of Phebe for the disguised Rosalind in *As You Like It* parallels in miniature that of Olivia for the disguised Viola; finally, the fatuity of Sir Andrew so recalls that of Slender in *The Merry Wives of Windsor* that it has frequently been suggested that the part was written for the same actor (see the Commentary at 2.3.18).

Though invoking incidents and techniques that had earlier served him well, Shakespeare has in *Twelfth Night* melded the sub-plot to the main plot with such deftness that this, the last of his festive comedies, seems a smooth amalgam of romance and realism. To many it has seemed the consummation of his comic vein. Perhaps for this reason he turned restively after *Twelfth Night* to exploring the complex issues that mark out the problem comedies – *All's Well That Ends Well, Measure for Measure* and *Troilus and Cressida*.

Critical commentary

After the theatres reopened in 1660, Pepys saw *Twelfth Night* on three occasions – in 1661, 1663 and 1668. Despite such familiarity, he seems to have missed the evocative and allusive quality of Shakespeare's alternative title, noting in his diary after the 1663 performance that this 'silly' play did not relate 'at all' to the name or to the day. Even for Shakespeare's contemporary audience its most memorable element was the character of the proud, self-loving steward Malvolio – witness a performance presented at court by Shakespeare's company in 1623 (again on Candlemas Day) under the title *Malvolio*. Leonard Digges, who had contributed commendatory verses to the First Folio, observed in a later and longer tribute:

> loe in a trice
> The Cockpit Galleries, Boxes, all are full
> To hear Malvoglio that cross-garter'd gull.

(Shakespeare's *Poems*, 1640)

Some time in 1632 (or later) King Charles inscribed 'Malvolio' against the printed title in his copy of the Second Folio. One may conclude that, so far as contemporary (and later) stage popularity was concerned, the whirligig of time did bring in the revenge on the 'whole pack' of the other characters that the discomfited steward promises as he exits in the final act.

But it is Sir Toby Belch, the Countess Olivia's perennially tipsy kinsman, who has the most lines to speak and who, despite his earlier 'fruitless pranks', contrives the means both to complicate the plot and to resolve it. From the outset the convivial Sir Toby is hard put to understand the countess's vow to abjure both the sight and the company of men in order to mourn her brother's death for seven long summers. This desire to cloister herself for so extended a period reveals, as John Russell Brown observes, that Olivia must be very young indeed;[1] so, too, if one judges from their

---

[1] *Shakespeare and His Comedies*, pp. 176–7 n. Elsewhere ('Directions for *Twelfth Night*', *Shakespeare's Plays in Performance*, 1967, pp. 207–19, and reprinted in Palmer, *Casebook*, pp. 188–203) John Russell Brown presents a more elastic charting of the characters' ages.

emotional predispositions and actions, all the characters must be, except perhaps for Feste – the Lady Olivia's father having taken much delight in him – and, possibly, the sprightly Sir Toby, though modern productions do not always take such evidence into account.

Shakespeare, in fact, is fairly specific in indicating the ages of the two pairs of lovers. The twins were thirteen when their father died (5.1.228–9, 232); the disguised Viola is described by Malvolio as 'not yet old enough for a man, nor young enough for a boy' (1.5.130) and an 'apple cleft in two' is not more like than the pair of them (5.1.207–8). Though obviously beardless, Sebastian is a skilful swordsman (even if Viola is not). Orsino is described as of 'fresh and stainless youth' though he has a beard (1.5.214, 3.1.38–9); since he believes that a husband should be older than his wife (2.4.27–8), he may be assumed to be a little older than both Olivia and Viola. Whether or not he is as young as the four lovers, Sir Toby, like Touchstone in *As You Like It* (5.4.55–6), pressing in among the 'country copulatives', anticipates the dénouement by taking the 'little villain' Maria as his wife, an action presaged in the jesting remarks of Feste at 1.5.22–4 and of Sir Toby himself at 2.5.150, and performed, it would seem, as early as 4.2, as line 57 suggests. Convinced, on any count, that 'care's an enemy to life', he has brought in a suitor for Olivia, even if it is the fatuous Sir Andrew Aguecheek. As incorrigible a 'gull-catcher' as Maria, Sir Toby also uses him as his own 'dear manikin' from whom he can extract a steady supply of money.

Sentiment, which motivates Olivia's desire to become a weeping recluse (though Feste soon prompts her to laugh again, and she is without a veil when Cesario arrives at her gate), is also characteristic of the moody Orsino, the duke or perhaps simply a count of Illyria – Shakespeare seems to have wavered in his conception.[1] Having loved the image of Olivia for a month before the play opens, he continues to protest his love for three more months even before he has a chance to speak to her directly[2] Like Romeo infatuated with fair Rosaline, he is obsessed with the idea of being in love. His inconstancy of mood is emphasised in the first seven lines of the play when, calling for an excess of music in order that his appetite for it may sicken, he at once demands that the musicians repeat one particular strain because of its 'dying fall', but before he has spoken three more lines his appetite has already sickened, and he orders them to desist altogether.[3] At the end of this opening speech he foreshadows the hasty replacement of the initial object of his affection that will occur in Act 5 by acknowledging here the capricious quality of love: whatever is held of greatest worth may 'fall into abatement and low price'. Yet as a result of the homage and solicitude of his young page, who bravely masks her own emotions in order to woo Olivia on his behalf, he comes by the end of the last act to recognise the value of the devotion she has tendered to him.

With Olivia and her o'erhasty marriage to Sebastian, the case is different. Shakespeare explains it with a metaphorical reference to bowling; in her case, 'nature

[1] See p. 16 below and n. 4, and Textual Analysis, p. 153.
[2] As in other of Shakespeare's plays, there is a double-time scheme: the action requires three months for its fulfilment, but two consecutive days serve for the sequence of scenes. See Brown, 'Directions for *Twelfth Night*', where he correlates the references to time with the action.
[3] See Commentary (1.1.4) for Joseph H. Summers's suggestion of some comic stage business here.

in her bias drew in that'. Although it may be Olivia's own tendency to sentiment that prompts her to become so quickly enamoured of the disguised Cesario, her counter-wooing has the function of predisposing her to love Sebastian in accord with nature's bias. The rationale behind this quite absurd situation is, Porter Williams notes, much like that of the lover in Donne's 'The Good-morrow':

> If ever any beauty I did see,
> Which I desired and got, 'twas but a dream of thee.[1]

Still, Olivia remains sufficiently cool-headed to take the wondering but infinitely pliable Sebastian-supposed-Cesario to a nearby chantry to plight their troth before a holy man.

Contrasting with the sentimental Orsino and Olivia is Viola, the charming but quite practical flotsam of the sea who quickly sets about improving her situation. Informed that she cannot serve Olivia, she at once determines to disguise herself as a page and serve the noble Orsino, known to her father and, fortuitously it seems, still a bachelor. Within three days she has endeared herself to him, so much so that he has unclasped to her the book even of his 'secret soul'. In the exchanges with Olivia and the 'lighter members' of her household, she conducts herself with great verbal skill, exhibiting a remarkable range of emotional responses, at times saucy, florid or outspoken, but in some situations she remains quite surprisingly taciturn. Though Antonio, having rescued her from the farcical duel with Sir Andrew, addresses her as Sebastian, she says nothing to interfere with his arrest as a pirate or to question him about the fate of her brother. She simply allows herself to hope that he is indeed alive. Her actions throughout can be said to be predicated on her view that time will untangle all things (2.2.37–8), this in accord with the commonplace doctrine (*topos*) that truth is the daughter of time (*veritas filia temporis*). Even in the final scene, when Orsino asks to take her hand and to see her in her woman's weeds, she says nothing more than that the captain who has them has been imprisoned at Malvolio's suit. When some forty lines later he again gives her his hand and declares that from this time on she is to be her 'master's mistress', she utters not a word. Nor does she say anything more for the remainder of the action. Yet underlying her variable responses and her taciturnity is an emotional constancy, well evoked in the lines beginning 'My father had a daughter loved a man' and culminating in the moving self-portrait of the figure of Patience smiling at grief (2.4.110–11).[2]

The clown Feste, mediating between the courtly milieu and Sir Toby's, is an irresistible figure. This results in large part from the fact that, actively engaged in both worlds, he distances himself from each by means of his witty and facetious comments. It is now accepted that Shakespeare's projection of the role of professional wit who wears the dress of the fool but does not wear motley in the brain, was the

---

[1] 'Mistakes in *Twelfth Night* and their resolution', p. 181, in Palmer, *Casebook*, originally published *PMLA* 76 (1961).

[2] Viola's taciturnity in the later part of Act 5 can, of course, be accounted for by the exigencies of the plot. Like his heroine earlier on, Shakespeare has a great many knots to untie. Having given her this moving speech when it applied so aptly to her emotional situation, he can assume (with the audience) that with its happy resolution, words are unnecessary.

2 Feste, by C. Walter Hodges

result of Robert Armin's entry into the Chamberlain's Company (probably in 1599). Early apprenticed to a goldsmith, Armin was also for some years a writer of ephemeral pamphlets and entertainments; these include an account of six 'natural' fools and a play exploiting the art of impersonation, in which he was adept. Two of the pamphlets he signed 'Clunnico del Curtanio Snuffe' and 'Clunnico del Mondo Snuffe', that is, Snuff, Clown of the Curtain Theatre and Snuff, Clown of the Globe. He was included in the list of actors in Jonson's *The Alchemist* in 1610, so at that date he was still a member of the King's Men, the title given to the Lord Chamberlain's Company on the accession of James I. He died five years later.[1] The following lines, addressed to 'Honest, gamesom Robin Armine', attest to his skill and echo Viola's comment on Feste: 'This fellow is wise enough to play the fool' (3.1.50):

> So play thy part, be honest still with mirth,
> Then, when th'art in the tiring-house of earth;

[1] For a biographical account of Armin, see Jane Belfield, 'Robert Armin, citizen and goldsmith of London', *N&Q* 225 (1980), 158–9, and M. C. Bradbrook, 'Robert Armin and *Twelfth Night*', in Palmer, *Casebook*, pp. 222–43 (originally published in *Shakespeare the Craftsman*, 1969).

Thou being his servant whom all kings do serve,
Mayest for thy part well-played like praise deserve:
For in that tiring-house when either be,
Y'are one man's men and equal in degree;
So thou in sport the happiest men dost school
To do as thou dost – wisely play the fool.

(John Davies, *Scourge of Folly* (1611))

Four years Shakespeare's junior, Armin would have been thirty or so when *Twelfth Night* was written, and the slightly wry speeches Feste is given seem intended to reflect a maturity of outlook that holds no illusions about the durable nature either of emotional situations or of practical circumstances. Hence his incorrigible begging and hence his stress both in words and in song on the transitory: youth is a stuff – a material thing – that will not endure; beauty is but a flower; present love is justified by present laughter since 'what's to come is still [i.e. always] unsure'. His wit is both corrective and apt. He uses his good fooling to remedy Olivia's displeasure at his truancy from her household and to persuade her of the folly of mourning a brother's soul which, after all, she *knows* is in heaven, and he pointedly remarks that Orsino's tailor should make him a doublet of changeable taffeta to accord with his changeable mind.

All in all, Feste seems to present through his nonsense a no-nonsense point of view. Accosting Cesario – though, ironically, it is in fact Sebastian – he speaks to him in his own highly ironic fashion:

No, I do not know you, nor I am not sent to you by my lady to bid you come speak with her; nor your name is not Master Cesario; nor this is not my nose neither. Nothing that is so is so. (4.1.4–7)

In the next scene, as he impersonates Sir Topas the curate come to visit Malvolio the lunatic, he observes of his disguise:

'That that is, is', so I, being Master Parson, am Master Parson; for what is 'that' but 'that' and 'is' but 'is'?

Yet Cesario has declared to Olivia, in all truth, 'I am not what I am'; Sir Toby has said to Sir Andrew, with some truth, that 'not to be abed after midnight is to be up betimes'; even the dénouement of the play seems to go contrary to Feste's claim. When the twins are seen together, they seem so like that it is as if there were but one face, one voice and one manner of dress – that is, the *same* face, voice and dress but still two flesh-and-blood persons. To the others, struck with wonder at the sight, the identical appearance of the twins is declared to be, in the words of Orsino, 'A natural perspective, that is and is not!' Yet in so far as theatrical illusion has been achieved, the dénouement gives substance to Feste's claim, 'That that is, is', at least in Illyria.

The dissembling of one's true nature (conscious with Viola and Feste, unconscious with Orsino and Olivia) is highlighted in the figure of the steward Malvolio. The chief officer in Olivia's household – and one that she would not have miscarry for half of her dowry – he takes to his duties with seriousness and some pomposity. That these responsibilities would have included the preserving of discipline is shown by the rules for his household which a young nobleman, Anthony Browne, the second Viscount Montague, set down in 1595, at the age of twenty-one. The steward should 'in civil sort' reprehend and correct 'negligent and disordered persons', reforming them by his 'grave admonitions and vigilant eye', among these the 'riotous, the contentious, and quarrelous persons of any degree' as well as 'the frequenters of tabling, carding, and dicing in corners and at untimely hours and seasons'.[1]

But when Malvolio breaks in on the carousing Sir Toby, Sir Andrew and Feste, called to do so, it seems, by the countess herself as Maria has forewarned, he cannot be said to chide them 'in civil sort'. Rather he accuses the two knights of gabbling like tinkers, squeaking out – this of the mellifluous-voiced Feste – cobblers' catches as if they were in an ale-house. Such a rebuke by a social inferior is enough to set off Sir Toby and he rounds on him, 'Art any more than a steward?'; he then follows this up with one of the most quoted lines in the play, incorporating in it what Hazlitt termed an 'unanswerable answer':

Does thou think because thou art virtuous there shall be no more cakes and ale?

Maria is also angered by his charge that she is at fault in providing the means for this 'uncivil rule', and she sums up for the others Malvolio's unpleasant qualities: he is a 'kind' of a puritan, that is, censorious, but one who is inconstantly so. He is, moreover, a time-server, an affected ass who imitates the behaviour of his betters, and is 'so crammed', she says, 'with his own excellencies' that he conceives of himself as worthy of the love of all. On these grounds she contrives the device of forging a love letter from the countess enjoining him to assume ridiculous behaviour and garb in order to secure her favour, a device which feeds his aspiration to become 'Count Malvolio'. Although Feste is not in the group which observes Malvolio's absurd response to the letter, he justifies his share in the 'interlude' on the grounds of Malvolio's having disparaged his ability as a jester, while Fabian justifies his on the grounds that Malvolio has brought him out of favour with his lady about a bear-baiting. The last of his officious actions, noted this time by Viola, is to have the kindly captain who has rescued her imprisoned on some unspecified charge. There is then in Malvolio's 'stubborn and uncourteous parts' sufficient motivation to justify Maria's trick. Intended 'to pluck on laughter', it begins to get out of hand with the confining of Malvolio in a dark room as a madman; at one moment, even Sir Toby wishes they were well rid of their knavery.

Yet Malvolio's lubricious self-projection, cunningly revealed in a day-dream-like soliloquy, is splendidly comic. He imagines himself as three months married to Olivia, now wearing a velvet gown and sitting in a chair of state, having just come from a day-bed where he has left her sleeping; he imagines how he will have 'seven' of his servants summon Sir Toby to his presence and how, after quenching his 'familiar smile' and saying, 'Cousin Toby, my fortunes having cast me on your niece', he will direct him to amend his ways. This fantasy on Malvolio's part is put into perspective when he appears before Olivia wearing yellow stockings and cross-garters,

---

[1] 'Booke of orders and rules', quoted by Muriel St Clare Byrne, 'The social background', in *A Companion to Shakespeare Studies*, ed. Granville-Barker and Harrison, pp. 204–5.

3　Act 2, Scene 5: Malvolio soliloquising. An engraving by C. Heath after the painting by J. M. Wright

4   Act 2, Scene 5: Malvolio with Maria's letter. An engraving by J. Quarterly after the painting by William Ralston

his face crimped into myriad lines by his incessant smiling. Even more startling to her than his dress is the 'ridiculous boldness' of his talk. Tipped off as she is by Maria's charge that he is 'for sure' tainted in his wits, she accepts his strange words as evidence that something is wrong and solicitously asks, 'Wilt thou go to bed, Malvolio?' Taking this in seriousness, since it accords with his secret desires, he responds, 'To bed? Ay, sweetheart, and I'll come to thee.'[1] The audacity of his response is further highlighted by Shakespeare's establishing the time-scheme by means of adroit references. At the end of the preceding scene (2.5), when Maria alerts the conspirators to hide in (or behind) a box-tree to spy on Malvolio, it is probably early morning since she comments that he has been 'yonder i'the sun practising behaviour to his own shadow this half hour'. In the exchange between Viola and the fool that opens this scene, Feste comments that foolery like the sun shines everywhere, which suggests that it is now midday. Thus Malvolio's avidity to go to bed at noon (as the Fool in *Lear* puts it) strikes an even more lubricious note.[2] From Shakespeare's time until the mid eighteenth century, the 'sportful malice' prompting the treatment of Malvolio seemed a just matter of comedy, but for Romantic and Victorian interpreters, as well as for some in the twentieth century, the ill-used steward came to seem a victim not of sport but of social discrimination.[3]

If Shakespeare's characterisation of Malvolio has stimulated a mixed reaction, so, too, has the structure of the play, some critics finding in it signs of hasty composition, though not so many as to distract a viewing audience. One discrepancy is the rank of Orsino, who is consistently called 'duke' in stage directions and speech headings and during two scenes of the first act but is otherwise called 'count'. In his careful analysis of the text, Robert K. Turner suggests that Shakespeare's conception of the character of Orsino changed during composition and that he decided to make him less of a figure of authority (such as Duke Theseus in *A Midsummer Night's Dream*) and more of a lover (like Count Claudio in *Much Ado about Nothing*).[4]

There are other inconsistencies and loose ends. On Viola's first entrance, when she resolves to serve Orsino, she gives as a qualification her ability to sing and to speak to him in many sorts of music, but when a song is required in the second act, it is Feste who performs. This has led some, including Dover Wilson, to postulate revision, a more radical explanation than is required in view of the favours Orsino has extended to Cesario, which have elevated him above the status of a mere performer: within three days' time (1.4.1–3) he is no longer a stranger to Orsino who has, within that short span, divulged to him his inmost sentiments (1.4.12–13).

Again one notes that it is Fabian who makes a 'third' in the espial of Malvolio's antics, rather than Feste as Maria had specified; yet at the end of Act 5, Feste is able to quote from the letter as if he, too, had been one of the eavesdroppers on Malvolio. In fact, what Maria first declares she intends for him – 'some obscure epistles of love, wherein by the colour of his beard, the shape of his leg, the manner of his gait, the

[1] For a reference in *SR* to a ballad entitled 'goo to bed swete harte', see Commentary at 3.4.28.
[2] See Brown, 'Directions for *Twelfth Night*'.
[3] For an account of the theatrical history of the part of Malvolio see pp. 28–33 below.
[4] 'The text of *Twelfth Night*', pp. 128–38. Turner explains the consistency of stage directions and speech headings as a scribal normalising of foul papers. See Textual Analysis, pp. 152–4 below.

expressure of his eye, forehead, and complexion, he shall find himself most feelingly personated' (2.3.131–4) – does not concur with the letter that Malvolio reads aloud two scenes later – except, that is, for its amatory suggestiveness. One small inconsistency is in the two accounts of Antonio's sea fight with Orsino's galleys: for his part, Antonio denies (3.3.30) that it was of a 'bloody nature' whereas Orsino (5.1.45) speaks of the 'scathful grapple' directed against the finest of their ships, though the speech is also intended to acknowledge Antonio's valour even as a pirate. Finally, the appearance of Sir Andrew and Sir Toby with bleeding heads must be the result of a second encounter with Sebastian-supposed-Cesario (see Commentary and stage direction at 5.1.160), but this is not provided for in the text.

In spite of these inconsistencies and loose ends, there is much subtlety in Shakespeare's handling of his complex plot which is particularly evident when an attitude or an action or situation relating to one character is duplicated by another. This creates a 'twinning' effect that reinforces the central situation brought about by a pair of identical twins.[1] It is as if – to adapt Ulysses' words in *Troilus and Cressida* – many touches of nature make the whole world kin.

Despite the difference in the situation of the two heroines there is a similarity: both have lost their fathers and both, it would appear, have recently lost their brothers, but whereas Olivia would extravagantly mourn (even as Orsino would extravagantly love), Viola, trusting to her own escape as a promise of Sebastian's, reacts practically. Yet in the matter of falling in love the two heroines act alike, in that Viola freely extends her affection to Orsino without invitation on his part, even as Olivia extends hers to Cesario without any invitation except that suggested by her role as surrogate wooer. This makes for a slight touch of irony at the end of the first wooing scene, for when Cesario says 'Love make his heart of flint that you shall love', Viola does not know that she herself will turn out to be the inadvertent object of Olivia's love. The wish is also ironically cancelled with Sebastian's arrival in Illyria and the stunning alacrity with which he assents to a betrothal.

The two heroines are alike in their personal orientation. Viola's conviction that time will 'untangle' all things (*veritas filia temporis*, or, as the English proverb has it, 'time brings the truth to light' (Tilley T324)) is comparable to Olivia's (and Malvolio's) belief in 'fate' which is commented on below. The two are also alike in possessing the virtue of constancy, Viola in her devotion to Orsino, Olivia in her refusal to accept his suit. To Orsino's query in Act 5, 'Still so cruel?', she responds, 'Still so constant'. The emotional impact the twins make is, quite expectedly, alike; Olivia terms it an 'enchantment', Antonio a 'witchcraft'; the harsh denunciation he levels at Cesario-supposed-Sebastian for his seeming ingratitude is paralleled by that which Orsino levels at Cesario for the seeming betrayal of his trust.

Perhaps the most ingenious duplication is that between Olivia and Malvolio. She herself acknowledges their similarity of deportment: he is 'sad and civil', a kind of behaviour that she feels suits well with her own fortunes in love. When Maria informs her that he is surely tainted in his wits since he does nothing but smile, she confesses:

[1] See L. G. Salingar's detailed and perceptive account of this aspect of the play or what he calls 'points of contact' among the characters, 'The design of *Twelfth Night*', pp. 117–39.

5   Cross-gartering in 1562. From John Heywood's *Workes*

6 Cross-gartering in 1628: an *inamorato*. An engraving by C. le Bon, from Robert Burton's *Anatomy of Melancholy*, 3rd edn, 1628

> I am as mad as he
> If sad and merry madness equal be.

And later she alludes to her own 'extracting frenzy', which has made her forget about his. Moreover, such sad and merry madness typifies the deportment of the other characters, whether it be the moody Orsino or the mad-brained Sir Toby; this is finely pinpointed in 4.1 when, out of the blue, Sir Andrew attacks Sebastian, who wonders incredulously: Are *all* the people mad? Again, in 4.3, Sebastian 'wrangles' with his reason, speculating in soliloquy whether it is he himself or Olivia who is mad. From the confines of the dark room Malvolio's words thus have special point when he asserts to Feste: 'I tell thee, I am as well in my wits as any man in Illyria.'

Malvolio also emphasises the similarity of his deportment to Olivia's when he writes assuring her that he has the benefit of his senses as well as she. But his assurance is comically belated; by the time Olivia hears the letter, read madly at first by Feste impersonating the 'mad' Malvolio and then straightforwardly by Fabian, she (like Orsino) has met with a happy corrective, first to her predisposition to grief and then to her infatuation with Cesario. In view of the psychological misrule prevailing in Illyria, it is not surprising that the word 'mad', together with its cognates (madness, madmen, madly), is used more frequently in this play than in any other in the canon, with *The Comedy of Errors,* and its double set of twins, a close rival.

Another point of likeness between Olivia and Malvolio is their willingness to justify their own desires by readily ascribing them to a power outside themselves called either 'fate' or 'fortune'. In the soliloquies following on Cesario's first visit, Olivia ponders how quickly she has caught the plague, questions her actions, and concludes:

> Fate, show thy force; ourselves we do not owe.
> What is decreed must be; and be this so. (1.5.265–6)

In writing to Malvolio, Maria simulates not only Olivia's hand but also this point of view when she specifies, 'Thy fates open their hands.' To Malvolio, willingly deluded by the letter's confirmation of his own desires, 'it is Jove's doing, and Jove make me thankful', a point he reiterates with supreme confidence after Olivia believes him to be mad:

What can be said? Nothing that can be can come between me and the full prospect of my hopes. Well, Jove, not I, is the doer of this, and he is to be thanked![1] (3.4.71–3)

Even before Maria drops the letter, Malvolio prefaces his rationalising hope that Olivia might indeed love him, by saying ''Tis but fortune; all is fortune.' When Olivia pleads with Cesario-supposed-Sebastian to admit their betrothal, she echoes this point of view, urging him 'Fear not, Cesario, take thy fortunes up.'

This is, of course, what all the central characters do. If somewhat bewildered by the fortuitous opportunity to marry Olivia after the earlier 'malignancy' of his fate,

---

[1] The frequency of references to Jove in a play not having a classical setting is often accounted for by the Act of Abuses (against profanity), but as Turner has pointed out ('Text of *Twelfth Night*', p. 136) 'God' appears about twice as often as the supposed substitute; this scarcely supports the notion of expurgation. See also Commentary at 2.5.142.

7   Act 4, Scene 2: Malvolio in the 'dark room', with Maria and Sir Topas. The earliest illustration of
Twelfth Night. From Rowe's edn, 1709

8 Act 4, Scene 2: Malvolio in the 'dark room', with Sir Topas and Maria looking on. An engraving by Bromley after the painting by Henry Fuseli

Sebastian at once accepts 'this accident and flood of fortune', an acceptance that twins with Viola's attitude when, resolved to serve Orsino, she awaits whatever may be the outcome: 'What else may hap, to time I will commit.' The untangling of circumstances by the passage of time and the reliance on fortune and fate create, for characters 'of fresh and stainless youth', the sense of wonder that is proper to the ending of romantic comedy. For the lovers, the result, as it was earlier for Maria and Sir Toby, is to be marriage when 'golden time convents'. For Antonio and Sir Andrew, what's to come is still unsure. For Malvolio, the whirligig of time having also brought in its revenges, there is the hint that he may be entreated to a peace. For Feste, there is still the pleasure he takes in singing.

And, fittingly, in place of an epilogue, he is given a final song. This, while promising that the actors for their part will strive each day to please their audience, also provides a somewhat cryptic ending to the dramatic action. Commentators have ranged widely in their response to it. Eighteenth-century editors, followed by Dover Wilson and others in this century, reacted strongly to its seeming lack of relevance to the play or to the character of Feste; more recent commentators extract a bawdy and sexual import,[1] while still others find a strain of melancholy that harkens back to the potential within the play for violence and unhappiness – the arrest of Antonio, the (short-lived) anger of Orsino towards Olivia and Viola, perhaps even Sir Toby's harsh dismissal of the 'thin-faced knave' Sir Andrew. But since this potential is never actualised, Feste's song is perhaps more properly viewed as a means of breaking away from the Illyrian world of illusions with a return to the real world where it may – or it may not – rain every day. The song's cryptic nature, with its catch-phrase 'that's all one', may be particularly appropriate for the ending of a play with the subtitle 'What You Will'.

CRITICAL FASHIONS

Changing taste and judgement over the generations affect both critical interpretations of the plays and their stage productions, and it is not easy to determine what effect they may have upon each other. Early in the twentieth century, when a return to early staging conditions seemed somewhat revolutionary, the Elizabethan Stage Society included critics and scholars among its members.[2] At that time scholarly investigation was concerned with restoring the integrity of the theatrical text, determining the historical basis for costuming and ascertaining the precise meaning of the language (particularly the bawdry). More recently the differences of orientation between 'theatrical' and 'literary' Shakespeareans have become a live topic for discussion. J. L. Styan, surveying the 'revolution' in twentieth-century theatrical productions, finds that it correlates with a 'less apparent but no less profound change in criticism', but he admits that it may be too soon to say whether the 'new' Shakespeare belongs to the actor or the critic.[3] Bernard Beckerman, seeing a new readiness on the part

---

[1] See Hotson, pp. 167–72, for example, and John Hollander, '*Twelfth Night* and the morality of indulgence', *Sewanee Review* 67 (1959), 220–38.
[2] See A. C. Sprague, *Shakespearian Players and Performances*, 1953, p. 143.
[3] J. L. Styan, *The Shakespeare Revolution*, 1977, pp. 3, 9.

of directors and performers to let the text guide the production, nonetheless finds contrarieties between theatrical and literary approaches. He concludes that the theatre should discover 'the limits within which a given work allows legitimate interpretation'.[1]

Legitimate interpretation is not easily defined, for the work of specialists and critics outside the theatre reflects academic and intellectual fashions, too. Thus John Draper's *The 'Twelfth Night' of Shakespeare's Audience* (1950), the only book-length study of the play, expresses the current interest in sociological and psychological modes of analysis. Taking Olivia's household as a representative Elizabethan establishment in transition from feudal paternalism to a more modern economy, Draper analyses each character in terms of social status, astrological complexion and psychological humour. Later essays have included psychological, anthropological and theological accounts, with some treatment of the topics of sexual identity and disguise.[2] Other studies have focused on language and imagery, and on thematic motifs of many kinds – fortune, providence, masking, revelry, misrule and folly.[3] Opinions often differ about the play's ending, some finding it 'double-edged' or 'bitter-sweet' or 'half-gay, half-sad', while others find a comic spirit with a happy reconciliation of much incongruous action. There have been markedly fewer critical studies of *Twelfth Night* than of its two predecessors *Much Ado About Nothing* and *As You Like It*. As Molly Mahood remarks in a summary of the work done on the middle comedies between the 1950s and the 1970s, critics may have retreated before the play's 'elusive grace'.[4]

Theatrical history

THE RESTORATION: DAVENANT, WYCHERLEY AND BURNABY

During the 1660s *Twelfth Night* was produced at least three times, as we remember from Pepys's somewhat jaundiced observations; he called it a 'silly play', perhaps because the text had been subject to Davenant's 'improvements'. However that may have been, the play's romantic character was not of the sort to appeal to the sophisticated audience of the Restoration theatre. A clever playwright, nevertheless (like a later actor-manager), might capitalise on an audience's capacity to recognise Shakespearean elements. This appears to have been the case with William Wycherley's harsh satire *The Plain-Dealer*, performed in 1674 and published three years later in a version dedicated to 'My Lady B—' (Mother Bennet, a well-known bawd). Though indebted to the *Misanthrope* of Molière for his concept of the plain-dealing, plain-speaking hero, Wycherley shapes his plot to recall that of *Twelfth Night* and to evoke in two of his main characters its two heroines.

The plot centres on the unrequited love of the manly protagonist – fittingly, or ironically, called 'Manly' – for Olivia and the equally unrequited love for him on the

---

[1] 'Explorations in Shakespeare's drama', *SQ* 29 (1978), 133–45.
[2] See Ralph Berry, '*Twelfth Night*: the experience of the audience', *S.Sur.* 34 (1981), 111–19; René E. Fortin, '*Twelfth Night*: Shakespeare's drama of initiation', *Papers on Language & Literature* 8 (1972), 135–46; Robert Kimbrough, 'Androgyny seen through Shakespeare's disguise', *SQ* 33 (1982), 17–33.
[3] See Reading List, pp. 157–8 below.
[4] 'Shakespeare's middle comedies: a generation of criticism', *S.Sur.* 32 (1979), 7.

part of Fidelia who (in spite of the feminine form of her name) is serving as his page. Her faithful service requires her to act not as his ambassador of love, like Viola, but in effect as his pimp, a situation made possible by the lust she arouses in the hypocritical, scheming Olivia. Having been abused by Olivia in manifold ways, Manly is thus able to have his 'revenge', or yield to his sexual desire, by taking on the role of surrogate lover, substituting himself for the page, who is left to weep outside the bedroom. Later in a sword fight (which takes place in a bedroom) between Olivia's husband and Manly, Fidelia is wounded in coming to his aid and her true sex revealed, thus prompting her master to acknowledge the basis of her long devotion to him.

This romantic dénouement vitiates the prevailing satiric tone of the earlier action in the same way that the patient Fidelia appears as a symbolic relic of a lost world of romance. Yet by debasing the main plot of *Twelfth Night* and by turning Olivia into a sordid character and Manly into a brutal one, Wycherley was able to point to the degradation of contemporary society. That his *Plain-Dealer* offers a novel interpretation of one of Shakespeare's heroines is supported by the comment of a recent critic who observes that although a seventeenth-century audience may never have idealised Shakespeare's Olivia, a modern-day audience needs Wycherley's 'parody' in order to demonstrate to us what the real-life colours of Shakespeare's original were.[1]

Though it was not a 'parody' of Shakespearean materials so much as a mis-appropriation of them, William Burnaby's *Love Betray'd; or, The Agreable Disapoint-ment* was performed at Lincoln's Inn Fields, under the management of Thomas Betterton, in February 1703. Since it was published a month later, it seems clearly to have been a failure, a situation the author himself accounts for by the failure of the management to supply a concluding masque; it was revived only once again for a single performance in 1705.[2] Burnaby's failure may be accounted for less by the absence of a splendid finale than by his attempt to blend the fashionable comedy of manners with romantic comedy so that the sentimental dénouement (like Wycherley's) jars badly with what has gone before.

As in Shakespeare's own source – Riche's *Farewell to Military Profession* – the disguised Cesario has been in love with the duke and so follows him to his home (in Venice) and is in turn followed by Sebastian. Villaretta (corresponding to Olivia) is also, like Riche's prototype, a beautiful wealthy widow, but Burnaby imbues her with the smart cynicism typical of the period, though the duke himself is still the moody, sentimental lover of *Twelfth Night*. To these fugitives from Shakespeare's play he adds some typically Restoration servant-types, deletes both Fabian and Feste, and fuses Sir Andrew and Malvolio into a character called 'Taquilet'. Together with the duel scene, the rest of the plot follows that of *Twelfth Night*. In the preface to the published version, Burnaby acknowledges that he has taken 'part' of the tale from Shakespeare and about fifty lines of the text, which, he declares, he has marked with

[1] Norman Suckling, 'Molière and English Restoration comedy', in *Restoration Drama*, Stratford-upon-Avon Studies 6, 1965, pp. 105–6.
[2] F. E. Budd, *The Dramatic Works of William Burnaby*, 1931, p. 61. The later quotation from the text of the play is from this edition.

inverted commas. In fact, he has taken something more than that, and his kind of appropriation may be judged by a passage from the second scene in the first act where the disguised Cesario (like Viola in *Twelfth Night*) first appears. Here Burnaby recalls something (perhaps justifying the lack of inverted commas) from the duel scene in Act 3 when Sir Toby is urging on the reluctant duellists, and Viola, in an aside, says 'Pray God defend me! A little thing would make me tell them how much I lack of a man.' In Burnaby's scene, a female attendant, having learnt of Cesario's secret love for the duke, questions the efficacy of her scheme:

Its like to be done well, if you carry it – But how can you do any thing for your self, Madam? 'Twill be impossible for him to see a Woman, as they say, thro' a Pair of Breeches.

To this Burnaby's Cesario answers:

No more than thro' a Nun's Habit – When I find a proper time for my purpose, a little thing will shew him what I am.

FROM MACKLIN TO OLIVIER

Through the Restoration and into the early eighteenth century, *Twelfth Night*, it seems, was thought to appeal on the stage only in its remodelled form.[1] It was off the stage for some thirty years before it was revived (along with *As You Like It* and *The Merchant of Venice*) by Charles Macklin, himself playing Malvolio, at Drury Lane in 1741. His performance helped to reintroduce the middle comedies to the stage, supplementing the current heavy emphasis upon the tragedies and some of the histories, and served to alert other actor-managers to the great theatrical potential of the character of Malvolio, which had been recognised in Shakespeare's own day when the play took on his name.[2] Thus, despite its brevity in comparison with the role, for example, of Sir Toby, it became one that important actors took as their own – Robert Bensley (so affectionately recalled by Lamb), John Philip Kemble, William Farren (affectionately recalled by Leigh Hunt), down to such recent popular stars as Laurence Olivier.[3]

The result of the hiatus of nearly seventy-five years between the third performance of *Twelfth Night* which Pepys saw and Macklin's production in 1741 was that theatrical tradition was lost, and it was up to the individual actor-manager to determine stage business and interpretation.[4] Accordingly, in this brief account of the

[1] Hallett Smith reminds me that Sheridan in *The Rivals* (1775) made most effective use of the duelling scene, with Bob Acres recalling something of Sir Andrew and with Mrs Malaprop, of course, looking back to the verbal licence of a number of Shakespearean characters.

[2] For historical accounts of casts, performances and theatres, see George C. D. Odell, *Shakespeare from Betterton to Irving*, 2 vols., 1920; C. B. Hogan, *Shakespeare in the Theatre, 1701–1800*, 2 vols., 1952 and 1957; *The London Stage, 1600–1800*, ed. W. van Lennep *et al.*, 5 parts in 11 vols., 1960–8. For the later nineteenth and early twentieth century, see William Winter, *Shakespeare on the Stage*, 2nd ser., 1915, the chapter on *Twelfth Night* originally published in *The Century Magazine*, Sept. 1914, in abridged form.

[3] Lamb's 'On Some of the Old Actors' is in *Essays of Elia* and is reprinted in Gāmini Salgādo, *Eyewitnesses of Shakespeare*, pp. 203–4; Leigh Hunt's is in his *Dramatic Criticism, 1808–31*, ed. L. H. and C. W. Houtchens, 1949, pp. 229–30. In contrast with Hunt's evaluation of Farren, another contemporary termed the production a 'patent puppet-show' (*Theatrical Inquisitor*, 1 Nov. 1820, p. 336).

[4] In America the first recorded performance was apparently in Boston in 1794; ten years later it was produced in New York (Winter, p. 47; Odell, *Annals of the New York Stage*, 15 vols., 1927–49, II, 204).

play's stage history, I shall consider some of the general trends in the handling of the play and then some of the different lines along which the character of Malvolio developed, together with the more conspicuous touches of stage business that came to encrust these interpretations.

If Wycherley and Burnaby had looked to *Twelfth Night* as source material, the trend among nineteenth-century adapters was to eke out the dramatic text by spectacle and by musical interpolations. The *festive* aspect of the comedy became even more festive by a kind of Shakespearean accretion. A notable instance was Frederic Reynolds's operatic version produced at Covent Garden in 1820. Although this adaptation, unlike his earlier treatments of *A Midsummer Night's Dream* and *The Comedy of Errors*, was not published, Odell (*Betterton to Irving*, II, 136) was able to cite the musical numbers that were interpolated into it, according to a playbill of 8 November:

Act 1	Full many a glorious morning (*Sonnets*)
	Who is Sylvia (*Two Gentlemen*)
	Even as the sun (*Venus and Adonis*)
	Orpheus with his lute (*Henry VIII*)
Act 2	Come o'er the brook (*King Lear* and *Poems*)
	A cup of wine (*2 Henry IV*)
Act 3	Crabbed age (*Passionate Pilgrim*)
	Cesario, by the roses of the spring (*Twelfth Night*)
	O, by rivers, by whose falls (*Passionate Pilgrim*)
Act 4	O how much more doth beauty (*Sonnets*)
	Take all my loves (*Sonnets*)
	Come unto these yellow sands (*Tempest*)
	Masque of Juno and Ceres (*Tempest*)
Act 5	In bowers of laurel (*Poems*)
	Bid me discourse (*Venus and Adonis*)
	Feste's song as finale

This extravaganza had seventeen performances and was revived again in 1825.

Nearly seventy-five years later Augustin Daly produced his musically embellished, scenically heightened, moonlit version of *Twelfth Night* which had originated in America, the last, and some judged the best, of his three productions of the play. As a prelude, fishermen and peasants sang 'Come unto these yellow sands', and at the end of Act 3 a group of Orsino's musicians sang 'Who is Olivia?' (to a rearrangement of Schubert's music); 'Come away death' and 'O mistress mine' were transposed, evidence of the ease with which the nineteenth-century producers altered the text to suit their conception of good theatre. An assiduous recorder of Shakespearean performances, William Winter (*Shakespeare on the Stage*, p. 67), justified Daly's musical insertions, declaring that every note was required by the text or authorised by the scheme of the play. Despite these additions, the play was reduced to four acts (with Beerbohm Tree it was reduced to three); Malvolio's scenes were condensed, the 'dungeon scene' and his final expostulation omitted altogether.

The tradition of elaborate spectacle and scenery was continued in Tree's production in 1901 which ran for more than three months to a capacity audience; by the end of the run 200,000 people had seen the production and had been entranced by the setting of broad grassy terraces and real fountains; this had been inspired by a garden-picture Tree had seen in *Country Life*, 'stumbling', so Lady Tree records, 'upon something that months at the British Museum could not have given him'.[1] 'When that I was and-a little tiny boy' became a final song and dance for the whole company, perhaps to represent a nineteenth-century elaboration of an Elizabethan jig.

The concept of spectacle was to be radically revised in this century under the influence of Gordon Craig, William Poel and Harley Granville-Barker in favour of non-illusory Shakespearean staging (see illustration 10). Yet in spite of the emphasis on a return to simplified staging, something of this operatic tradition seems to have lingered, influencing Poel. Wishing to reveal the music of Shakespeare's verse, he cast a play as one would an opera, with, for example, Viola mezzo-soprano, Olivia contralto, Maria high soprano, Orsino tenor, Malvolio baritone, Toby bass, Sir Andrew falsetto, and a vocal range of two octaves demanded of each speaker.[2]

Whatever the vagaries of some of their productions, nineteenth-century actor-managers merit applause for having introduced Shakespeare to a wide popular audience. Samuel Phelps, actor-manager of Sadler's Wells from 1844 to 1862, deserves much credit in this respect. Replacing with Shakespeare the fare that had appealed to a rough and ready suburban audience remote from the fashions of London, he ultimately gave them some thirty plays from the canon for a total of 4,000 performances, appearing himself to much acclaim in many of them.[3]

In 1848 and again in 1857, Phelps took on the role of Malvolio. His performance fell into what may be termed the Spanish-Malvolio tradition – a tradition, it appears from Lamb's comments, that looked back to Bensley's interpretation (or one of them) during the years that he had essayed the role. Lamb stressed Bensley's air of Spanish loftiness, seeming in appearance, speech and movement to be an 'old Castilian', starched, spruced and opinioned, twirling his gold chain with 'ineffable carelessness'. Phelps's Malvolio, on the other hand, was achieved in part by his own 'natural gravity' of manner, deepening at times to formality. He displayed in his performance a sort of 'frozen calm', a 'solidified presumption' that conveyed his sense of his own 'elevated consciousness' which altogether approved of his lady's supposed infatuation.[4]

Yet there could be more than one kind of deportment imagined for a Spanish type. Bensley's stage-walk reminded James Boaden of the 'one, two, three, hop' of a dancing

---

[1] Maud Tree, 'Herbert and I', in *Herbert Beerbohm Tree*, compiled by Max Beerbohm [1921], p. 117.

[2] John Styan, *The Shakespeare Revolution*, p. 49; Robert Speaight, *William Poel and the Elizabethan Revival*, 1954, p. 111. In 1897 Poel produced *Twelfth Night* at the Middle Temple, site of the earliest recorded performance, and it was revived twice in 1903 when he himself took on the role of Malvolio. In his early period Poel advocated adherence to the text (though cutting Malvolio's dark-room scene), and he opposed the current tendency to play Sir Toby in a leather jerkin and stuffed breeches as if he were an innkeeper, Maria in the dress of a kitchen maid, and Malvolio in cross-garters which imitated those of a brigand out of Italian opera. See his *Shakespeare in the Theatre*, 1913, pp. 212–13.

[3] *Macready and Forrest and Their Contemporaries*, ed. Brander Matthews and Laurence Hutton, 1900, p. 76.

[4] From a review in the *Weekly Dispatch*, 1857, cited in W. May Phelps and John Forbes-Robertson, *The Life and Life-Work of Samuel Phelps*, 1886, p. 162.

master; once he had donned his yellow stockings and garters it became a 'sliding, zigzag advance and retreat' topped off by a 'horrible laugh of ugly conceit'.[1] Phelps, in contrast, was described as walking 'not with a smirk and a light comic strut', but with the heaviness of grandeur, his grave face empty of all expression, his eyes 'nearly covered with their heavy lids' as if there were nothing in the external world worthy of his regard compared with his own excellence.[2]

When ten months later (in October 1857) Phelps took on the role of Don Armado in *Love's Labour's Lost*, it, too, showed a general resemblance to his Malvolio (Morley, *Journal*, p. 166). It is hard to account for the Spanish style, which might more readily have been attributed to Sir Andrew on the basis of Sir Toby's phrase *Castiliano vulgo*, but in 1884 (some thirty-five years after the previous London production with Charles Kean), it was again adopted for Malvolio, this time by Henry Irving.

Lean and lank, with a peaked Spanish beard, he entered dressed in a 'close garb of black striped with yellow', with a steward's wand, his nose in the air, his eyes half shut. Another contemporary described him as looking like 'some great Spanish hidalgo' out of a painting by Velasquez and therefore appearing much too superior a person to be gulled by Maria and her band[3] (see illustration 9). The play's music and songs were dropped, but the scenery with its sixteen sets was costly and romantic, clogging the action, so the critics said; but what they found even more disturbing was the tragic aura that Irving gave to Malvolio's scene in the 'dark house' where he had collapsed on the straw in a 'nerveless state of prostrate dejection'.[4] Of this 'tragic and pitiable' ending, Irving's grandson Laurence speculates that, as Irving had never seen the play performed, it probably derived from his reading of Lamb's description of Bensley.[5] Since the soundness of Lamb's recollection has been questioned,[6] it is ironic that Irving's interpretation was admired neither in England nor in America.

Despite its jarring tone, Irving's conception elicited an aspect of the play to which the American E. H. Sothern responded in two productions (with his wife Julia Marlowe a much admired Viola) and to which criticism has since responded again. Though Sothern sought historical accuracy in the 1905 production at the Knicker-bocker Theatre in New York, he also aimed to do Shakespeare in a novel way. Hence his Malvolio was invested with a 'pitiful and comic dignity', amounting, it was said, to a new interpretation of the character.[7] Two years later, when he took four of his productions, including *Twelfth Night*, to England, his Malvolio stirred Arthur Symons to enthusiastic praise. Sothern, he felt, carried technique to a supreme point:

[1] Cited in Winter, *Shakespeare on the Stage*, p. 24.
[2] Henry Morley, *Journal of a London Playgoer*, 1891, pp. 139–40, repr. in Salgādo, *Eyewitnesses*, pp. 208–10, and Winter, *Shakespeare on the Stage*, pp. 28–30.
[3] *Fortnightly Review*, 1 Sept. 1884, reprinted in Furness, p. 400, and Palmer, *Casebook*, pp. 54–5; Frank Benson, 'Irving as Malvolio', in *We Saw Him Act*, ed. H. A. Saintsbury and Cecil Palmer, 1939, reprinted 1969, p. 245.
[4] William Archer, '*Twelfth Night* at the Lyceum', *Macmillan's Magazine*, 1884, 2, p. 279.
[5] Laurence Irving, *Henry Irving, The Actor and His World*, 1951, p. 439.
[6] For a reconsideration of Lamb's view, see Sylvan Barnet, 'Charles Lamb and the tragic Malvolio', *PQ* 33 (1954), 178–88.
[7] *The Theatre*, Dec. 1905, pp. 290–1.

9 Henry Irving as Malvolio, with supporting cast, 1884

10   Act 2, Scene 3: *Twelfth Night* performed in a single, non-illusory setting in New York, 1904. Ben Greet as Malvolio, Millicent McLaughlin as Maria, B. A. Field as Sir Toby

He acts with his eyelids, which move while all the rest of the face is motionless; with his pursed, reticent mouth, with his prim and pompous gestures; with that self-consciousness which brings all Malvolio's troubles upon him. It is a fantastic, tragically comic thing, done with rare calculation, and it has its formal, almost cruel share in the immense gaiety of the piece. The play is great and wild, a mockery and a happiness; and it is all seen and not interpreted, but the mystery of it deepened, in the clown's song at the end, which, for once, has been allowed its full effect, not theatrical, but of pure imagination.[1]

Though Beerbohm Tree's production fell into a tradition – that of elaborate stage setting and spectacle – his interpretation of Malvolio did not, as it moved beyond comedy to farce. George Bernard Shaw remarks that since Tree did not inherit the theatrical tradition handed down from Phelps he had to make a style and technique of his own personality. This may account for the fact that in place of the image of Spanish gravity and hauteur, Tree projected the character as an 'intolerably condescending blue-eyed peacock with a red twirl of beard'[2] (see illustration 11). Shaw also remarks that the only unforgettable passages in Tree's Shakespearean performances were those of which he and not Shakespeare was the author, and he gives as example the four small Malvolios in the production who aped the large one in dress and deportment. When majestically descending a magnificent flight of stairs, Tree regularly slipped and fell with a crash; he showed no discomfiture but raised his eyeglass and surveyed the scene as if he had done it on purpose. This, like the four smaller Malvolios, Shaw thought not only funny but subtle.[3] It was to counter Tree's

---

[1] A. Symons, 'Great acting in English', *Plays, Acting, and Music*, 1909, pp. 191–2.
[2] J. C. Trewin, *Shakespeare on the English Stage, 1900–1964*, p. 18.
[3] 'The point of view of a playwright', in *Herbert Beerbohm Tree*, pp. 247–9.

11 Act 3, Scene 4: Beerbohm Tree as Malvolio, Maud Jefferies as Olivia, in the tradition of elaborate stage setting and spectacle, 1901

tour de force, according to G. Wilson Knight, that in 1912 Granville-Barker directed
Henry Ainley as a 'dry puritan'. According to a contemporary review, his dress and
demeanour were sombre, his movements few and simple, his discourse studied but
quietly spoken.[1]

Whether Malvolio was played 'straight' (as with Phelps) or given a tragic aura (as
with Irving and Sothern) or burlesqued (as with Tree), the stage business was
modified accordingly. Bensley, it will be remembered, twirled his gold chain of office
with 'ineffable carelessness'; in the last act Tree tore his off in order to symbolise
his defiance as well as his servitude. Phelps maintained his self-satisfied posture after
learning of the trickery, retiring without a word until on hearing Feste's taunt he
stormed back to utter his imprecation on the 'whole pack'. Sothern tore the letter
to bits.

Most Malvolios carried a staff of office, but Irving apparently first used the trick
of slipping Olivia's ring over the end of it and churlishly dropping it at Viola's feet.[2]
When he appeared to the revellers, his rebuke was heightened by his wearing a
'marvellously spectral night-dress' in a scenic arrangement that threw the 'grim
grotesqueness of his appearance' into relief[3] (see illustration 9). Stage business for
the so-called kitchen scene (2.3) tended to become increasingly extravagant, with many
absurdities on the part of Sir Toby and Sir Andrew, such as their smoking long pipes
and generally horsing about.

These diverse interpretations and productions elicited strong divisions of opinion.
There were those who, like William Winter justifying Daly's musical version of
Twelfth Night, wished to keep up the spectacular and festive traditions of theatre.
Those who dissented did not necessarily look for old-style alternatives. Max
Beerbohm admired Gordon Craig's use of mystery and fantasy but did not think the
Victorian 'science of scenic productions' was therefore necessarily outmoded and
mocked a 1903 performance of *Twelfth Night* by the Elizabethan Stage Society for
its lifeless pursuit of archaeological correctness: 'The epithet "owlish" is inevitable
of a Society which finds in the darkness of the dark ages its natural element.'[4] Yet
in the decades that followed, the dominance of the director as independent artist was
often exercised on sets that displaced scenery with movement and lighting, allowing
an Elizabethan rapidity and continuity of staging. Thus Terence Gray, who directed
the Festival Theatre at Cambridge (1926–33), had it both ways. In his production
of *Twelfth Night* on a plain (but revolving) stage, Sir Toby and Sir Andrew entered
on roller-skates.[5]

---

[1] *Shakespearian Production,* 1964, p. 207; like Shaw, Knight (though he had not seen the production)
thought Tree's Malvolio 'extremely subtle burlesque'. The description of Ainley's performance is from
the *Morning Post,* 16 Nov. 1912, cited in Trewin, *Shakespeare on the English Stage,* p. 55.

[2] Percy Fitzgerald, *Shakespearean Representation,* 1908, cited in A. C. Sprague, *Shakespeare and the
Actors,* 1944, p. 5.

[3] Archer, '*Twelfth Night*', p. 279. Winter records a 1904 American performance in which the Malvolio
(John Blair) appeared wearing dressing-gown and nightcap, his beard and moustache crimped in long
curl-papers (*Shakespeare on the Stage,* pp. 76–7). It is difficult to imagine Sir Toby telling a Malvolio
in a night-shirt to go rub his chain with crumbs unless he were wearing the chain at the time.

[4] *Around Theatres,* 1924, reprinted 1953, p. 258.

[5] Styan, *The Shakespeare Revolution,* p. 153.

Some twenty years later there were signs that 'Director's Shakespeare' was giving way to 'Actor's Shakespeare'. John Gielgud reports that in his own production of *Twelfth Night* Laurence Olivier played Malvolio like a Jewish hairdresser with a lisp and insisted in spite of his director on falling backwards off a bench in the garden scene.[1]

E.S.D.

RECENT YEARS

Since 1955, when Olivier's broad comic initiatives were thought by some to prevail over the cool and beautiful felicities of Gielgud's production,[2] directors and players have had many opportunities to refine, refresh or challenge the historical traditions of the play's performance.

Peter Hall directed what was to become the first Royal Shakespeare Company production from 1958 to 1960, starting with Dorothy Tutin as Viola, Geraldine McEwan as Olivia, Derek Godfrey as Orsino and Mark Dignam as Malvolio. The sets, by Lila de Nobili, included glowing gauze prospects of clouded and towered landscape, a rich Elizabethan gallery and a great gateway to Olivia's Tudor mansion. Cavalier costumes offset the puritanism of a Malvolio who was allowed some gentlemanly status and even (in Eric Porter's later rendering) efficiency, dignity and good sense. Olivia was a young coquette with a mischievous wit, while Feste was required to break down and sob in the course of his final song. Max Adrian, playing Feste in 1960, was seen to be 'nursing the secret of an insoluble melancholy'[3] and in the prison scene appeared less to be teasing Malvolio than trying to save him from the damnation attending his folly. The performance ended on 'a dying fall' with the distant sound of trumpets.

In 1966 Clifford Williams directed for the RSC a long-running production of the play which was revived for the last time in 1972. A Renaissance-style arcaded stage with a musicians' gallery, designed by Sally Jacobs, served an Italianate performance which frequently alluded in its styles and spectacle to the *commedia dell'arte*. Alan Howard's Orsino provoked the comment that 'a bad performance' was 'on its way to being a striking one';[4] 'an uncomfortable parody', said another reviewer, 'indeed, he gives us excess of it'.[5] Ian Holmes's very English Malvolio, on the other hand, spoke with 'a complex mongrel accent' made out of 'eccentric gentility and a basis of raw bullying cockney'.[6] His appearance was close enough to the Droeshout portrait of Shakespeare to suggest to one reviewer that Malvolio's revenge upon the whole pack was perhaps the writing of the play itself.[7]

Of the next RSC production, by John Barton in 1969, one critic said that he could remember 'no production that held all the comedy's elements in such harmony'. It

[1] *An Actor and His Time*, 1980, cited in Thomas Kiernan, *Sir Larry*, 1981, pp. 254–5.
[2] See John Russell Brown, *Shakespeare's Plays in Performance*, 1966, p. 207.
[3] Robert Speaight, 'The 1960 season at Stratford-upon-Avon', *SQ* 11 (1960), 445–53 (p. 450).
[4] Ronald Bryden, 'A long way to Illyria', *The Observer*, 19 June 1966.
[5] J. C. Trewin, *The Birmingham Post*, 17 June 1966.
[6] 'Twelfth Night without pathos', *The Times*, 17 June 1966.
[7] Alan Brien, 'The Illyrian business', *The Sunday Telegraph*, 19 June 1966.

12   Judi Dench, 1969: 'And what should I do in Illyria?' Set designed by Christopher Morley

was set in a deep wattle cage, designed by Christopher Morley, which allowed an
enchanting (or disenchanting) play of light upon simple but decorative properties (see
illustration 12). Judi Dench's Viola was said to be 'sturdy, steadfast and – if the word
doesn't sound absurd – spiritual at the same time'.[1] She and Emrys James's Feste
'bickering on a bench' seemed 'to discover in each other the same bewildered
hard-pressed sense of life'.[2] Donald Sinden played Malvolio as a pitiful figure but
with great comic zest. 'There is more joyousness in Donald Sinden's pride of office
than in any of those who oppose him', said one experienced playgoer: 'The outraged
dignity with which he gasps "Run, Madonna?" would be the comic highspot of the
evening, if it weren't for the Zulu lope at which he proceeds to carry out her order.'[3]
Malvolio's repetition of Olivia's word 'run' and intrusion of Feste's 'Madonna' are
not in the text and in earlier performances Sinden only mouthed them without voicing.
The comic run and the turning about on the word 'revolve' (2.5.119) were already
part of the stage tradition observed and recreated by Laurence Olivier. Like others
before him Sinden flung down the ring at Viola's feet, but only after getting it stuck
on his own finger. On a touring occasion he rotated the garden sundial to make it
conform with the watch he carried on his chain of office. In the prison scene, however,
high conceit and despairing sanity collapsed into sobs that could still be heard from

[1] J. W. Lambert, 'The wind and the rain', *The Sunday Times,* 24 August 1969.
[2] J. W. Lambert, as above.
[3] Ronald Bryden, 'In Illyrian neverland', *The Observer,* 24 August 1969.

13   Royal Shakespeare Company, 1974. Set designed by William Dudley

under the stage when Sebastian in the next scene speaks the words 'Yet 'tis not
madness.' Malvolio's 'shattered but dignified' exit was meant, by Sinden's own
account, to be a prelude to suicide.[1]

Peter Gill from the Royal Court Theatre directed *Twelfth Night* for the RSC in
1974, using a domestic set, by William Dudley, which was sometimes dominated by
a picture of Narcissus (see illustration 13). Orsino, Olivia and Malvolio were equally
'sick of self-love', but Nicol Williamson's Malvolio alone had the 'distempered
appetite'. He was 'a full-blooded Welsh puritan', his 'huge heels adding an impression
of overwhelming height and authority'. His smile in the letter scene was described
as 'spreading like cracks over paving stones', and his voice was 'reedy, Welsh and
ridiculous'.[2] His valedictory threat was disturbingly malignant and four times
repeated as (like Sothern before him) he tore the letter to shreds, putting an end at
once to the 'sportful' mood of Maria's comedy and of Shakespeare's.

The 1979 RSC production, directed by Terry Hands, moved in its design (by John
Napier) from winter to spring but hinted too at that arrival in autumn and prospect
of winter which had determined the mood of Barton's production (see illustration 14).
As the play advanced, Geoffrey Hutchings's austere Feste decorated the scene with
narcissi. The graces, tendernesses and resolute energies of Viola were played by Cheri

[1] See Donald Sinden, 'Malvolio in *Twelfth Night*', in Philip Brockbank (ed.), *Players of Shakespeare*,
    1985, pp. 41–66.
[2] Peter Ansorge, *Plays and Players*, October 1974, 30–3.

14   Royal Shakespeare Company, 1979. Cheri Lunghi, Kate Nicholls, John Woodvine: 'Alas, Malvolio, this is not my writing.' Set designed by John Napier

15   John Woodvine, 1979: 'I will smile'

Lunghi in an Illyria which otherwise owed more to the grossness of the flesh than
to its frailty. John Woodvine's Malvolio was an unimaginative and wooden puritan
(in a high black hat) lapsing into cross-gartered and heavily codpieced bravado. He
studied his smile in a rectangular looking-glass, first held upright and then rotated
sideways (see illustration 15). Upon the word 'revolve' he turned, not himself, but
Maria's letter. From his under-stage prison he reached his hands through the trap-door
and Feste banged it down on his fingers.

In 1983 the spectator at John Caird's Stratford production might have reflected
that neither director nor actor dominated a performance which was largely shaped by
the designer. Robin Don devised a vast and intricate tree set in a landscape whose
ruins, moods and dispositions owed much to Giorgione's famous painting *La Tempesta*
(see illustration 16). It was not the 'box-tree' specified in the text (2.5.13), which is
traditionally square-cut to form a wall or maze, but rather a symbolic expression of
the play's concern with the at once simple and complex laws of growth and decay
in the natural and human world. The performers required considerable agility to
accommodate themselves to the symbols, however, and (as in 1979) the action lost
its household setting and therefore something of what might be called its interior
significance; the structures of pastoral idyll prevailed over those of domestic comedy.
Emrys James, who had played Feste to Sinden's Malvolio, played Malvolio in the
tradition Sinden had followed, and the audience's sympathies were deeply engaged

16   Royal Shakespeare Company, 1983. Set designed by Robin Don

in the last scene. An Illyria surrendered to affectation and self-indulgence was much in need of the spirited good sense of Zoë Wanamaker's Viola. An ageing, slightly brutal but still patrician Sir Toby (John Thaw) was attended by a wistful and winning Sir Andrew (Daniel Massey) who was contemptuously discarded in the last scene. The production made much of their transient fellowship with the fool (Richard O'Callaghan), especially in their rendering of 'O mistress mine' in tipsy but exquisite accord. Sir Andrew's wispy radiance on the line 'I was adored once, too' (2.3.153) was owed (said Daniel Massey) to his recollection of his mother. The play's attentiveness to self-love was sensitively realised, both in the Malvolio comedy and in the reunion of the twins. Maria's letter makes 'a contemplative idiot' of a Malvolio imprisoned first in a false self and then in a dark cell; but when the joke has gone far enough and he has been 'most notoriously abused', a way must be found to recall him to the community. In the meeting of Viola and Sebastian the true self seemed to find itself in the other ('Do I stand there?') in what might indeed be taken as a playful perspective upon the Narcissus story.

These RSC productions are only a tiny sample, of course, of stagings of the play in recent years. There have been many London versions – at the Royal Court, for example, in Regent's Park, at Hampton Court and in the Middle Temple; and provincial performances have included Bristol, Cambridge, Darlington, Leeds, Liverpool, Malvern, Windsor and York. The BBC television version (1981) is now familiar to audiences all over the world, and the history of performance is no longer co-extensive with that of the theatre. The play, like Viola herself, can sing and speak to us in many sorts of music, but she would have been much surprised by the 'smash-hit rock musical' by Hal Hester and Danny Apolinar, first staged in New York in 1967–8 (the book of the production, by Donald Driver, now stands more in need of explanatory annotation than the original text).

J.P.B.

NOTE ON THE TEXT

Twelfth Night was first published in the First Folio in 1623 where it is placed next to the last of the comedies, *The Winter's Tale*. It is a superior text, but for an account of some 'short-lived' trouble during the sequence of printing and for the nature of the copy, see Textual Analysis, pp. 151–4 below.

In this edition, acts and scenes correspond with the divisions in the Folio.[1] The somewhat anomalous clearing of the stage at 3.4.231 which, in accord with the law of re-entry, should mark a new scene but is instead immediately followed by the re-entry of Sir Toby and Sir Andrew, has been retained;[2] this allows for some business off-stage that is visible at least to Sir Toby and Sir Andrew (and perhaps to the audience through an open stage door), as is evident from Sir Toby's remark, 'Fabian can scarce hold him yonder.' Locations of scenes, traditional from eighteenth-century editions on, are given in the Commentary. Requisite entrances and exits not in the Folio have been inserted in square brackets, as have some few other stage directions and indications of 'asides'.

Because of the discrepancy in the rank of Orsino between what is given in the stage directions and in the text (pointed out at p. 16 above) and because of the general practice of referring to Shakespearean characters by name, all speech headings involving him (*Du.*) have been regularised to Orsino. On the same grounds, speech headings for the clown (*Clo.*) have been regularised to Feste, though he is named only once in the text.

The frequent contractions (*th', o'th'*, etc.) have been retained in accord with the colloquial character of much of the dialogue; *h'as* (i.e. *he has*) has been retained as indicating the two words contracted and the variant *ha's* has been regularised; *an* meaning *if* has been regularised to *and* and *ta'en* to *tane*.

The punctuation in the Folio is not generally troublesome though there is a generous use of colons, and these have frequently been silently replaced by periods or by commas or dashes in the comic scenes; quotation marks have been inserted when required. When a final *-ed* is pronounced because of the requirement of metre, it is indicated by a *grave* accent; some few other differences from modern stress are indicated in the notes. Finally, the seventeenth-century practice of italicising proper names within the dialogue has been ignored.

In addition to substantive readings, the collation includes a number of punctuation changes, largely in the comic scenes, that have been introduced from the eighteenth century on; they serve to indicate how editors have gradually come to interpret the

---

[1] Furness gives Henry Irving's acting version with act and scene divisions, and it is still common for modern directors to transpose the first two scenes in Act 1.

[2] See C. M. Haines, 'The law of re-entry in Shakespeare', *RES* 1 (Oct. 1925), 449–51, where he notes sixteen occasions, excluding battle scenes, when the convention is disregarded.

text. The authority for the reading comes immediately after the square bracket, followed by the reading in F (the First Folio, the sole authority); other readings, if any, follow in chronological order.

The following abbreviations are used: *subst.* for *substantively*, followed by the name of the editor who introduced the change, usually of a stage direction or a mark of punctuation, and which is, in the main, adopted in this edition; *This edn* for a modification, again usually of a stage direction or mark of punctuation, that does not appear in earlier standard editions though it may be indicated as earlier having been *conjectured (conj.)*. An asterisk preceding the lemma in the Commentary is used to call attention to a word or phrase that has been emended in the text.

Twelfth Night
or What You Will

LIST OF CHARACTERS

ORSINO, *Duke (or Count) of Illyria*
SEBASTIAN, *twin brother to Viola*
ANTONIO, *captain, a friend to Sebastian*
SEA CAPTAIN, *a friend to Viola*
VALENTINE ⎫
CURIO   ⎭ *gentlemen attending Orsino*
SIR TOBY BELCH, *a kinsman of Olivia's*
SIR ANDREW AGUECHEEK, *a companion of Sir Toby's*
MALVOLIO, *steward to Olivia*
FABIAN, *a gentleman of Olivia's household*
FESTE, *a jester in Olivia's household*

OLIVIA, *a countess*
VIOLA, *twin sister to Sebastian, later called Cesario*
MARIA, *a gentlewoman in Olivia's household*

PRIEST
Musicians, Lords, Sailors, Officers and other attendants
Scene: Illyria

Notes

The List of Characters is based mainly on that of Rowe, the first to appear in print, and on the Douai MS.

ORSINO For the variation between 'duke' and 'count' in F's stage directions and the text, see p. 16 above.

CURIO A frequent name for a courtier, from Latin *curia*, court.

VIOLA The first syllable receives the stress. For a discussion of the symbolism of the name, see Winfreid Schleiner, 'Orsino and Viola: are the names of serious characters in *Twelfth Night* meaningful?', *S.St.* 16 (1984), 135–41.

MARIA Olivia specifies that Maria is one of her gentlewomen at 1.5.135 and Malvolio confirms this at 1.5.136.

44

TWELFTH NIGHT OR WHAT YOU WILL

1.1 [*Music.*] *Enter* ORSINO, *Duke of Illyria*, CURIO, *and other Lords*

ORSINO If music be the food of love, play on;
        Give me excess of it, that surfeiting,
        The appetite may sicken and so die.
        That strain again, it had a dying fall;
        O it came o'er my ear like the sweet sound   5
        That breathes upon a bank of violets,
        Stealing and giving odour. Enough; no more.
        'Tis not so sweet now as it was before.
        O spirit of love, how quick and fresh art thou,
        That, notwithstanding thy capacity,   10

Title] *Twelfe Night, Or what you will.* F   **Act 1, Scene 1**   1.1] *Actus Primus, Scæna Prima.* F   0 SD *Music*] *Mahood; Musick attending.* / *Capell; not in* F

Title: TWELFTH F's form 'twelfe' here (and again at 2.3.73) for 'twelfth' appears nowhere else in the canon though *Ham.* (Q2), thought to be set from Shakespeare's autograph, has 'twelfe' for 'twelve'.

WHAT YOU WILL For the sense of this catchphrase, see p. 4 above.

Act 1, Scene 1
1.1 Acts and scenes divided as in F.
Location A room in the duke's palace (Capell).
0 SD *Duke of Illyria* Though consistently called 'duke' in stage directions and speech headings in F, after 1.4 he is called 'count' in the text for the rest of the play. See p. 16 above and Textual Analysis, pp. 151 ff.
0 SD *Illyria* On the eastern coast of the Adriatic.
1 **music...love** Compare *Ant.* 2.5.1–2: 'music, moody food / Of us that trade in love'. The sentiments in 1–11 receive their own ironic comment in Orsino's words to Viola, 2.4.91–7, where it is women's love that is said to suffer 'surfeit, cloyment, and revolt'.
4 **That strain again** Having specified a 'surfeit' of music, here Orsino demands that the musicians (probably a household consort) stop and repeat the musical phrase. Joseph Summers calls the effect here, and in line 7 when the demand is countered, 'a comic bit of stage business which is rarely utilised in production' ('The masks of *Twelfth Night*', p. 88).
4 **fall** cadence.
5–7 **like the sweet sound...odour** A substitution of the effect for the cause (a form of metonymy); a rhetorically mannered style marks Orsino's speech. For a comparable instance of this figurative use, see *Comus* 555–7: 'At last a soft and solemn-breathing sound / Rose like a stream of rich distill'd Perfumes, / And stole upon the Air' (Halliwell).
9 **quick and fresh** alive and vigorous. For 'fresh', see *OED* sv *a* 10.
10–14 **That...minute** i.e. the lover's sensibility has the sea's capacity to take in everything, but everything that enters, no matter how high its value, quickly loses its worth. Orsino has taken in the music which has now lost its significance for him, leaving his love still 'quick and fresh'; compare his words at 2.4.15–18.
10 **capacity** ability to take in (and contain) impressions (*OED* sv 4).

Receiveth as the sea. Nought enters there,
Of what validity and pitch soe'er,
But falls into abatement and low price
Even in a minute. So full of shapes is fancy,
That it alone is high fantastical.   15
CURIO Will you go hunt, my lord?
ORSINO   What, Curio?
CURIO The hart.
ORSINO Why so I do, the noblest that I have.
O when mine eyes did see Olivia first,
Methought she purged the air of pestilence;   20
That instant was I turned into a hart,
And my desires like fell and cruel hounds
E'er since pursue me.

Enter VALENTINE

How now, what news from her?
VALENTINE So please my lord, I might not be admitted,
But from her handmaid do return this answer: 25
The element itself, till seven years' heat,
Shall not behold her face at ample view;

---

23 SD] *As Dyce; follows* her? *in* F

11 **Receiveth** For another of the frequent
instances of a third-person singular used with a
second-person antecedent (Abbott 247), see *AYLI*
3.5.52–3: ''Tis such fools as you [foolish shepherd]
/ That makes the world full of ill-favor'd children.'
11 **there** With the immediate antecedent 'sea',
the statement here and in the next two lines
characterises what happens to objects in the
'never-surfeited sea' (*Temp.* 3.3.55). Many, however, take 'there' to refer to the 'capacity' of love,
which of course it does by the analogy.
12 **validity and pitch** i.e. high value. This use
of two nouns in place of a noun and an adjective
(hendiadys) is another example of Orsino's rhetorical
manner; 'pitch' (from falconry, describing the
highest point of a flight) is frequently metaphorical,
as in *Ham.* (Q2) 1740 (3.1.85): 'enterprises of great
pitch and moment'.
14–15 **So...fantastical** So full of imagined
forms is love ('fancy') that (like the sea) it is the
most capricious of all things. 'Fantastical' in
Shakespeare is generally derogatory, though it can
simply mean 'imaginary'. Compare *LLL* 5.2.762–3,

where love is said to be 'Form'd by the eye and
therefore like the eye, / Full of straying shapes, of
habits, and of forms', and *MND* 5.1.3–22.
17–18 **hart...I have** Punning on hart/heart,
the latter being his 'noblest' part.
20 **purged...pestilence** Though Olivia
purged the air, Orsino caught the plague of love; she
is thus both remedy and cause. Compare her similar
response in 1.5.250: 'Even so quickly may one catch
the plague?'
22–3 **desires...pursue me** Like the hunter
Actaeon who, having seen Diana bathing, was
turned into a stag and pursued by his own hounds
(Ovid, *Metamorphoses* III, 138 ff.). Orsino is thus
both hunter and quarry. The identification of erotic
desires with pursuing hounds was common. See
Daniel's *Delia* (1592), Sonnet 5, for an elaboration
of the conceit.
22 **fell** fierce.
26 **element** sky.
26 **heat** i.e. the heat of seven summers (an
example of synecdoche, taking the part for the
whole).

But like a cloistress she will veilèd walk,
And water once a day her chamber round
With eye-offending brine; all this to season   30
A brother's dead love, which she would keep fresh
And lasting, in her sad remembrance.

ORSINO O she that hath a heart of that fine frame
To pay this debt of love but to a brother,
How will she love, when the rich golden shaft   35
Hath killed the flock of all affections else
That live in her; when liver, brain, and heart,
These sovereign thrones, are all supplied and filled
Her sweet perfections with one selfsame king!
Away before me to sweet beds of flowers: 40
Love-thoughts lie rich when canopied with bowers.

                                Exeunt

1.2 *Enter* VIOLA, *a* CAPTAIN, *and Sailors*

VIOLA What country, friends, is this?
CAPTAIN This is Illyria, lady.
VIOLA And what should I do in Illyria?
      My brother, he is in Elysium.
      Perchance he is not drowned: what think you, sailors?   5

---

39 selfsame] F2 ; selfe F   Act 1, Scene 2   1.2] *Scena Secunda*. F

28 cloistress A nun cloistered in her chamber.

30 season preserve with brine. This play on 'season' and 'brine' is used in Shakespeare either for a rhetorical or a comic effect, as in *The Rape of Lucrece* 796: 'Seasoning the earth with show'rs of silver brine', and *Rom.* 2.3.69–70: 'Jesu Maria, what a deal of brine / Hath wash'd thy sallow cheeks for Rosaline!' Other instances are in *A Lover's Complaint* 17–18 and *AWW* 1.1.48–9.

32 remembrance An obsolete form, pronounced as four syllables.

33 that fine frame Compare *AWW* 4.2.4: 'In your fine frame hath love no quality?'

35 golden shaft Cupid's 'best arrow' (*MND* 1.1.170) induced love, the one tipped with lead, hatred (Ovid, *Metamorphoses* 1, 468–71).

36 affections else other feelings.

37–8 liver...thrones The liver was the throne of the passions, the brain of reason, and the heart of emotion.

38 filled (hath) satisfied. Paralleling 'Hath killed' at 36. See *OED* sv *v* 10, 17.

39 *selfsame An intensive. F's omission of 'same' is corrected in subsequent folios both for metre and clarity of meaning. Shakespeare uses the form 'selfsame' most frequently. Kökeritz observes that in everyday speech '-ion' was normally a monosyllable (p. 293).

40–1 Away...bowers Orsino's directive to his attendants allows him to express the final sentiment of the couplet as they are leaving the stage. For its significance in relation to the projected season of the play's action and the metaphorical nature of its title, see pp. 3–4 above.

Act 1, Scene 2
Location The sea coast (Capell)

4 Elysium Equivalent to heaven as the abode of the blessed; the similarity of initial sound with 'Illyria' points up the difference in locales that Viola wishes to emphasise.

5–7 Perchance Viola uses the term to mean 'perhaps', the Captain uses it to mean 'by chance', and Viola then plays upon both senses.

CAPTAIN It is perchance that you yourself were saved.

VIOLA O my poor brother! And so perchance may he be.

CAPTAIN True, madam, and to comfort you with chance,
　　　　　Assure yourself, after our ship did split,
　　　　　When you, and those poor number saved with you,   10
　　　　　Hung on our driving boat, I saw your brother
　　　　　Most provident in peril, bind himself
　　　　　(Courage and hope both teaching him the practice)
　　　　　To a strong mast that lived upon the sea;
　　　　　Where like Arion on the dolphin's back   15
　　　　　I saw him hold acquaintance with the waves
　　　　　So long as I could see.

VIOLA For saying so, there's gold.
　　　　　Mine own escape unfoldeth to my hope,
　　　　　Whereto thy speech serves for authority,   20
　　　　　The like of him. Know'st thou this country?

CAPTAIN Ay, madam, well, for I was bred and born
　　　　　Not three hours' travel from this very place.

VIOLA Who governs here?

CAPTAIN A noble duke in nature as in name.   25

VIOLA What is his name?

CAPTAIN Orsino.

VIOLA Orsino! I have heard my father name him.
　　　　　He was a bachelor then.

CAPTAIN And so is now, or was so very late;   30
　　　　　For but a month ago I went from hence,
　　　　　And then 'twas fresh in murmur (as you know
　　　　　What great ones do, the less will prattle of)
　　　　　That he did seek the love of fair Olivia.

VIOLA What's she?   35

---

15 Arion] *Pope;* Orion F

8 **chance** possibility of good fortune.

11 **driving** drifting. A nautical term.

14 **lived** floated. Another nautical term.

15 *****Arion** After leaping into the sea to escape some murderous sailors, Arion climbed on the back of a dolphin; both paying his fare and charming the waves by the music of his lyre, he was brought to shore in safety (Ovid, *Fasti* II, 93–118). Herodotus (I, 24) also tells the story.

19–20 **Mine...authority** My escape gives me hope for his to which your words give sanction.

22 **bred and born** This looks like an inversion of sequence (the figure hysteron proteron), but 'bred' meaning 'begotten' is frequent in Shakespeare, as in *The Rape of Lucrece* 1188: 'So of shame's ashes shall my fame be bred.'

32 **murmur** rumour.

33 **the less** those of inferior degree.

35 **What's she** i.e. of what quality or rank (Abbott 254).

CAPTAIN A virtuous maid, the daughter of a count
        That died some twelvemonth since, then leaving her
        In the protection of his son, her brother,
        Who shortly also died; for whose dear love
        (They say) she hath abjured the sight   40
        And company of men.

VIOLA   O that I served that lady,
        And might not be delivered to the world
        Till I had made mine own occasion mellow
        What my estate is!

CAPTAIN   That were hard to compass,
        Because she will admit no kind of suit,   45
        No, not the duke's.

VIOLA There is a fair behaviour in thee, captain,
        And though that nature with a beauteous wall
        Doth oft close in pollution, yet of thee
        I well believe thou hast a mind that suits   50
        With this thy fair and outward character.
        I prithee (and I'll pay thee bounteously)
        Conceal me what I am, and be my aid
        For such disguise as haply shall become
        The form of my intent. I'll serve this duke.   55
        Thou shalt present me as an eunuch to him –
        It may be worth thy pains – for I can sing,
        And speak to him in many sorts of music
        That will allow me very worth his service.

40–1 sight / And company] F; company / And sight *Hanmer*   50 well] *Conj. Walker;* will F

40–1 sight...company The F reading is
satisfactory though most editors, ignoring the
logical sequence but thinking the versification
improved, follow Hanmer's transposition 'company
/ And sight'. There is in this period and earlier in
Shakespeare a pervasive insecurity of verse form
with a tendency to move into prose.

42–4 delivered...is i.e. I wish that my position
(estate) should not become known until the time is
ripe. Compare *LLL* 4.2.69–70: 'delivered upon the
mellowing of occasion'.

44 compass bring about.

46 not not even.

48–51 And though...character The possible
disjunction between the outward character (appearance) and inner nature of an individual is

commented on again at 3.4.317–19 and at 5.1.120.
It is a frequent motif in the *Sonnets*.

50 *well Walker conjectured an e:i confusion
as occasioning the reading 'will' in F. There is a
similar confusion in *Lear* 1.4.1: Q1 and Q2 read 'If
but as well I other accents borrow' where F reads
'will'.

53 am i.e. conceal that I am a woman. For the
redundant object ('me'), see Abbott 414.

54 become suit.

56 eunuch *castrato*, male soprano. In fact, Viola
disguises herself as a page. Since this first idea is not
picked up, some argue for a revision of the text; see
p. 16 above.

59 allow me...service prove me worthy to
serve him.

What else may hap, to time I will commit, 60
Only shape thou thy silence to my wit.
CAPTAIN Be you his eunuch, and your mute I'll be;
When my tongue blabs, then let mine eyes not see.
VIOLA I thank thee. Lead me on.

Exeunt

1.3 *Enter* SIR TOBY [BELCH] *and* MARIA

SIR TOBY What a plague means my niece to take the death of her
brother thus? I am sure care's an enemy to life.
MARIA By my troth, Sir Toby, you must come in earlier o'nights. Your
cousin, my lady, takes great exceptions to your ill hours.
SIR TOBY Why, let her except, before excepted. 5
MARIA Ay, but you must confine yourself within the modest limits of
order.
SIR TOBY Confine? I'll confine myself no finer than I am: these clothes
are good enough to drink in, and so be these boots too; and they
be not, let them hang themselves in their own straps. 10
MARIA That quaffing and drinking will undo you: I heard my lady talk
of it yesterday and of a foolish knight that you brought in one night
here to be her wooer.
SIR TOBY Who, Sir Andrew Aguecheek?
MARIA Ay, he. 15
SIR TOBY He's as tall a man as any's in Illyria.

Act 1, Scene 3 1.3] *Scæna Tertia.* F 0 SD BELCH] *Malone; not in* F 3 o'] *Capell;* a F

61 wit invention. As in *Oth.* 4.1.189–90: 'Of so
high and plenteous wit and invention!'
62 mute A dumb (i.e. silent) servant, as at the
Turkish court. Suggested by 'eunuch'. In *H5*
1.2.232, a 'Turkish mute' is said to have a
'tongueless mouth'.

Act 1, Scene 3
Location Olivia's house (Rowe).
3 By my troth By my pledged faith. A mild
oath.
4 cousin There are seventeen references to
Olivia as Sir Toby's 'niece', six references to either
of them as 'cousin'; this latter term was widely used
to denote an imprecise degree of kinship.
5 except...excepted with the exceptions that
have already been named. From the Latin *exceptis
excipiendis*, a legal phrase which Sir Toby uses to

deride Olivia's having already taken 'exception', in
Maria's words (4), to his earlier deportment.
6 modest moderate.
8 confine...finer (1) 'I will accept no further
constraints', (2) 'I refuse to dress more finely.' Sir
Toby plays upon chimes of sound and sense
between 'confines' and 'finer'.
9 and if. In this period 'and' frequently
appears as 'an'; for another instance, see 5.1.276.
10 let them...straps Similar expressions
are recorded in Tilley (G42), but all of them follow
Shakespeare's earlier use in *MND* (1595/96), in
1H4 (1597), and in this play (? 1601). *ODEP* gives
one citation from 1591, scarcely an indication of its
proverbial nature before Shakespeare.
16 tall brave. Ironic in view of Sir Andrew's own
words at 3.4.237 and 240–3. In her reply Maria
wilfully takes it as a reference to height.

MARIA What's that to th'purpose?

SIR TOBY Why, he has three thousand ducats a year.

MARIA Ay, but he'll have but a year in all these ducats. He's a very fool
and a prodigal.   20

SIR TOBY Fie, that you'll say so! He plays o'th'viol-de-gamboys, and
speaks three or four languages word for word without book, and
hath all the good gifts of nature.

MARIA He hath indeed all, most natural: for besides that he's a fool,
he's a great quarreller; and but that he hath the gift of a coward   25
to allay the gust he hath in quarrelling, 'tis thought among the
prudent he would quickly have the gift of a grave.

SIR TOBY By this hand, they are scoundrels and substractors that say
so of him. Who are they?

MARIA They that add, moreover, he's drunk nightly in your company.   30

SIR TOBY With drinking healths to my niece! I'll drink to her as long
as there is a passage in my throat and drink in Illyria; he's a coward
and a coistrill that will not drink to my niece till his brains turn
o'th'toe like a parish top. What, wench! *Castiliano vulgo*: for here

---

24 indeed all, most] *Mahood, conj. Furness;* indeed, almost F; indeed, – all most *Collier, conj. Upton*   34 *Castiliano vulgo*]
F; *Castiliano volto / Hanmer*

---

18 **three thousand ducats** According to
Thomas Coryat, in 1611 a Venetian ducat was worth
four shillings and eightpence (i.e. twenty-three
pence).

19 **he'll...ducats** i.e. he will use up his estate
within a year.

19 **very true.**

21 **viol-de-gamboys** *viola da gamba* or bass
viol. The bawdy implication of playing this
instrument is discussed by Gustav Ungerer, 'The
viol da gamba as a sexual metaphor in Elizabethan
music and literature', *Renaissance and Reformation*
8:2 (May 1984), 79–90.

22 **without book** by memory. Again ironic in
view of Sir Andrew's words at 77–9.

24 *indeed all, ...natural* (1) from nature, (2)
like a natural born idiot. Upton's conjecture allows
for Maria's play on 'natural' in these two senses.

25 **gift** natural ability. Affording a quibble at 27
on 'gift' as 'present'.

26 **gust...in** taste...for.

28 **By this hand** An oath derived from shaking
hands when making a promise; used also by
Malvolio at 2.3.105.

28 **substractors** i.e. detractors. This nonce
usage points up Sir Toby's wayward diction,
perhaps underscoring his tipsy behaviour.

33 **coistrill** knave. Literally, a groom. This

word, like the later 'gaskins', 'pavin' and 'galliard'
(subsequently used three times), represents Shakespeare's earliest usage, with 'gaskins' and 'pavin'
not used again. Kenneth Muir (*Shakespeare's
Sources*, 1957, revised as *The Sources of Shakespeare's
Plays*, 1978) points out that the four words appear
in Riche's *Farewell to Military Profession*, which
includes the story of 'Apolonius and Silla',
Shakespeare's main source for this play.
J. J. M. Tobin ('Gabriel Harvey in Illyria', *ES* 61
(1980), 318–28) emphasises the remarkable similarity
of diction in *TN* to that found in several works of
Nashe, particularly in the controversy with Harvey;
for evidence of similar Nashean vocabulary in
Hamlet, close in date to *TN*, see Harold Jenkins
(ed.), *Ham.*, 1982, pp. 104–6.

34 **parish top** A large top for public use which
was kept spinning by being lashed with a whip (a
diversion called 'top-scourging'). See *OED* sv *sb*²

34 **What, wench!** Sir Toby may be seeking
Maria's approval for his drinking resolution,
responding to some reproof of his deportment, or
warning her of Sir Andrew's approach.

34 *Castiliano vulgo* There have been several
attempts to explain or emend Sir Toby's tipsy
cosmopolitan phrase. Hanmer's *volto* would yield 'a
Castilian countenance', and argue for sedate and
proper behaviour in Sir Andrew's presence. Others

comes Sir Andrew Agueface.   35

Enter SIR ANDREW [AGUECHEEK]

SIR ANDREW Sir Toby Belch! How now, Sir Toby Belch?
SIR TOBY Sweet Sir Andrew!
SIR ANDREW Bless you, fair shrew.
MARIA And you too, sir.
SIR TOBY Accost, Sir Andrew, accost.   40
SIR ANDREW What's that?
SIR TOBY My niece's chambermaid.
SIR ANDREW Good Mistress Accost, I desire better acquaintance.
MARIA My name is Mary, sir.
SIR ANDREW Good Mistress Mary Accost –   45
SIR TOBY You mistake, knight. 'Accost' is front her, board her, woo
  her, assail her.
SIR ANDREW By my troth, I would not undertake her in this company.
  Is that the meaning of 'accost'?
MARIA Fare you well, gentlemen. [*Leaving*]   50
SIR TOBY And thou let part so, Sir Andrew, would thou mightst never
  draw sword again.
SIR ANDREW And you part so, mistress, I would I might never draw
  sword again. Fair lady, do you think you have fools in hand?
MARIA Sir, I have not you by th'hand.   55

35 SD AGUECHEEK] *Malone; not in* F   43 SH SIR ANDREW] F2 *(An.); Ma.* F   45 Mary Accost –] *Theobald subst.;*
Mary, accost. F   50 SD *Leaving*] *This edn; not in* F

have supposed Sir Toby to be calling for a kind of
wine (*Castiglione voglio*) or thinking of a Spanish
ducat (*Castigliano volgo*). J. F. Killeen (*SQ* 28
(1977), 92–3) argues for its meaning 'the devil' in
vulgar speech and suggests that '*Castiliano*' was
perhaps a cant Italian term.

35 **Agueface** Like Aguecheek, the name accords
with Sir Andrew's physical appearance; he is later
described by Sir Toby as a 'knave, a thin-faced
knave, a gull' (5.1.190–1).

38 **shrew** A generic usage: compare the carol at
2H4 5.3.32–6, which has the line, 'For women are
shrows [contemporary pronunciation of "shrew"],
both short and tall.' Often in Shakespeare the term
designates a 'scold'; for this, see the adverbial use
at 1.5.133.

40 **Accost** A verb, though Sir Andrew persists
in mistaking the word for a proper name; at 46–7
Sir Toby dilates on the word's other meanings.

42 **My...chambermaid** Sir Toby wilfully
misunderstands in order to jest at Maria's expense;

a gentlewoman attending the countess, she is later
to become Lady Belch.

43 SH *SIR ANDREW F's assignment of the SH
to *Ma.* rather than to Sir Andrew (corrected to *An.*
in F2) is perhaps the result of eyeskip. For later
errors in speech headings, see 2.5.29, 33, 69–70 and
3.4.23, 78 nn.

46–7 **front...assail** 'front' = confront, come
alongside (a nautical term); 'board' = to enter a
ship by force (also nautical, but with a sexual innuendo as with 'woo'); 'assail' = attack (a military
term).

48 **undertake** have to do with. Also with a
sexual innuendo.

48 **in this company** i.e. before this audience.
An interruption of dramatic illusion for comic
effect. For another instance of this technique, see
3.4.108–9.

51 **And...so** If you let her leave thus.

54 **in hand** to deal with.

SIR ANDREW Marry, but you shall have, and here's my hand.

MARIA Now, sir, thought is free. I pray you bring your hand to th'buttery-bar and let it drink.

SIR ANDREW Wherefore, sweetheart? What's your metaphor?

MARIA It's dry, sir.   60

SIR ANDREW Why, I think so: I am not such an ass but I can keep my hand dry. But what's your jest?

MARIA A dry jest, sir.

SIR ANDREW Are you full of them?

MARIA Ay, sir, I have them at my fingers' ends; marry, now I let go   65
your hand, I am barren.   *Exit*

SIR TOBY O knight, thou lack'st a cup of canary. [*Hands him a cup*] When did I see thee so put down?

SIR ANDREW Never in your life, I think, unless you see canary put me
down. Methinks sometimes I have no more wit than a Christian   70
or an ordinary man has, but I am a great eater of beef, and I believe
that does harm to my wit.

SIR TOBY No question.

SIR ANDREW And I thought that, I'd forswear it. I'll ride home
tomorrow, Sir Toby.   75

---

67 SD *Hands...cup*] This edn; not in F

---

56 Marry Mild expletive here and elsewhere; originally 'by the Virgin Mary'.

57 thought is free Proverbial; see Tilley T244, who cites Lyly's *Euphues and His England*, II, 60: 'Why then quoth he, doest thou thinke me a fool, thought is free my Lord quoth she.' See also *Temp.* 3.2.123, where it is the last line of a catch or part-song.

57–8 bring...drink The dialogue suggests that Maria is toying with his hand. Compare 'Didst thou not see her paddle with the palm of his hand?' (*Oth.* 2.1.253–4) and 'paddling palms and pinching fingers' (*WT* 1.2.115).

58 buttery-bar The ledge on the top of the buttery hatch on which to rest tankards.

59 your metaphor i.e. of a drinking hand.

60 dry Both 'thirsty' and 'lacking sexual vigour'. To Othello (3.4.36 ff.), Desdemona's 'moist' hand indicates her libidinous nature; to Charmian (*Ant.* 1.2.52–3), an 'oily palm' is a sign of fertility.

61–2 an ass...dry Tilley (F537) cites Shakespeare's usage here as a variation of the proverb 'Fools have wit enough to come in out of the rain.'

63 dry jest caustic joke. Otherwise called a

'privy taunt', a 'dry bob' or a 'dry mock'. Elsewhere Shakespeare plays on the alternative meaning 'insipid', as in the repartee in *LLL* 5.2.371–3 where Rosaline says, 'this I think, / When they are thirsty, fools would fain have drink', to which Berowne replies, 'This jest is dry to me.'

65 at my fingers' ends in readiness and in hand. Proverbial; Tilley F245.

66 barren i.e. bereft both of Sir Andrew's hand, which she drops, and of jests.

67 canary A sweet wine colloquially referred to by the name of the islands where it was produced. Compare Mistress Quickly's observation of Doll's rosy colour: 'i' faith, you have drunk too much canaries' (*2H4* 2.4.26).

68 put down baffled, deflated.

69–70 unless...put me down i.e. unless you should see drink (1) baffle my wits and (2) lay me flat. An ironic assertion in view of his nightly carousing.

71–2 beef...wit Beef was proverbially supposed to make a man stupid (Dent B215.1). Shakespeare's Thersites calls Ajax 'beef-witted' (*Tro.* 2.1.13).

SIR TOBY *Pourquoi*, my dear knight?

SIR ANDREW What is '*pourquoi*'? Do, or not do? I would I had
bestowed that time in the tongues that I have in fencing, dancing,
and bear-baiting. O had I but followed the arts!

SIR TOBY Then hadst thou had an excellent head of hair.   80

SIR ANDREW Why, would that have mended my hair?

SIR TOBY Past question, for thou seest it will not curl by nature.

SIR ANDREW But it becomes me well enough, does't not?

SIR TOBY Excellent; it hangs like flax on a distaff; and I hope to see
a huswife take thee between her legs and spin it off.   85

SIR ANDREW Faith, I'll home tomorrow, Sir Toby; your niece will not
be seen, or if she be, it's four to one, she'll none of me. The count
himself here hard by woos her.

SIR TOBY She'll none o'th'count; she'll not match above her degree,
neither in estate, years, nor wit. I have heard her swear't. Tut,   90
there's life in't, man.

SIR ANDREW I'll stay a month longer. I am a fellow o'th'strangest mind
i'th'world: I delight in masques and revels sometimes altogether.

SIR TOBY Art thou good at these kickshawses, knight?

SIR ANDREW As any man in Illyria, whatsoever he be, under the degree   95
of my betters, and yet I will not compare with an old man.

SIR TOBY What is thy excellence in a galliard, knight?

SIR ANDREW Faith, I can cut a caper.

---

82 curl by] *Theobald;* coole my F   83 me] F2; we F   83 does't] *Rowe;* dost F

76–7 Pourquoi Why. Despite his ignorance of
French at this point, Sir Andrew is able to muster
a few words at 3.1.61. Here and elsewhere
Shakespeare's French has been regularised.

78 tongues languages. There is a pun (picked up
in 82) on 'tongs' (i.e. curling tongs); in Elizabethan
English the two were homophones as indicated by
the rhymes tongues/songs in *Venus and Adonis*
775–7 and tongue/long, *Rape of Lucrece* 1465–8
(NS).

79 the arts learning. Sir Toby thinks 'the arts'
signifies something artificial as opposed to natural.

81 mended improved.

82 *curl by Theobald's reading is preferred to
F's 'coole my', a possible but meaningless
misreading of the copy.

84 distaff A staff for spinning the straight,
straw-coloured fibres of flax.

85 huswife (1) housewife (pronounced
'hussif'); (2) hussy or prostitute (with a suggestion
of venereal disease causing the hair to fall out).

88 hard near.

89 degree rank. Since Olivia is a countess, Sir
Toby's remark would seem to confirm Shakespeare's
original intention of making Orsino a duke – unless
Toby is, as usual, gulling the fatuous Sir Andrew.

91 there's...in't Tilley (L265) records the
expression as proverbial, though Shakespeare's
usage here is the earliest one cited; L269 is perhaps
its origin: 'While there's life there's hope.'

92 strangest most singular.

94 kickshawses (1) elegant trifles, (2) tidbits
served with mutton. The second meaning prompts
Sir Toby's allusion in 99. Compare *2H4* 5.1.27–8:
'a joint of mutton, and any pretty little tiny
kickshaws'. The form 'kickshaws', derived from
French *quelque chose*, is a singular.

95–6 under...old man i.e. provided he is
not above me in social rank (in accord with the
proverb 'Compare not with thy betters', Tilley
C578) and provided he is not more experienced
because of his age.

97 galliard A lively dance in triple time.

98 cut a caper leap.

SIR TOBY And I can cut the mutton to't.

SIR ANDREW And I think I have the back-trick simply as strong as any   100
man in Illyria.

SIR TOBY Wherefore are these things hid? Wherefore have these gifts
a curtain before 'em? Are they like to take dust, like Mistress Mall's
picture? Why dost thou not go to church in a galliard and come
home in a coranto? My very walk should be a jig; I would not so   105
much as make water but in a sink-a-pace. What dost thou mean?
Is it a world to hide virtues in? I did think, by the excellent
constitution of thy leg, it was formed under the star of a galliard.

SIR ANDREW Ay, 'tis strong, and it does indifferent well in a dun-coloured
stock. Shall we set about some revels?   110

SIR TOBY What shall we do else? Were we not born under Taurus?

SIR ANDREW Taurus? That's sides and heart.

SIR TOBY No, sir, it is legs and thighs. Let me see thee caper. Ha,
higher; ha, ha, excellent!

Exeunt

109 dun-coloured] *Collier*² ; dam'd colour'd F ; flame-colour'd *Rowe*³   110 set] *Rowe*³ ; sit F   112 That's] F3 ; That F

99 **cut the mutton** Mutton is a slang term for
a strumpet, a *double entendre* which Sir Andrew
recognises in his response.

100 **back-trick** Backward steps in a dance.
There is also the innuendo of sexual vigour.
Compare Marston, *Certaine Satyres*, 5, 47:

> When strong backt Hercules in one poore night
> With great, great ease, and wondrous delight
> In strength of lust and Venus surquedry
> Rob'd fifty wenches of virginity.

A. Davenport (ed.), *The Poems of Marston*, 1961, p.
251 n., gives instances of this usage in the drama.

103 **curtain** Curtains were used to protect
pictures from dust and sunlight.

103 **Mistress Mall's** Mall is a diminutive of
Mary, perhaps used here generically, perhaps in
reference to Maria.

105 **coranto** A running dance.

106 **sink-a-pace** A dance with five steps, as its
name (cinque pace) indicates, but with a quibble on
'sink' = a receptacle for filth and ordure.

107 **virtues** abilities.

108 **leg…galliard** i.e. determined by the
stars to dance. Compare *Ado* 2.1.335: 'there was a
star danc'd, and under that was I born'.

109 **indifferent** moderately.

109–10 *****dun-coloured stock** mouse-coloured
stocking. This emendation of F's 'dam'd colour'd'
provides a plausible explanation for Compositor B's
misreading 'dunne' or 'donne' as 'dam'd' by the
common confusion of d/e and variable minims.
Though some editors doubt that Sir Andrew would
choose dark-coloured stockings, one may note that
Augustine Phillips, a fellow sharer with Shakespeare
in the company of the Lord Chamberlain's–King's
Men, in 1605 bequeathed to his apprentice his
'mouse colloured Velvit hose'. (The will is printed
in Var. 1821, III, 472.)

111 **Taurus** The twelve signs of the zodiac were
believed to govern distinct areas of the body.
Taurus, the sign of the bull, was generally said to
govern the neck and throat, but Sir Toby's
correction to legs and thighs in 113 accords with his
earlier sexual innuendoes.

1.4 *Enter* VALENTINE, *and* VIOLA *in man's attire*

VALENTINE If the duke continue these favours towards you, Cesario,
you are like to be much advanced; he hath known you but three
days, and already you are no stranger.

VIOLA You either fear his humour, or my negligence, that you call in
question the continuance of his love. Is he inconstant, sir, in his   5
favours?

VALENTINE No, believe me.

VIOLA I thank you. Here comes the count.

Enter DUKE [ORSINO], CURIO, *and Attendants*

ORSINO Who saw Cesario, ho?

VIOLA On your attendance, my lord, here.   10

ORSINO [*To Curio and Attendants*] Stand you awhile aloof. Cesario,
Thou know'st no less but all: I have unclasped
To thee the book even of my secret soul.
Therefore, good youth, address thy gait unto her,
Be not denied access; stand at her doors,   15
And tell them there thy fixèd foot shall grow
Till thou have audience.

VIOLA   Sure, my noble lord,
If she be so abandoned to her sorrow
As it is spoke, she never will admit me.

ORSINO Be clamorous, and leap all civil bounds,   20
Rather than make unprofited return.

VIOLA Say I do speak with her, my lord, what then?

ORSINO O then unfold the passion of my love,
Surprise her with discourse of my dear faith;

Act 1, Scene 4   1.4] *Scena Quarta.* F   8 SD] *Follows 7 in* F   11 SD *To...Attendants*] Mahood; *not in* F

Act 1, Scene 4
   Location The duke's palace (Cam.).
   2–3 but three days For an account of the
double-time scheme, see p. 9 above, n. 2.
   4 his humour...negligence his volatility or
my neglect of duty.
   10 On your attendance Ready and waiting to
do service.
   11 aloof aside. So that Curio and attendants will
not hear his directives to Viola-Cesario.
   14 address thy gait go. Another instance of
Orsino's mannered style.

   15 access Accented on the second syllable.
   16 them i.e. servants, not doors; 'there' serves
as a fulcrum, referring to those at the doors and to
the place.
   20 leap...bounds exceed the limits of proper
behaviour. An indecorum paralleling that of Sir
Toby.
   21 unprofited return without advantage (to his
suit).
   24 Surprise her Take her (heart) by force. A
military image (Ard.).
   24 dear heartfelt.

It shall become thee well to act my woes: 25
She will attend it better in thy youth
Than in a nuncio's of more grave aspect.

VIOLA I think not so, my lord.

ORSINO   Dear lad, believe it;
For they shall yet belie thy happy years
That say thou art a man: Diana's lip   30
Is not more smooth and rubious; thy small pipe
Is as the maiden's organ, shrill and sound,
And all is semblative a woman's part.
I know thy constellation is right apt
For this affair. Some four or five attend him –   35
All if you will, for I myself am best
When least in company. Prosper well in this,
And thou shalt live as freely as thy lord
To call his fortunes thine.

VIOLA   I'll do my best
To woo your lady. [*Aside*] Yet a barful strife!   40
Whoe'er I woo, myself would be his wife.

                                              Exeunt

1.5 *Enter* MARIA *and* CLOWN [FESTE]

MARIA Nay, either tell me where thou hast been, or I will not open my
    lips so wide as a bristle may enter in way of thy excuse. My lady
    will hang thee for thy absence.

25 **become** suit.
26 **attend** pay attention to.
27 **nuncio's...aspect** messenger of more dignified countenance; 'aspect' is accented on the
second syllable.
29 **yet** as yet.
31 **rubious** ruby-coloured. A Shakespearean
coinage (Onions).
31–2 **small pipe...sound** i.e. Cesario has a
piping voice, like that of a eunuch or a virgin (as
in *Cor.* 3.2.114), still clear and uncracked. Compare
also *Wiv.* 1.1.48, where Anne Page (not yet
seventeen) is said to speak 'small like a woman'.
33 **semblative** like. Properly 'semblative to'. A
Shakespearean coinage (Onions).

33 **part** (1) nature, (2) role. The double meaning
reflects both the dramatic and the feigned theatrical
situation: a boy playing the part of a girl who then
disguises herself as a boy and so serves as a fitting
surrogate wooer of Olivia.
34 **constellation** The determining configuration
of the stars at a nativity.
38 **freely** readily.
40 **barful strife** a striving full of obstacles. This
striving is specified in the next line as singular.

Act 1, Scene 5
    Location Olivia's house (Rowe).

FESTE Let her hang me: he that is well hanged in this world needs to
fear no colours. 5

MARIA Make that good.

FESTE He shall see none to fear.

MARIA A good lenten answer. I can tell thee where that saying was born,
of 'I fear no colours.'

FESTE Where, good Mistress Mary? 10

MARIA In the wars, and that may you be bold to say in your foolery.

FESTE Well, God give them wisdom that have it; and those that are
fools, let them use their talents.

MARIA Yet you will be hanged for being so long absent – or to be turned
away: is not that as good as a hanging to you? 15

FESTE Many a good hanging prevents a bad marriage; and for turning
away, let summer bear it out.

MARIA You are resolute then?

FESTE Not so neither, but I am resolved on two points –

MARIA That if one break, the other will hold, or if both break, your 20
gaskins fall.

---

4 SH FESTE] F *reads* / *Clo.* / *throughout*   14 absent – or] *This edn;* absent, or F   19 points –] *NS;* points F

---

5 **fear no colours** have no fear of an enemy's
flag. Proverbial (Tilley C520). Feste quibbles on
'colours' as 'flags' and as 'false pretexts' (as in
'colorable colors', *LLL* 4.2.149–50) and 'collars',
the hangman's nooses. The same set of puns occurs
in *2H4* 5.5.85–8: '*Fal.* This that you heard was but
a color [false pretext]. *Shal.* A color that I fear you
will die in, Sir John. *Fal.* Fear no colors...'
  6 **Make that good** Prove it.
  8 **lenten** less than sufficient, as in the season for
fasting. Compare the reference to 'lenten entertainment' in *Ham.* 1363 (2.2.316).
  8–9 **saying...colours** Colloquial transposition
'that saying of "I fear no colours" was born'.
  11 **In the wars** From the literal meaning of the
proverb.
  11 **that...bold to say** 'say with confidence', as
opposed to the quibbling on 'false pretexts' and
'hangman's nooses'.
  12 **God give...have it** Echoing the Biblical
statement, 'For unto everie man that hathe, it shal
be given' (Matt. 25.29, and elsewhere). This
chapter of St Matthew, which includes the parable
of the talents, may have prompted Feste's pun in
the next line.
  13 **talents** natural gifts of a born fool (as against
the gifts that a professional fool like Feste exploits).
There is an orthographic pun on 'talons' = claws,

which are equally natural. A similar pun occurs in
LLL 4.2.63–4: 'If a talent be a claw, look how he
claws him with a talent.'
  14–15 **to be turned away** to be dismissed, with
a hint of 'turned off', hanged (*OED* Turn *v* 73d).
Abbott (416) justifies the change of construction
with 'to' on grounds of clarity.
  16 **Many...marriage** Shakespeare may be
recalling his use in *MV* 2.9.82–3 of 'The ancient
saying... / Hanging and wiving goes by destiny'
(Tilley W232).
  17 **bear it out** make it endurable. For the
significance of Feste's remark in relation to the
projected season of the play's action see p. 4
above.
  19 **points** (1) matters, (2) laces that tied the
breeches (upperstocks) to the doublet. Punctuation
is lacking in F, apparently because of the scant
margin.
  20 **the other will hold** With a glance perhaps at the proverb (Tilley R119), 'Good riding
at two anchors...for if the one fall, the other may
hold.'
  21 **gaskins** Wide breeches reaching to the knee.
They were usually loose, but some were inflated by
padding (bombasted), a pair made for the court fool
in 1575 requiring six yards of material (Linthicum,
p. 208 and n.).

FESTE Apt, in good faith, very apt. Well, go thy way; if Sir Toby would
leave drinking, thou wert as witty a piece of Eve's flesh as any in
Illyria.

MARIA Peace, you rogue, no more o'that; here comes my lady: make   25
your excuse wisely, you were best.   [*Exit*]

              Enter LADY OLIVIA [*attended,*] *with* MALVOLIO

FESTE Wit, and't be thy will, put me into good fooling! Those wits that
think they have thee do very oft prove fools, and I that am sure I
lack thee may pass for a wise man. For what says Quinapalus?
'Better a witty fool than a foolish wit' – God bless thee, lady.   30

OLIVIA Take the fool away.

FESTE Do you not hear, fellows? Take away the lady.

OLIVIA Go to, y'are a dry fool: I'll no more of you; besides, you grow
dishonest.

FESTE Two faults, madonna, that drink and good counsel will amend: 35
for give the dry fool drink, then is the fool not dry; bid the dishonest
man mend himself; if he mend, he is no longer dishonest; if he
cannot, let the botcher mend him. Anything that's mended is but
patched: virtue that transgresses is but patched with sin, and sin
that amends is but patched with virtue. If that this simple syllogism   40
will serve, so; if it will not, what remedy? As there is no true cuckold

---

26 SD.1 *Exit*] *Pope; not in* F   26 SD.2 OLIVIA *attended,*] *Capell; Olivia,* F   30 wit' –] *This edn; wit.* F

22–4 if...Illyria Feste's seeming *non sequitur*
assumes the validity of the Porter's observation in
Mac. 2.3.30–2: 'Therefore much drink may be said
to be an equivocator with lechery.' Except for the
conditional about Sir Toby's drinking, he implies
that Maria and Sir Toby would make a good match
and sexual partnership.

26 SD.2 As a countess, Olivia should be well
attended on her first entrance, as Feste's reference
to 'fellows' (32) and 'gentlemen' (59) indicates.

27 Wit...will In invoking 'Wit, if it be thy will'
to give him 'good fooling', Feste hopes by that
means (1) to chide his mistress for her folly in
grieving and (2) to placate her for his 'dishonest'
(34) absence. This is perhaps to be accounted for
by his presence at Orsino's palace: Viola sees him
there and he too has seen her (3.1.31, 34–5); by Act
5, Orsino also acknowledges that he knows him well
(8).

27–8 Those...fools Compare the proverb
(Tilley C582), 'He that is wise in his own conceit
is a fool', which echoes Prov. 26.5.

29 Quinapalus An example of Feste's mock
learning, as in 2.3.20–1.

31 Take...away Olivia's order indicates that
she has overheard his barbed innuendoes. If not
quite the 'bitter fool' of *Lear*, Feste is capable of
many sharp passes, as Cesario remarks at 3.1.36; see
also his mocking of Malvolio in 4.2 and at
5.1.349–50.

33 Go to Here and elsewhere a term of reproof
or impatience.

33 dry See 1.3.63 n.

34 dishonest dishonourable (in absenting
himself).

35 madonna my lady. Italian *mia donna*: Feste's
characteristic manner of addressing Olivia.

35–8 amend...mend him Feste plays on the
moral sense 'to make better' and on the material
sense 'to make useful again'; 'mend' is simply an
aphetic form of 'amend'. For other examples in *TN*
of Shakespeare's use of the stem of a word in a
different sense from the word itself, see 5.1.240 and
265 and nn.

38 botcher mender of old clothes.

41 so As in *TGV* 2.1.131: 'And if it please you,
so; if not, why, so.'

41–2 As...calamity This perhaps means that

but calamity, so beauty's a flower. The lady bade take away the fool;
therefore I say again, take her away.

OLIVIA Sir, I bade them take away you.

FESTE Misprision in the highest degree! Lady, *cucullus non facit* 45
monachum: that's as much to say as I wear not motley in my brain.
Good madonna, give me leave to prove you a fool.

OLIVIA Can you do it?

FESTE Dexteriously, good madonna.

OLIVIA Make your proof. 50

FESTE I must catechise you for it, madonna. Good my mouse of virtue,
answer me.

OLIVIA Well, sir, for want of other idleness, I'll bide your proof.

FESTE Good madonna, why mourn'st thou?

OLIVIA Good fool, for my brother's death. 55

FESTE I think his soul is in hell, madonna.

OLIVIA I know his soul is in heaven, fool.

FESTE The more fool, madonna, to mourn for your brother's soul being
in heaven. Take away the fool, gentlemen.

OLIVIA What think you of this fool, Malvolio? Doth he not mend? 60

MALVOLIO Yes, and shall do, till the pangs of death shake him;
infirmity, that decays the wise, doth ever make the better fool.

FESTE God send you, sir, a speedy infirmity, for the better increasing
your folly! Sir Toby will be sworn that I am no fox, but he will
not pass his word for twopence that you are no fool. 65

---

58 soul being] *Rowe;* soul, being F

whereas the marital state of a husband may
alter – for the worse – to that of a cuckold, a
calamitous state of affairs necessarily alters – for the
better; the first is potential; the second inevitable
and hence 'true'.

42–3 beauty's...take her away Feste's comment that youthful beauty fades, taken together
with his comment that misfortune can change to its
opposite, draws attention to Olivia's folly of
grieving for seven years apart from the 'sight / And
company of men'.

45 Misprision Error (Shakespeare's most frequent usage) but also a legal term for a
misdemeanour; 'in the highest degree' emphasises
the gravity of the offence.

45–6 cucullus...monachum 'The hood makes
not the monk.' Proverbial (Tilley H586).

46 motley The particoloured costume worn by
fools; hence the frequency of their being called
'Patch', as in the string of epithets in *Err.* 3.1.32:
'Mome, malt-horse, capon, coxcomb, idiot, patch!'

49 Dexteriously An Elizabethan form, not a
malapropism; the only appearance of the adverbial
form in Shakespeare.

51 Good...virtue 'Good' used as a vocative,
as in 'good my lord'; 'mouse', a term of
endearment – but Feste's modifying phrase may
glance at Olivia's small virtue of prolonged
mourning. In catechising her, Feste anticipates his
later impersonation of Sir Topas the curate.

53 idleness pastime.

60 mend improve (in his fooling). Olivia's
laughter here will account for Malvolio's marvelling
at the 'delight' (67) she takes in Feste's fooling.

62 infirmity...fool Perhaps a glance at William
Wager's interlude (entered in *SR* in 1569) *The
Longer Thou Livest, the More Fool Thou Art*, where
the main character, Moros, is an irredeemable fool.

65 pass give.

OLIVIA How say you to that, Malvolio?

MALVOLIO I marvel your ladyship takes delight in such a barren rascal.
I saw him put down the other day with an ordinary fool that has
no more brain than a stone. Look you now, he's out of his guard
already. Unless you laugh and minister occasion to him, he is   70
gagged. I protest I take these wise men that crow so at these set
kind of fools no better than the fools' zanies.

OLIVIA O you are sick of self-love, Malvolio, and taste with a
distempered appetite. To be generous, guiltless, and of free
disposition is to take those things for bird-bolts that you deem   75
cannon bullets. There is no slander in an allowed fool though he
do nothing but rail; nor no railing in a known discreet man though
he do nothing but reprove.

FESTE Now Mercury endue thee with leasing, for thou speak'st well
of fools!   80

Enter MARIA

MARIA Madam, there is at the gate a young gentleman much desires
to speak with you.

OLIVIA From the Count Orsino, is it?

MARIA I know not, madam; 'tis a fair young man and well attended.

OLIVIA Who of my people hold him in delay?   85

MARIA Sir Toby, madam, your kinsman.

68–9 with an ordinary…stone i.e. by one
who was born a fool and who entertained in an
ordinary, or tavern. An apparent topical allusion:
Stone was the name of a tavern-fool known for his
caustic remarks and frequently referred to in
popular literature; Nashe, for example, comments
that *aqua fortis*, or nitric acid, has almost spoiled
his nose (*Works*, III, 25). Stone is mentioned in Ben
Jonson's *Volpone*; two of his barbed witticisms are
recorded in Jonson, *Works*, ed. C. H. Herford and
P. and E. Simpson, 11 vols., 1925–52, IX, 701.

69 out of his guard used up his tricks of
defence. A term in fencing.

71 wise men…crow i.e. sane persons who
laugh uproariously. A 'palpable hit' in respect to his
mistress.

71–2 set kind artificial sort (as opposed to those
who are 'born fools').

72 zanies Subordinates who mimicked a professional clown (from Italian *zanni*, a character in the
commedia dell'arte).

73 of because of; 'self-love' is Malvolio's
'humour'.

74 distempered unwholesome, morbid.

74–5 free disposition generous temper or
character.

75 bird-bolts Blunt arrows used for shooting
small birds, perhaps with a glance at the proverb 'A
fool's bolt is soon shot' (Tilley F515). Olivia's
diction anticipates other allusions to the art of
bird-catching, used generally in reference to
Malvolio (2.5.39, 2.5.69, 4.2.45–6), and so gives
point to his later triumphant vaunt about Olivia, 'I
have limed her' (3.4.66).

76 allowed licensed.

77–8 railing…reprove A 'palpable hit' in
respect to her steward, whose duty it was to
'reprove' in civil fashion. See pp. 12–13 above.

79 Mercury…leasing let Mercury, the god of
deception, endow you with the art of lying. The
word 'leasing' appears only one other time in
Shakespeare – *Cor.* 5.2.22.

OLIVIA Fetch him off, I pray you; he speaks nothing but madman. Fie
on him.

[Exit Maria]

Go you, Malvolio. If it be a suit from the count, I am sick, or not
at home – what you will to dismiss it.   90

Exit Malvolio

Now you see, sir, how your fooling grows old, and people dislike
it.

FESTE Thou hast spoke for us, madonna, as if thy eldest son should be
a fool: whose skull Jove cram with brains, for – here he comes –

Enter SIR TOBY *[staggering]*

one of thy kin has a most weak *pia mater*.   95

OLIVIA By mine honour, half drunk! What is he at the gate, cousin?

SIR TOBY A gentleman.

OLIVIA A gentleman? What gentleman?

SIR TOBY 'Tis a gentleman here – *[Hiccuping]* a plague o'these pickle
herring! How now, sot?   100

FESTE Good Sir Toby –

OLIVIA Cousin, cousin, how have you come so early by this lethargy?

SIR TOBY Lechery! I defy lechery. There's one at the gate.

OLIVIA Ay, marry, what is he?

SIR TOBY Let him be the devil and he will, I care not: give me faith,   105
say I. Well, it's all one.   *Exit*

OLIVIA What's a drunken man like, fool?

FESTE Like a drowned man, a fool, and a madman: one draught above

---

88 SD *Exit Maria*] *Capell; not in* F   94 for – …comes –] *Cam.; for…comes.* F   94 SD *staggering*] *This edn; not in* F
99 here – *[Hiccuping.]*] *Rann subst.; heere,* F   101 Toby –] *This edn; Toby.* F

---

87 speaks…madman Analogues to this construction are: 'She speaks poniards', *Ado* 2.1.247; 'I
will speak daggers', *Ham.* 2267 (3.2.396); and 'He
speaks plain cannon-fire, and smoke, and bounce',
John 2.1.462 (Furness).

90 what you will For the significance of this
catch-phrase, see p. 4 above.

91 old stale.

93–4 Thou hast spoke…fool i.e. 'wisely', in
accord with the proverb 'A wise man commonly has
a fool to his heir' (Tilley M421). Commentators
have misunderstood Feste's remark, interpreting it
(in the words of one of them) as 'at best a left-handed
compliment'; see Jenkins, p. 32.

95 pia mater brain. Physiologically, its covering
membrane (metonymy).

100 sot Both 'fool' and 'drunkard'. Armin, who
is generally believed to have played Feste, uses the
double meaning in his *Foole upon Foole or Six Sortes
of Sottes* (1600) (NS).

102 lethargy stupor.

104 what is he of what quality or rank is he. As
in 1.2.35.

105 give me faith i.e. as opposed to good
works as a means of salvation – a source of
theological debate (NS).

106 it's all one it doesn't matter. For the
repeated use of this catch-phrase, see p. 5 above
and 5.1.181 and 351 nn.

108–9 above heat beyond bodily warmth. Compare *Tim.* 1.1.261: 'Ay to see meat fill knaves, and
wine heat fools'.

heat makes him a fool, the second mads him, and a third drowns
him.   110

OLIVIA Go thou and seek the crowner, and let him sit o'my coz, for
he's in the third degree of drink: he's drowned. Go look after him.

FESTE He is but mad yet, madonna, and the fool shall look to the
madman.   [*Exit*]

Enter MALVOLIO

MALVOLIO Madam, yond young fellow swears he will speak with you.   115
I told him you were sick; he takes on him to understand so much
and therefore comes to speak with you. I told him you were asleep;
he seems to have a foreknowledge of that too, and therefore comes
to speak with you. What is to be said to him, lady? He's fortified
against any denial.   120

OLIVIA Tell him he shall not speak with me.

MALVOLIO H'as been told so; and he says he'll stand at your door like
a sheriff's post, and be the supporter to a bench, but he'll speak
with you.

OLIVIA What kind o'man is he?   125

MALVOLIO Why, of mankind.

OLIVIA What manner of man?

MALVOLIO Of very ill manner: he'll speak with you, will you or no.

OLIVIA Of what personage and years is he?

MALVOLIO Not yet old enough for a man, nor young enough for a boy: 130
as a squash is before 'tis a peascod, or a codling when 'tis almost
an apple. 'Tis with him in standing water, between boy and man.
He is very well-favoured and he speaks very shrewishly. One would
think his mother's milk were scarce out of him.

OLIVIA Let him approach. Call in my gentlewoman.   135

MALVOLIO Gentlewoman, my lady calls.   *Exit*

114 SD *Exit*] *Rowe; not in* F   122 H'as] *Staunton;* Ha's F

111 **crowner** Old form of 'coroner'; not a
vulgarism.
111 **sit o'** hold an inquest on.
117 **therefore** for that reason.
118 **foreknowledge** prescience. A theological
term; used only this once by Shakespeare.
122 **H'as** Staunton's alteration of F's 'ha's' is in
accord with F at 5.1.164 and with Rowe's alteration
of F's 'has' at 5.1.181 and 269, thus retaining the
colloquial flavour of the speeches that a modernisa-
tion to 'he's' largely dissipates.
123 **sheriff's post** Posts were set before the

houses of mayors and sheriffs and were often
elaborately carved and coloured (Halliwell, cited in
Furness).
123 **supporter** prop.
131 **squash** unripe peapod (peascod).
131 **codling** unripe apple.
132 **in standing water** at the turn of the tide.
133 **well-favoured** good-looking.
133 **shrewishly** i.e. like a scold.
133–4 **One…him** Listed in Tilley (M1204) as
proverbial, but the only example antedating this
instance comes from a manuscript source.

Enter MARIA

OLIVIA Give me my veil; come throw it o'er my face.
We'll once more hear Orsino's embassy.

Enter VIOLA

VIOLA The honourable lady of the house, which is she?

OLIVIA Speak to me; I shall answer for her. Your will? 140

VIOLA Most radiant, exquisite, and unmatchable beauty – I pray you
tell me if this be the lady of the house, for I never saw her. I would
be loath to cast away my speech: for besides that it is excellently
well penned, I have taken great pains to con it. Good beauties, let
me sustain no scorn; I am very comptible, even to the least sinister 145
usage.

OLIVIA Whence came you, sir?

VIOLA I can say little more than I have studied, and that question's out
of my part. Good gentle one, give me modest assurance if you be
the lady of the house, that I may proceed in my speech. 150

OLIVIA Are you a comedian?

VIOLA No, my profound heart; and yet, by the very fangs of malice,
I swear, I am not that I play. Are you the lady of the house?

OLIVIA If I do not usurp myself, I am.

VIOLA Most certain, if you are she, you do usurp yourself: for what is 155
yours to bestow is not yours to reserve. But this is from my
commission. I will on with my speech in your praise, and then show
you the heart of my message.

OLIVIA Come to what is important in't: I forgive you the praise.

VIOLA Alas, I took great pains to study it, and 'tis poetical. 160

---

138 SD VIOLA] F2; *Uiolenta.* F   141 beauty –] *Rowe;* beautie. F   152–3] yet, by…fangs of malice, I swear, I am] *This edn;* yet (by…phangs of malice, I sweare) I am F

---

143 cast…speech waste my efforts (on the wrong auditor, e.g. Maria).

144 con it learn it by heart.

145 sustain no scorn suffer no derision.

145 comptible sensitive. A nonce use.

145 sinister wrong.

149 modest satisfactory.

151 comedian stage player. This picks up Cesario's own theatrical diction.

152 my profound heart my wise dear one; 'heart' or 'my heart' is a familiar term of affection, as in Falstaff's address to Prince Hal, 'I speak to thee, my heart' (*2H4* 5.5.46). Cesario is still being saucy.

152–3 very fangs…play i.e. I swear, by the very teeth of spite, I am not what I impersonate (as the audience well knows). Note that 'I swear' can serve as a fulcrum, governing both the prepositional phrase and 'I am not'. See 1.4.16 for a similar construction.

154 usurp myself wrongfully possess myself.

155–6 usurp…reserve i.e. by acting wrongly in not giving yourself to a husband.

156–7 from my commission outside my mandate.

159 important significant.

159 forgive you excuse you from.

OLIVIA It is the more like to be feigned; I pray you keep it in. I heard
you were saucy at my gates, and allowed your approach rather to
wonder at you than to hear you. If you be not mad, be gone; if
you have reason, be brief. 'Tis not that time of moon with me to
make one in so skipping a dialogue.   165

MARIA Will you hoist sail, sir? Here lies your way.

VIOLA No, good swabber, I am to hull here a little longer. Some
mollification for your giant, sweet lady! Tell me your mind, I am
a messenger.

OLIVIA Sure you have some hideous matter to deliver, when the   170
courtesy of it is so fearful. Speak your office.

VIOLA It alone concerns your ear. I bring no overture of war, no
taxation of homage; I hold the olive in my hand; my words are as
full of peace as matter.

OLIVIA Yet you began rudely. What are you? What would you?   175

VIOLA The rudeness that hath appeared in me I learned from my
entertainment. What I am, and what I would, are as secret as
maidenhead: to your ears, divinity; to any other's, profanation.

OLIVIA Give us the place alone; we will hear this divinity.

                    [*Exeunt Maria and Attendants*]
Now, sir, what is your text?   180

VIOLA Most sweet lady –

---

179 SD *Exeunt Maria and Attendants*] Capell; *not in* F   181 lady –] Theobald subst.; Ladie. F

---

161 feigned fictive because 'poetical', in contrast to the deeds recorded in historical writings. See Tilley P28: 'Painters (Travelers) and poets have leave to lie.'

163 not mad i.e. not altogether mad (though the negative has puzzled editors). Elsewhere Shakespeare uses intensives to qualify the degree of madness: 'stark mad' (*Err.* 2.1.59); (*Shr.* 1.1.69; *WT* 3.2.183; and 'very mad, exceeding mad' (*H8* 1.4.28).

164–5 'Tis…dialogue i.e. I am not so under the influence of the moon – therefore lunatic – as to take part in such a wanton or flighty conversation. Compare the same metaphorical reference to love in *LLL* 5.2.760–1: 'love… / All wanton as a child, skipping and vain'.

166 Here…way Proverbial (Tilley D556).

167 swabber cleaner of decks.

167 hull lie adrift. Cesario continues the nautical diction introduced by Maria's 'hoist sail'.

167–8 Some mollification…giant Somewhat appease your huge protectress. A mocking allusion

to Maria's diminutive size, later twice commented on by Sir Toby – 2.5.11 and 3.2.52.

168 mind message (Schmidt). As in *TGV* 1.1.136–40: 'Sir, I could perceive nothing at all from her; no, not so much as a ducat for delivering your letter: and being so hard to me that brought your mind, I fear she'll prove as hard to you in telling your mind.' Many editors adopt Warburton's division of the Folio text by giving 'I am a messenger' to Olivia, but 'mind' as 'message' appropriately introduces Viola's identification of herself as a 'messenger'.

170–1 when…fearful i.e. when the show of politeness (on your part) induces apprehension. A reference back to the report of Cesario's 'ill manner' in 133–4.

171 Speak…office Report what you are charged to report.

173 taxation of homage demand for tribute.

177 entertainment reception.

178 maidenhead virginity.

178 divinity sacred doctrine.

OLIVIA A comfortable doctrine, and much may be said of it. Where lies
your text?

VIOLA In Orsino's bosom.

OLIVIA In his bosom? In what chapter of his bosom?   185

VIOLA To answer by the method, in the first of his heart.

OLIVIA O I have read it. It is heresy. Have you no more to say?

VIOLA Good madam, let me see your face.

OLIVIA Have you any commission from your lord to negotiate with my
face? You are now out of your text, but we will draw the curtain   190
and show you the picture. [*Unveiling*] Look you, sir, such a one I
was this present. Is't not well done?

VIOLA Excellently done, if God did all.

OLIVIA 'Tis in grain, sir; 'twill endure wind and weather.

VIOLA 'Tis beauty truly blent, whose red and white   195
    Nature's own sweet and cunning hand laid on.
    Lady, you are the cruell'st she alive,
    If you will lead these graces to the grave,
    And leave the world no copy.

OLIVIA O sir, I will not be so hard-hearted: I will give out divers   200
schedules of my beauty. It shall be inventoried and every particle
and utensil labelled to my will, as, *item*, two lips, indifferent red;
item, two grey eyes, with lids to them; *item*, one neck, one chin,
and so forth. Were you sent hither to 'praise me?

VIOLA I see you what you are. You are too proud;   205

---

191 SD *Unveiling*] Rowe; not in F

182–7 Much as Feste does at 51 ff., Olivia here
'catechises' Viola.

182 **comfortable** full of comfort, like a religious
text. In this interchange, the diction conforms to
that of the secular religion of love.

186 **by the method** (1) according to the stylistic
form of her catechism, (2) according to its contents.
Compare *1H6* 3.1.12–13: 'I...am not able /
Verbatim to rehearse the method of my pen.'

190 **out of** departing from.

190–1 **draw...picture** Compare Pandarus's
words in *Tro.* 3.2.46–7: 'Come, draw this curtain,
and let's see your picture.'

192 **this present** i.e. just now, this present time.
Not used before Shakespeare (Onions).

193 **God...all** Perhaps with a wry suggestion of
the proverb 'God has done his part' (Tilley G188).

194 **in grain** fast-dyed.

195 **blent** blended.

197 **she** Compare Orlando's verses in *AYLI*

3.2.9–10: 'carve on every tree / The fair, the chaste,
and unexpressive she'.

198–9 **If...copy** Compare *Rom.* 1.1.219–20:
'For beauty starv'd with her [Rosaline's] severity /
Cuts beauty off from all posterity.' The first
fourteen *Sonnets* also treat this theme.

201 **schedules** detailed listings. A deliberate
wresting of 'copy' from 'posterity' back to its literal
meaning.

201–2 **particle...will** every particular and
every furnishing added as a codicil to my will.

202 *item* Latin, 'likewise'; used in
enumerations.

202 **indifferent** somewhat.

204 **'praise** appraise. This usage (*OED* v[1])
continued until at least 1886, perhaps the result of
its being treated as an apheitic form of 'appraise',
a form which Shakespeare never uses. In 159 Olivia
excused Cesario from any charge to extol or praise
her.

But if you were the devil, you are fair!
My lord and master loves you. O such love
Could be but recompensed, though you were crowned
The nonpareil of beauty.

OLIVIA   How does he love me?

VIOLA With adorations, fertile tears,   210
With groans that thunder love, with sighs of fire.

OLIVIA Your lord does know my mind. I cannot love him.
Yet I suppose him virtuous, know him noble,
Of great estate, of fresh and stainless youth;
In voices well divulged, free, learned, and valiant,   215
And in dimension, and the shape of nature,
A gracious person. But yet I cannot love him.
He might have took his answer long ago.

VIOLA If I did love you in my master's flame,
With such a suff'ring, such a deadly life,   220
In your denial I would find no sense;
I would not understand it.

OLIVIA   Why, what would you?

VIOLA Make me a willow cabin at your gate,
And call upon my soul within the house;
Write loyal cantons of contemnèd love,   225
And sing them loud even in the dead of night;
Hallow your name to the reverberate hills,
And make the babbling gossip of the air
Cry out 'Olivia!' O you should not rest
Between the elements of air and earth   230

206 **if...devil** even if you were as proud as
Lucifer. See Dent L572 for a reference antedating
those in Tilley.

208–9 **be but recompensed...beauty** be no
more than requited even if you were crowned the
paragon of beauty.

210 **fertile** abundant.

215 **In...free** Publicly proclaimed as generous.

216 **dimension...nature** form and physical
appearance.

217 **A gracious** An attractive.

219 **flame** Figuratively, 'passion'.

220 **deadly life** death-like life. An oxymoron
characteristic of love poetry.

223 **willow cabin** Hut of willows as a symbol of
unrequited love. Compare *Ado* 2.1.217–19: 'I
off'red him my company to a willow-tree...to make
him a garland, as being forsaken...'

224 **my soul** i.e. Olivia.

225 **loyal...love** duteous songs of unrequited
love; 'canton', a variant form of 'canto', is used
only this once by Shakespeare.

227 **Hallow** Shout, halloo. The F spelling,
retained here, also suggests the meaning 'conse-
crate' as in *Sonnets* 108.8: 'Even as when first I
hallowed thy fair name'.

227 **reverberate** reverberating. Philip Brockbank (ed.), *Cor.*, 1976, compares it with the use of
'participate' for 'participating' in *Cor.* 1.1.102.

228 **babbling...air** The prating woman of the
air is the nymph Echo who wasted away for love of
Narcissus until nothing was left but her voice.

229 **rest** (1) remain, (2) have peace of mind.

230 **Between...earth** i.e. anywhere.

But you should pity me!

OLIVIA   You might do much.
What is your parentage?

VIOLA Above my fortunes, yet my state is well:
I am a gentleman.

OLIVIA   Get you to your lord.
I cannot love him. Let him send no more –   235
Unless (perchance) you come to me again,
To tell me how he takes it. Fare you well.
I thank you for your pains. Spend this for me.

VIOLA I am no fee'd post, lady; keep your purse;
My master, not myself, lacks recompense.   240
Love make his heart of flint that you shall love,
And let your fervour like my master's be
Placed in contempt. Farewell, fair cruelty.   *Exit*

OLIVIA 'What is your parentage?'
'Above my fortunes, yet my state is well: 245
I am a gentleman.' I'll be sworn thou art;
Thy tongue, thy face, thy limbs, actions, and spirit
Do give thee five-fold blazon. Not too fast! Soft, soft!
Unless the master were the man – How now?
Even so quickly may one catch the plague?   250
Methinks I feel this youth's perfections
With an invisible and subtle stealth
To creep in at mine eyes. Well, let it be.
What ho, Malvolio!

Enter MALVOLIO

MALVOLIO   Here, madam, at your service.
OLIVIA Run after that same peevish messenger,

249 man –] man...*NS*; man. F   255

233 state social condition.
239 fee'd post A messenger who expects
payment.
241 heart of flint Proverbial (Tilley H311).
241 that whom.
246 thou art While soliloquising, Olivia thinks
of Cesario in the familiar second person.
248 five-fold blazon A heraldic coat-of-arms,
proclaimed here five times over in terms of beauty
of speech, of face, of body, of demeanour, of spirit.

248 Soft, soft Here and elsewhere = 'Slowly,
slowly'.
249 Unless...man Unless the servant were the
master.
253 To...eyes The standard doctrine was that
love entered through the eyes. Prospero comments
on the instant enamourment of Miranda and
Ferdinand: 'At the first sight / They have chang'd
eyes' (*Temp.* 1.2.441–2).
255 peevish perverse.

The county's man. He left this ring behind him,
Would I, or not. Tell him, I'll none of it.
Desire him not to flatter with his lord,
Nor hold him up with hopes; I am not for him.
If that the youth will come this way tomorrow,   260
I'll give him reasons for't. Hie thee, Malvolio!
MALVOLIO Madam, I will.   *Exit*
OLIVIA I do I know not what, and fear to find
Mine eye too great a flatterer for my mind.
Fate, show thy force; ourselves we do not owe.   265
What is decreed must be; and be this so.   [*Exit*]

2.1 *Enter* ANTONIO *and* SEBASTIAN

ANTONIO Will you stay no longer? Nor will you not that I go with you?
SEBASTIAN By your patience, no. My stars shine darkly over me; the
malignancy of my fate might perhaps distemper yours; therefore
I shall crave of you your leave that I may bear my evils alone. It
were a bad recompense for your love to lay any of them on you.   5
ANTONIO Let me know of you whither you are bound.
SEBASTIAN No, sooth, sir. My determinate voyage is mere extravagancy.
But I perceive in you so excellent a touch of modesty that you will
not extort from me what I am willing to keep in. Therefore it
charges me in manners the rather to express myself. You must know 10

---

256 county's] *Capell;* Countes F   266 SD *Exit*] *Rowe; Finis, Actus primus.* F   Act 2, Scene 1 2.1] *Actus Secundus, Scæna prima.* F

256 county's count's. Capell's emendation keeps the metrical pattern. For the alternation with 'duke', see 1.1.0 SD n.
258 flatter with encourage.
261 Hie thee Hasten.
264 My quick emotional response has subdued my judgement.
265 owe own.

Act 2, Scene 1
Location The sea coast (Capell).
1 Nor will...you? Do you not wish me to go with you? The use of a double negative is common in the period; for an example of a triple negative, see 3.1.144 and n.
3 malignancy...fate my malevolent destiny. An astrological phrase in accord with 2 but also suggesting disease in accord with the verb 'dis-

temper' = infect. Sebastian's negative view here is countered by Antonio's invoking the 'gentleness' of the gods at 32. The influence of the heavens (here, the stars) ties in with the motifs of time, fate and fortune which run throughout the play.
4 evils ills.
7 sooth indeed, truly.
7 determinate voyage intended walk (nautical diction). As a sea captain, Antonio uses it in turn at 3.3.7. His use of 'bound' at 6 above is also nautical.
7 extravagancy vagrancy. Not pre-Shakespeare (Onions).
8 touch feeling. As in *Temp.* 5.1.21–2: 'Hast thou...a touch, a feeling / Of their afflictions...?'
9–10 it...manners i.e. in courtesy, I am charged.

of me then, Antonio, my name is Sebastian (which I called
Roderigo); my father was that Sebastian of Messaline whom I know
you have heard of. He left behind him myself and a sister, both
born in an hour: if the heavens had been pleased, would we had
so ended! But you, sir, altered that, for some hour before you took   15
me from the breach of the sea was my sister drowned.

ANTONIO Alas the day!

SEBASTIAN A lady, sir, though it was said she much resembled me, was
yet of many accounted beautiful; but though I could not with such
estimable wonder overfar believe that, yet thus far I will boldly   20
publish her: she bore a mind that envy could not but call fair. She
is drowned already, sir, with salt water, though I seem to drown
her remembrance again with more.

ANTONIO Pardon me, sir, your bad entertainment.

SEBASTIAN O good Antonio, forgive me your trouble.   25

ANTONIO If you will not murder me for my love, let me be your servant.

SEBASTIAN If you will not undo what you have done, that is, kill him
whom you have recovered, desire it not. Fare ye well at once; my
bosom is full of kindness, and I am yet so near the manners of my
mother that, upon the least occasion more, mine eyes will tell tales   30
of me. I am bound to the Count Orsino's court. Farewell.   *Exit*

ANTONIO The gentleness of all the gods go with thee!
I have many enemies in Orsino's court,
Else would I very shortly see thee there.
But come what may, I do adore thee so   35
That danger shall seem sport, and I will go.   *Exit*

11–12 **I...Roderigo** No explanation is given
for Sebastian's earlier use of an alias.

12 **Messaline** The reference is uncertain,
though the 'Massilians' (i.e. people of ancient
Massila, now Marseilles) are mentioned with the
Illyrians in Plautus's *Menaechmi* I, 235, in the
context of one twin searching for his fellow
(L. G. Salingar, *TLS*, 3 June 1955, p. 235).

14 **in an hour** within the same hour.

15 **some hour** about an hour.

16 **breach** surf.

19–20 **with...wonder** with such an admiring
judgement (Schmidt, Onions). Such disordered
sequence (the rhetorical figure hysteron proteron)
Puttenham describes as putting the cart before the
horse. Sebastian's locution serves both to call
attention to Viola's beauty and to depreciate it with

becoming modesty, the audience having seen that
brother and sister are identical in appearance.

21 **publish** proclaim. A link with Olivia's giving
out 'divers schedules' of her beauty at 1.5.200–1.

22–3 **with salt water...more** The drowning-
in-tears image is frequent in Shakespeare, as in *The
Rape of Lucrece* 1680: 'To drown one woe, one pair
of weeping eyes'.

24 **your...entertainment** my bad hospitality.

26 **murder me...love** i.e. cause me to die of
grief as the result of separation.

28 **recovered** rescued.

29 **kindness** emotion.

29–31 **the manners...me** Sebastian acknowledges the proclivity of women to weep; compare
H5 4.6.30–2: 'I had not so much of man in me, /
And all my mother came into mine eyes / And gave
me up to tears.'

2.2 *Enter* VIOLA *and* MALVOLIO *at several doors*

MALVOLIO Were you not even now with the Countess Olivia?

VIOLA Even now, sir; on a moderate pace, I have since arrived but
hither.

MALVOLIO She returns this ring to you. You might have saved me my
pains to have taken it away yourself. She adds, moreover, that you   5
should put your lord into a desperate assurance: she will none of
him. And one thing more, that you be never so hardy to come again
in his affairs, unless it be to report your lord's taking of this. Receive
it so.

VIOLA She took the ring of me. I'll none of it.   10

MALVOLIO Come, sir, you peevishly threw it to her; and her will is,
it should be so returned. If it be worth stooping for, there it lies,
in your eye; if not, be it his that finds it.   *Exit*

VIOLA I left no ring with her: what means this lady?
    Fortune forbid my outside have not charmed her!   15
    She made good view of me, indeed so much
    That, methought, her eyes had lost her tongue,
    For she did speak in starts distractedly.
    She loves me sure; the cunning of her passion
    Invites me in this churlish messenger.   20
    None of my lord's ring? Why, he sent her none;
    I am the man; if it be so, as 'tis,

Act 2, Scene 2   2.2] *Scæna Secunda*. F   17 That, methought,] F; That sure methought F2

Act 2, Scene 2
  Location A street (Capell).
  0 SD *several* separate.
  6 desperate assurance certainty that there is
no hope.
  7 so hardy so bold as. See Abbott 281 for the
frequent omission of 'as' in this construction.
  8 taking of this response (1) to this ultimatum
and (2) to the ring.
  8–9 Receive it so Take the ring back on this basis.
  10 Having left no ring behind, Cesario, sensitive
to Olivia's predicament, dissembles in the presence
of her messenger.
  11 peevishly ill-manneredly. Although Malvolio
appropriates Olivia's diction (1.5.255) here, he then
develops it in accordance with his own sense of
Cesario's earlier unseemly deportment (1.5.128).
  11 threw it Malvolio's elaboration; Olivia
simply said that he had 'left' it (1.5.256).

  13 in your eye in plain sight.
  15 charmed enchanted. A fact Olivia later
acknowledges (3.1.97).
  16 made...of me looked at me closely.
  17–18 her eyes...distractedly i.e. as a result
of her fixed staring, Olivia spoke only disjointedly,
by fits and starts.
  19 sure certainly (adverb).
  19–20 the cunning...messenger i.e. she
shows the crafty aspect of her emotional state in
soliciting me by means of this rude messenger.
Compare *A Lover's Complaint* 295. 'For lo his
passion, [is] but an art of craft.'
  21 None of...ring *Not* what Malvolio says but
what Olivia has said at 1.5.257: 'I'll none of it.'
  22 I...man i.e. of her choice. As in *AYLI*
3.3.2–4: 'And how, Audrey? am I the man yet?
Doth my simple feature content you?'

Poor lady, she were better love a dream.
Disguise, I see thou art a wickedness,
Wherein the pregnant enemy does much.   25
How easy is it for the proper-false
In women's waxen hearts to set their forms!
Alas, our frailty is the cause, not we,
For such as we are made of, such we be.
How will this fadge? My master loves her dearly,   30
And I (poor monster) fond as much on him
As she (mistaken) seems to dote on me.
What will become of this? As I am man,
My state is desperate for my master's love;
As I am woman – now alas the day! –   35
What thriftless sighs shall poor Olivia breathe?
O time, thou must untangle this, not I;
It is too hard a knot for me t'untie.   [*Exit*]

2.3 *Enter* SIR TOBY *and* SIR ANDREW

SIR TOBY Approach, Sir Andrew. Not to be abed after midnight is to
    be up betimes, and *diluculo surgere*, thou know'st –
SIR ANDREW Nay, by my troth, I know not; but I know to be up late
    is to be up late.

28 our] F2; O F   29 made of,] *Rann, conj. Tyrwhitt*; made, if F   32 As] *Dyce²*; And F   36 breathe] F2; breath F
38 SD *Exit*] *Rowe; not in* F   **Act 2, Scene 3**   2.3] *Scæna Tertia.* F   2 *diluculo*] *Rowe; Deliculo* F   2 know'st –] *Theobald
subst.*; know'st. F

25 **pregnant enemy** ready foe. Perhaps Cupid, perhaps the devil – the two perhaps not differentiated at this point. The adjective is used again at 3.1.74.
26 **proper-false** goodlooking but deceitful (men).
27 To impress their images on women's soft hearts.
28–9 **Alas…be** Viola accounts for women's susceptibility to love on the basis of their nature, thus excusing both Olivia's enamourment and her own (expressed at 31–2).
30 **fadge** turn out well.
31 **monster** i.e. responding both as a man (33) and as a woman (35).
31 **fond** dote. Among illustrative examples (sv v 2), *OED* cites a line from John Palsgrave's translation of the comedy *Acolastus* (1540): 'I fonde, or dote upon a thyng for inordynate love.'

32 *As F's reading 'And' seems a clear instance of dittography from the preceding line, blurring the sharp parallelism of the rest of the passage.
33 **As I am man** i.e. since I am disguised as a man.
34 **My state…for** My condition is hopeless in respect to.
36 **thriftless** unprofitable.
36 **breathe** 'breath', F's spelling, is frequently not distinguished in this period from 'breathe' as in *LLL* 5.2.722 (F): 'I breath free breath.'

Act 2, Scene 3
Location Olivia's house (Rowe).
2 **betimes** early.
2 *diluculo surgere* From William Lily's Latin *Grammar*: *diluculo surgere saluberrimum est* (to rise at daybreak is extremely healthful). Lily's *Grammar* was a standard school textbook from the sixteenth century to the nineteenth.

SIR TOBY A false conclusion: I hate it as an unfilled can. To be up after   5
    midnight and to go bed then is early; so that to go to bed after
    midnight is to go to bed betimes. Does not our lives consist of the
    four elements?
SIR ANDREW Faith, so they say, but I think it rather consists of eating
    and drinking.   10
SIR TOBY Th'art a scholar; let us therefore eat and drink. Marian, I
    say, a stoup of wine!

Enter CLOWN [FESTE]

SIR ANDREW Here comes the fool, i'faith.
FESTE How now, my hearts? Did you never see the picture of 'We
    Three'?   15
SIR TOBY Welcome, ass. Now let's have a catch.
SIR ANDREW By my troth, the fool has an excellent breast. I had rather
    than forty shillings I had such a leg, and so sweet a breath to sing,
    as the fool has. In sooth, thou wast in very gracious fooling last
    night, when thou spok'st of Pigrogromitus, of the Vapians passing   20
    the equinoctial of Queubus. 'Twas very good, i'faith: I sent thee
    sixpence for thy leman; hadst it?

---

12 SD FESTE] *This edn; not in* F   22 leman] *Theobald;* Lemon F

5 **unfilled can** empty drinking-vessel.

8 **four elements** i.e. fire, air, water and earth,
which were believed to compose all matter; the four
humours (choler, blood, phlegm and melancholy or
black bile) which composed the fluids of the human
body corresponded to them, providing an analogy
between the little world of man (the microcosm) and
the universe (the macrocosm).

11 **Th'art a scholar** i.e. in confirming Sir
Toby's own predilection.

11 **Marian** i.e. 'Maid Marian', a reference to the
disreputable character who led morris dances and
May games, popular diversions opposed by the
puritans. Another sobriquet for Maria, whom Sir
Toby earlier called his 'niece's chambermaid'
(1.3.42).

14 **my hearts** See 1.5.152 n.

14-15 **picture...Three** A sign-board representing two fools or two asses and inscribed 'We
Three', the spectator making the third (NS).

16 **Welcome, ass** Sir Toby's salutation to the
'fool' plays on the two forms (fool or ass) which the
sign-board might carry. See above.

16 **catch** A song with three successive vocal
parts.

17 **breast** voice. Synonymous with 'breath'
(18).

18 **forty shillings** The precise amount that
Slender (*Wiv.* 1.1.198–9) would give to have his
copy of the 'Book of Songs and Sonnets' at hand
in his attempt to woo Mistress Page. To the NS
editors, the similarity of details of character in the
two plays suggests that the same actor played both
Sir Andrew and Slender. This was perhaps John
Sincler, Sincklo or Sinklo, a member of Shakespeare's company at this time who was conspicuous
for his thinness.

18 **such a leg** Probably said in admiration of
Feste's ability to dance, the complementary feature
of his ability to sing. In commending the 'excellent
constitution' of Sir Andrew's leg at 1.3.107–8, Sir
Toby had attributed it to the astral influence of a
'galliard' at his birth. Still, there are other admiring
references in Shakespeare simply to a well-turned
leg; Romeo's, for example, according to the Nurse,
'excels all men's' (*Rom.* 2.5.41).

20-1 **Pigrogromitus...Queubus** Further instances of Feste's mock learning (see 1.5.29).

21 **equinoctial** The equinoctial line; terrestrial
equator. Used figuratively and humorously.

22 **leman** sweetheart.

FESTE I did impeticos thy gratillity: for Malvolio's nose is no whipstock;
my lady has a white hand, and the Myrmidons are no bottle-ale
houses.   25

SIR ANDREW Excellent! Why this is the best fooling, when all is done.
Now a song.

SIR TOBY Come on, there is sixpence for you. Let's have a song.

SIR ANDREW There's a testril of me, too; if one knight give a –

FESTE Would you have a love song or a song of good life?   30

SIR TOBY A love song, a love song.

SIR ANDREW Ay, ay. I care not for good life.

(Clown [Feste] sings)

O mistress mine, where are you roaming?
O stay and hear, your true love's coming,
That can sing both high and low.   35
Trip no further, pretty sweeting;
Journeys end in lovers meeting,
Every wise man's son doth know.

SIR ANDREW Excellent good, i'faith.

SIR TOBY Good, good.   40

29 a –] F2; a F   32 SD *Feste*] *This edn; not in* F

23 **impeticos** Burlesque word meaning 'im-
pocket', perhaps intending to suggest 'impetticoat',
a form that many editors adopt.

23 **gratillity** little tip. A perversion of 'gratuity'
to emphasise its smallness.

23 **for...whipstock** This perhaps means
that Malvolio's nose (for smelling out faults in
others) does not give him the right to punish; hence
Feste need have no fear of him. Literally, his nose
is no handle to a whip.

24 **my lady...hand** This perhaps means that
my lady (the Countess Olivia) is a gentlewoman, the
term to be taken in two senses: (1) of noble birth
and (2) kindly (in contrast to the just-mentioned
Malvolio). See 66 below and n.

24–5 **Myrmidons...houses** Meaning uncertain, often explained simply as the fool's 'nonsense'. The Myrmidons were the followers of
Achilles; 'bottle-ale' is used as a term of abuse in
2H4 (2.4.131), which suggests that it refers to
the inferior kind of beer served in low taverns.

26 **when...done** Proverbial (Dent A211.1)
for 'when all is said and done'.

29 **testril** A perversion of 'tester', a sixpence;
'unconscious imitation' of Feste's 'gratillity' (NS).

29 **give a –** The line in F ends at the margin
without punctuation; either the mark or, as
some think, words have been dropped from the
text.

30 **song of good life** A generic reference to the
extolling of the shepherd's life in contrast to that of
kings and worldlings. See Hallett Smith's chapter on
the pastoral in *Elizabethan Poetry*, 1952, pp. 13, 30
and n., where he alludes to more than forty-five
Elizabethan examples based on this topos.

32 **Ay...life** Not having 'followed the arts', Sir
Andrew understands Feste to mean a song having
a moral import, perhaps even a metrical psalm.

33–8, 41–6 Though there are three contemporary
musical settings for 'O mistress mine', the words
are thought to be Shakespeare's own. The difficulty
in reconciling the settings with the text suggests that
a popular tune antedated the earliest of these and
that each of three composers reworked it in turn.
See Seng (pp. 94–100) for a full discussion of the
issues frequently debated. The words would seem
to have a particular relevance to Olivia's folly in
shunning the 'sight / And company of men', to
which Feste alluded in 1.5.27–30.

FESTE [*Sings*]   What is love? 'Tis not hereafter;
                       Present mirth hath present laughter;
                       What's to come is still unsure.
                       In delay there lies no plenty,
                       Then come kiss me, sweet and twenty;   45
                       Youth's a stuff will not endure.

SIR ANDREW A mellifluous voice, as I am true knight.

SIR TOBY A contagious breath.

SIR ANDREW Very sweet, and contagious, i'faith.

SIR TOBY To hear by the nose, it is dulcet in contagion. But shall we   50
make the welkin dance indeed? Shall we rouse the night owl in a
catch that will draw three souls out of one weaver? Shall we do
that?

SIR ANDREW And you love me, let's do't: I am dog at a catch.

FESTE By'r lady, sir, and some dogs will catch well.   55

SIR ANDREW Most certain. Let our catch be, 'Thou knave'.

FESTE 'Hold thy peace, thou knave', knight? I shall be constrain'd in't
to call thee knave, knight.

SIR ANDREW 'Tis not the first time I have constrained one to call me
knave. Begin, fool. It begins, 'Hold thy peace.'   60

FESTE I shall never begin if I hold my peace.

SIR ANDREW Good, i'faith. Come, begin.

                                                          (*Catch sung*)

---

41 SD *Sings*] *Cam.; not in* F   57 knight?] *Capell;* knight. F

43 **still** 'always', here and frequently elsewhere.

45 **sweet and twenty** sweet and twenty times
sweet. An intensive, as in *Wiv.* 2.1.195–6: 'Good
even and twenty, good Master Page!' Substantiation
for this reading is provided by its use in *The Wit
of a Woman* (1604, sig. D2ᵛ): 'Sweet and twenty, all
sweet and sweet, why thou sweet Schoolemaster, all
my lesson is of Love, a sweet Love lesson…' (cited
by R. Proudfoot, *S.Sur.* 29 (1976), 179, but with
a different reference).

48 **contagious breath** A 'catchy voice' (Furness) but with a play on 'contagious' or 'pestilent'
(in reference to the plague) and breath or
'exhalation', as in *JC* 1.2.244–7: 'the
rabblement…utter'd such a deal of stinking
breath'.

50 **To hear…contagion** If one *hears* through
the nose in the same way that one catches the
pestilence through it, the voice is (indeed) sweetly
infectious.

51 **make…dance** make (the stars) in the sky
dance. Compare *Cor.* 5.4.49–51: 'The trumpets,
sackbuts, psalteries, and fifes, / Tabors and

cymbals, and the shouting Romans, / Make the sun
dance' (Kittredge).

52 **catch…weaver** Compare *Ado* 2.3.59–60:
'Is it not strange that sheep's guts should hale souls
out of men's bodies?' As refugees from the Low
Countries and frequently Calvinists, weavers were
accustomed to singing psalms, not catches; compare
1H4 2.4.133–4: 'I would I were a weaver, I could
sing psalms, or any thing.'

54 **dog** an adept. As in *TGV* 4.4.11–13: 'I
would have (as one should say) one that takes upon
him to be a dog indeed, to be, as it were, a dog at all
things.' Feste then literalises the metaphor in the
next line.

55 **By'r lady** By Our Lady.

57 **Hold…knave** The words of the round are
'Hold thy piece, thou knave, and I prithee hold thy
piece', with the result that each of the singers is
called 'knave' in turn. The text derives from
Thomas Ravenscroft's *Deuteromelia* (1609, sig. C4),
as printed in Seng, p. 101, who also notes (p. 103)
that an earlier musical version (*c.* 1580) exists in
King's College, Cambridge, MS. KC 1, no. 32.

Enter MARIA

MARIA What a caterwauling do you keep here! If my lady have not
called up her steward Malvolio and bid him turn you out of doors,
never trust me. 65

SIR TOBY My lady's a Cataian, we are politicians, Malvolio's a
Peg-a-Ramsey, and [*Sings*] 'Three merry men be we.' Am not I
consanguineous? Am I not of her blood? Tilly vally! 'Lady!'
[*Sings*] 'There dwelt a man in Babylon, lady, lady.'

FESTE Beshrew me, the knight's in admirable fooling. 70

SIR ANDREW Ay, he does well enough if he be disposed, and so do I,
too; he does it with a better grace, but I do it more natural.

SIR TOBY [*Sings*] O'the twelfth day of December –

67 SD *Sings*] NS; *not in* F   68 'Lady!'] NS, *conj. Furness;* Ladie F   69 SD *Sings*] Rowe *subst.; not in* F
73 SD *Sings*] Rowe *subst.; not in* F   73 O'] NS, *conj. Walker;* O F   73 December –] Theobald *subst.;* December. F

66 **Cataian** A form of 'Cathayan', i.e. native of
Cathay (China), used as a term of reproach in *Wiv.*
2.1.144–6: 'I will not believe such a Cataian, though
the priest o'th'town commended him for a true
man.' Although in his cups, Sir Toby seems
unlikely to mean anything more than that the
countess can be relied on not to execute the order
to which Maria has just referred, even as Feste, who
also risked being turned out, has just implied that
she was both of noble birth and kind (24 above).
Ard. usefully quotes a contemporary description
that accounts for the opprobrium of the name: 'the
Cathaiens...knowe not what we meane, when we
speake of faithfulnesse, or trustinesse' (John
Boemus, trans. William Watreman, *Fardle of
Facions* (1555), sig. M4ᵛ).
66 **politicians** schemers.
67 **Peg-a-Ramsey** A generic reference that has
occasioned much editorial debate; it was the name
both of a popular tune (the music is given in
William Chappell's *Old English Popular Music*, rev.
H. Ellis Woolridge, 2 vols., 1893, I, 248) and of a
dance to which Nashe alludes (*Works*, III, 122).
67 **Three...we** Four lines of what may be the
source of this fragment of song appeared in Peele's
The Old Wives' Tale (1595), where it is called an 'old
proverb' (Tilley M590):

Three merrie men, and three merrie men,
And three merrie men be wee.
I in the wood, and thou on the ground,
And Jacke sleeps in the tree.

A musical version, deriving from a manuscript commonplace book in the hand of John
Playford (*c.* 1650), is given in Chappell, *Popular
Music of the Olden Time*, 2 vols., 1855–9, I, 216
(reprinted in E. W. Naylor, *Shakespeare and Music*,
1931, p. 182, and John H. Long, *Shakespeare's Use
of Music*, 1955, p. 174); another version (given in

Louis C. Elson, *Shakespeare in Music*, 1901, p. 214)
seems to have been used for a number of Robin
Hood ballads (Seng, pp. 102–3, where he also
indicates the popularity of the song from frequent
allusions to it in the seventeenth century).
67–8 **Am I...'Lady'** Since Sir Toby is of
Olivia's blood – i.e. 'consanguineous' – he reacts
with some fervour ('Tilly vally!' = 'Fiddle-
faddle!') when Maria refers to her in formal terms
as 'my lady' rather than as earlier 'Your cousin, my
lady' (1.3.3–4).
69 **There...lady** Based on the Biblical story
of Susanna and the Elders, the ballad exists in
numerous versions, one of which was entered in
SR for Thomas Colwell in 1562/3. A version of it
is included in *Roxburghe Ballads*, ed. William
Chappell and J. W. Ebsworth, 9 vols., 1871–99, I,
190–3 (Seng, pp. 103–4). Claude M. Simpson (*The
British Broadside Ballad and Its Music*, 1966) gives
the tune as that of a popular ballad on King
Solomon by William Elderton, typified by the use
of a short refrain 'Lady, Lady' (pp. 410–12).
70 **Beshrew me** Curse me. Used here as a
simple asseveration.
71 **disposed** inclined to merriment.
72 **natural** naturally. The adjectival form is
used instead of the adverbial in order to play on
'born idiot' as at 1.3.24.
73 **O'...December** Not certainly identified.
Kittredge suggests it is a line from the ballad of
'Musselburgh Field' (*The English and Scottish
Popular Ballads*, ed. F. J. Child, 10 parts, 1882–98,
VI, 378) which reads 'the tenth day of December'.
Shakespeare could conceivably have altered this to
suit the title of the play, though a later version of
it (*Choyce Drollery: Songs & Sonnets* (1656), p. 78)
reads 'twelfth' (Seng, p. 103).

MARIA For the love o'God, peace!

Enter MALVOLIO

MALVOLIO My masters, are you mad? Or what are you? Have you no   75
   wit, manners, nor honesty but to gabble like tinkers at this time
   of night? Do ye make an alehouse of my lady's house, that ye squeak
   out your coziers' catches without any mitigation or remorse of
   voice? Is there no respect of place, persons, nor time in you?
SIR TOBY We did keep time, sir, in our catches. Sneck up!   80
MALVOLIO Sir Toby, I must be round with you. My lady bade me tell
   you that, though she harbours you as her kinsman, she's nothing
   allied to your disorders. If you can separate yourself and your
   misdemeanours, you are welcome to the house; if not, and it would
   please you to take leave of her, she is very willing to bid you farewell.   85
SIR TOBY [*Sings*] Farewell, dear heart, since I must needs be gone.
MARIA Nay, good Sir Toby.
FESTE [*Sings*] His eyes do show his days are almost done.
MALVOLIO Is't even so?
SIR TOBY [*Sings*] But I will never die.   90
FESTE [*Sings*] Sir Toby, there you lie.

86, 88, 90, 91 SD *Sings*] Hanmer *subst.*; *not in* F

76 wit...honesty judgement, breeding,
decency.
77–8 squeak out shrill out.
78 coziers' cobblers'.
78 mitigation or remorse abating or
softening.
79 respect of regard for.
80 Sneck up Shut up. Literally, 'shut the
doors', in reference to Malvolio's duty to secure the
house. From the time of Robert Nares's *Glossary*
(1822) the word, which *OED* gives as chiefly
Scottish and Northern, has usually been identified
with 'snick' or 'sneck up', meaning 'be hanged'.
82–3 nothing...disorders no kin to your bad
conduct. As Jessica says of Shylock (*MV*
2.3.18–19): 'But though I am a daughter to his
blood, / I am not to his manners.'
83 and from.
86–96 Farewell...dare not From 'Corydon's
Farewell to Phyllis' in Robert Jones's *The First
Booke of Songes and Ayres* (1600, sigs. D4ᵛ–E1). Sir
Toby and Feste sing a composite of the first two
stanzas:

(1)

Farewel dear love since thou wilt needs be gon,
mine eies do shew my life is almost done,

nay I will never die,
so long as I can spie,
there be many mo
though that she do go
there be many mo I feare not,
why then let her goe I care not.

(2)

Farewell, farewell, since this I finde is true,
I will not spend more time in wooing you:
But I will seeke elswhere,
If I may find her there,
Shall I bid her goe,
What and if I doe?
Shall I bid her go and spare not,
Oh no no no no I dare not.

For a listing of texts and settings, see Seng,
pp. 106–7.
87 Nay...Toby Maria is still remonstrating
with Sir Toby and his vocalising, but the 'nay'
perhaps refers to some amorous stage business here
on the part of Sir Toby.
91 Sir...lie The stichomythic exchange would
seem to preclude any stage business here, such as
Sir Toby's falling down.

MALVOLIO This is much credit to you.

SIR TOBY [*Sings*] Shall I bid him go?

FESTE [*Sings*] What and if you do?

SIR TOBY [*Sings*] Shall I bid him go, and spare not?   95

FESTE [*Sings*] O no, no, no, no, you dare not.

SIR TOBY Out o'time, sir? Ye lie! Art any more than a steward? Dost
thou think because thou art virtuous there shall be no more cakes
and ale?

FESTE Yes, by St Anne, and ginger shall be hot i'th'mouth too.   100
                                                              [*Exit*]

SIR TOBY Th'art i'th'right. Go, sir, rub your chain with crumbs. A
stoup of wine, Maria!

MALVOLIO Mistress Mary, if you prized my lady's favour at anything
more than contempt, you would not give means for this uncivil rule;
she shall know of it, by this hand.   *Exit*   105

MARIA Go shake your ears.

SIR ANDREW 'Twere as good a deed as to drink when a man's a-hungry,
to challenge him the field, and then to break promise with him, and
make a fool of him.

SIR TOBY Do't, knight. I'll write thee a challenge, or I'll deliver thy   110
indignation to him by word of mouth.

93–6 SD *Sings*] *Rowe subst.; not in* F   97 time, sir?] *Theobald; tune, sir,* F   100 SD *Exit*] *Ard.; not in* F

97 *Out o'time Sir Toby is reverting to his
original riposte to Malvolio in 80. F's 'tune' can be
accounted for on the grounds of frequent misreading
in Secretary hand of i:u followed by a nasal. Q2
Ham. 1814 (3.1.158) has 'Like sweet bells jangled
out of time' where F reads 'tune'; the reverse error
occurs in *Mac.* 4.3.235: 'This tune [F 'time'] goes
manly.' Compare also *R2* 5.5.42–3: 'How sour
sweet music is / When time is broke, and no
proportion kept!' On the other hand, Dent (T598.1)
gives 'out of tune' as proverbial, referring to *OED*
Tune *sb* 3b and meaning 'out of order'; while this
reading accords in general with Malvolio's
remonstrations in 75–85, it does not pick up any
specific charge with which Sir Toby can quibble.

98–9 cakes and ale Metaphoric for parish
celebrations at Christmas and Easter time; in the
view of a strict puritan like Phillip Stubbes
(*Anatomy of Abuses*, ed. F. J. Furnivall, 1877–9, I,
151) these included 'swilling and gulling, night and
day'.

100 St Anne Mother of the Virgin, according to
the apocryphal Book of James. St Anne was
venerated in the Middle Ages but her cult was
derided by Luther and later reformers; thus Feste's

asseveration is a further dig at Malvolio's would-be
puritan tendencies. It is used only here and in *Shr.*
1.1.250.

100 ginger Used to spice ale; 'canded, greene,
or condited', it was considered an aphrodisiac
according to Gerard's *Herball* (1633 edn), p. 62
(Furness).

100 SD F gives no exit for Feste, who clearly is
not present at 146 when Maria outlines her plot.

101 rub...crumbs i.e. polish up the insignia of
your steward's office with crumbs from the buttery.

104 give...rule provide drink to encourage
this unmannerly regimen.

106 Go...ears A contemptuous dismissal
(Tilley E16). Compare 'turn him off / (Like to the
empty [unburdened] ass) to shake his ears / And
graze in commons' (*JC* 4.1.25–7).

107 a-hungry This conjunction Abbott (24)
explains as the result of a corruption of Anglo-Saxon
intensive 'of' and compares Matt. 25.35: 'For I was
an hungred and ye gave me meat.' It is another
verbal mannerism that Sir Andrew shares with
Slender (*Wiv.* 1.1.270). See 2.3.18 n.

108 the field to single combat.

MARIA Sweet Sir Toby, be patient for tonight. Since the youth of the count's was today with my lady, she is much out of quiet. For Monsieur Malvolio, let me alone with him. If I do not gull him into an ayword, and make him a common recreation, do not 115 think I have wit enough to lie straight in my bed. I know I can do it.

SIR TOBY Possess us, possess us, tell us something of him.

MARIA Marry, sir, sometimes he is a kind of puritan.

SIR ANDREW O if I thought that, I'd beat him like a dog! 120

SIR TOBY What, for being a puritan? Thy exquisite reason, dear knight?

SIR ANDREW I have no exquisite reason for't, but I have reason good enough.

MARIA The devil a puritan that he is, or anything constantly but a time-pleaser, an affectioned ass, that cons state without book and 125 utters it by great swarths. The best persuaded of himself: so crammed (as he thinks) with excellencies, that it is his grounds of faith that all that look on him love him; and on that vice in him will my revenge find notable cause to work.

SIR TOBY What wilt thou do? 130

MARIA I will drop in his way some obscure epistles of love, wherein by the colour of his beard, the shape of his leg, the manner of his gait, the expressure of his eye, forehead, and complexion, he shall find himself most feelingly personated. I can write very like my lady

---

114 **let me alone** leave him to me. An idiom used again at 3.4.84, 95 and 153.

114 **gull** deceive. The compatibility of Maria and Sir Toby is highlighted: she has in mind a trick to gull Malvolio, while Sir Toby is gulling Sir Andrew throughout the action. Both victims are labelled 'gulls'.

115 **an ayword** a proverb. Maria threatens to make Malvolio's name synonymous with 'gull'. Kökeritz explains this nonce usage (p. 313) as equivalent to 'a nayword', with detached 'n' on the analogy of the modern 'adder' (formed by erroneous word-division in the Middle Ages so that 'a nadder' became 'an adder'). Though editors frequently emend to 'nayword', they do so by reference to *Wiv.* 2.2.126 and 5.2.5, where it means 'password' and hence represents a homonym.

115 **recreation** sport, diversion.

118 **Possess** Inform.

119 **kind of puritan** i.e. morally straitlaced, but not an adherent of a specific religious group, as Maria makes clear at 124. Sir Andrew, however, understands him to be a party member.

121 **exquisite** excellent.

124 **constantly** consistently.

125 **time-pleaser** time-server. As in *Cor.* 3.1.43–5: 'you repin'd...call'd them / Time-pleasers, flatterers, foes to nobleness'.

125 **affectioned** affected.

125–6 **cons state...swarths** memorises the rules for appearing dignified in speech and deportment and discloses them in great sweeps. A 'swarth' = swath, the quantity of corn etc. that can be cut down with one sweep of the scythe.

126 **The best persuaded** Having the best opinion.

127–8 **it is...of faith** i.e. all the elements of his creed are united in this opinion (Kittredge). The lack of concord between subject and verb is not unusual in Elizabethan English.

131 **obscure** ambiguously worded.

131 **epistles** Plural for singular. Similarly with 'letters' (139), though at 147 and elsewhere in the play a single missive is specified. Shakespeare's general practice as to singular and plural form is divided.

133 **expressure** expression.

134 **feelingly personated** precisely represented.

your niece; on a forgotten matter we can hardly make distinction   135
of our hands.

SIR TOBY Excellent, I smell a device.

SIR ANDREW I have't in my nose, too.

SIR TOBY He shall think by the letters that thou wilt drop that they
come from my niece, and that she's in love with him.   140

MARIA My purpose is indeed a horse of that colour.

SIR ANDREW And your horse now would make him an ass.

MARIA Ass, I doubt not.

SIR ANDREW O 'twill be admirable!

MARIA Sport royal, I warrant you: I know my physic will work with   145
him. I will plant you two, and let the fool make a third, where he
shall find the letter. Observe his construction of it. For this night,
to bed, and dream on the event. Farewell.   *Exit*

SIR TOBY Good night, Penthesilea.

SIR ANDREW Before me, she's a good wench.   150

SIR TOBY She's a beagle, true bred, and one that adores me. What
o'that?

SIR ANDREW I was adored once, too.

SIR TOBY Let's to bed, knight. Thou hadst need send for more money.

SIR ANDREW If I cannot recover your niece, I am a foul way out.   155

SIR TOBY Send for money, knight; if thou hast her not i'th'end, call
me 'cut'.

---

135 on a forgotten matter i.e. when we have forgotten the circumstances in which it was written or the topic it concerned.

136 hands handwriting.

137 smell perceive. A frequent metaphor in Shakespeare; see *WT* 4.4.642–3: 'I smell the trick on't', and *1H4* 1.3.277, where Hotspur says of Worcester's plot 'I smell it.'

137 device clever stratagem or invention. It is also the term Fabian uses (5.1.339) to refer to the plot against Malvolio.

143 Ass Used either (1) as a vocative or (2) as an object; some editors suggest a play on 'ass' and 'as'.

145 physic medicine (for purging Malvolio's self-love).

146 let…third Maria's language makes clear that the fool is not now present, and it is Fabian, in fact, who makes up the trio of observers in 2.5.

147 construction interpretation.

148 event outcome.

149 Penthesilea Queen of the Amazons. Another of Sir Toby's playful sobriquets for Maria, commenting again on her diminutive size, as at 1.5.167–8, 2.3.151, 2.5.11 and 3.2.52.

150 Before me On my soul. Modelled on 'before my God' (Onions).

151 beagle A small hunting-dog noted for its keenness of smell. Again a comment on Maria's diminutive size. The choice of diction says something again about Sir Toby's idiosyncratic speech since the term 'beagle' was generally one of opprobrium, as in *Tim.* 4.3.174–5 and many times elsewhere in drama.

153 I was…too Compare Sir Andrew's plaintive statement with that of Menelaus (*Tro.* 4.5.26): 'I had good argument for kissing, once' (Kenneth Palmer (ed.), *Tro.*, 1982).

155 recover obtain (and so regain expenses).

155 a foul way out grievously out of pocket.

156 Send for money Sir Toby has successfully importuned him 'some two thousand strong, or so' (3.2.43–4); at 1.3.18 he is said to have three thousand ducats a year.

157 cut Proverbial term of abuse (Tilley C940). It refers either to a horse with a cut tail or to one that has been gelded. It was considered a stupid beast; hence Falstaff's remark in *1H4* 2.4.193–4: 'if I tell thee a lie, spit in my face, call me horse'. For the obscene usage, see 2.5.72–3 and n.

SIR ANDREW If I do not, never trust me; take it how you will.

SIR TOBY Come, come, I'll go burn some sack; 'tis too late to go to
bed now. Come, knight, come, knight.   160

Exeunt

2.4 *Enter* DUKE [ORSINO], VIOLA, CURIO, *and others* [*both Lords and
Musicians*]

ORSINO Give me some music –
[*Musicians step forward*]
Now good morrow, friends;
Now, good Cesario – but that piece of song,
That old and antique song we heard last night;
Methought it did relieve my passion much,
More than light airs and recollected terms   5
Of these most brisk and giddy-pacèd times.
Come, but one verse.

CURIO He is not here, so please your lordship, that should sing it.

ORSINO Who was it?

CURIO Feste, the jester, my lord, a fool that the Lady Olivia's father   10
took much delight in. He is about the house.

ORSINO Seek him out, and play the tune the while.

[*Exit Curio*]

Act 2, Scene 4   2.4] *Scena Quarta.* F   0 SD *both Lords and Musicians*] *This edn; not in* F   1–2 music – [*Musicians step
forward.*] Now...friends; / ...Cesario –] *This edn;* Musick; Now...friends. / ...Cesario, F; music. Now – [*musicians
enter* good morrow, friends.... / ...Cesario, NS; music – [*to others*] Now...friends; / [*to Viola*] Now...Cesario –
conj. Ard.   12 SD.1 *Exit Curio*] Pope; *not in* F

159 burn...sack heat some canary wine with
sugar.

Act 2, Scene 4
Location The palace (Rowe).
0 SD *and...Musicians* Possibly lords or
musicians but better both lords *and* musicians;
'lords' corresponds to the directive at 1.1.0 SD
and again at 5.1.5; 'and musicians' solves the problem
presented in the first two lines. See next note.
1–2 The punctuation of these lines in F offers
difficulties as to whom the duke is addressing and,
consequently, as to the staging. If F's 'and others'
(0 SD) is taken to refer both to 'lords' and
'musicians' (as here) there is an easy solution: the
musicians come forward after the duke's opening
call for music, whereupon he interrupts his demand
for a specific piece in order to greet them and

Cesario. Such an arrangement removes any notion
that Cesario is being asked to sing and thus obviates
the revisionist theory that makes Feste a substitute
singer. See p. 16 above. This solution concurs in
part with that in NS (though it is offered there in
support of revision) and in part with the suggestions
of Ard. (which, however, except for the correction
in 1 follows F's punctuation of a full stop in place of
a semi-colon).
2 but only.
3 antique old and quaint. Frequently not
distinguished from 'antic' in pronunciation (as
here), meaning or orthography; compare 'these antic
fables' (*MND* (Q2; F 1793) 5.1.3).
4 passion pangs of unrequited love.
5 recollected artificial. In contrast with the 'old
and plain' song, which is the way Orsino
characterises it in 41.

(*Music plays*)

Come hither, boy; if ever thou shalt love,
In the sweet pangs of it, remember me:
For such as I am, all true lovers are,   15
Unstaid and skittish in all motions else,
Save in the constant image of the creature
That is beloved. How dost thou like this tune?

VIOLA It gives a very echo to the seat
Where love is throned.

ORSINO   Thou dost speak masterly.   20
My life upon't, young though thou art, thine eye
Hath stayed upon some favour that it loves;
Hath it not, boy?

VIOLA   A little, by your favour.

ORSINO What kind of woman is't?

VIOLA   Of your complexion.

ORSINO She is not worth thee then. What years, i'faith?   25

VIOLA About your years, my lord.

ORSINO Too old, by heaven! Let still the woman take
An elder than herself; so wears she to him;
So sways she level in her husband's heart;
For, boy, however we do praise ourselves,   30
Our fancies are more giddy and unfirm,
More longing, wavering, sooner lost and worn,
Than women's are.

VIOLA   I think it well, my lord.

ORSINO Then let thy love be younger than thyself,
Or thy affection cannot hold the bent: 35

15–18 For...beloved Compare 1.1.9–15 where, by his analogy of love and the 'never-surfeited sea', Orsino suggests the inconstancy of (male) lovers, a point that he (inconstantly) denies here and (inconstantly) reaffirms at 31–3.

16 motions else other thoughts and feelings.

19 seat i.e. the heart.

22 stayed...favour fixed upon some countenance.

23 by your favour if you please. A courteous formula, but also a quibble on 'near to your countenance' (Abbot 145).

24 complexion temperament. Dictated by a mixture of the four humours; see 2.3.8 n.

27 still Carries here the two senses: (1) nonetheless and (2) ever.

28 wears...him becomes fit to (and for) him

like a garment. Perhaps echoing the proverb 'Win it and wear it' (Tilley w408).

29 sways she level (1) rules, (2) swings in perfect balance (NS).

31 fancies loves.

32 worn worn out. Following Hanmer, many editors emend to 'won', but the duke is continuing his earlier metaphorical use of 'wear'; see 28 and n.

33 I...well I believe it. The expression appears again in *MM* 2.4.130, where Angelo is agreeing with Isabella's comment that women are frail, soft and 'credulous to false imprints'. Her attitude agrees with that expressed in Viola's soliloquy at 2.2.26–9.

35 hold the bent keep its intensity. A metaphor from the extent to which a bow can be made taut.

For women are as roses, whose fair flower,
Being once displayed, doth fall that very hour.
VIOLA And so they are. Alas, that they are so:
To die, even when they to perfection grow!

Enter CURIO *and* CLOWN [FESTE]

ORSINO O fellow, come, the song we had last night.   40
Mark it, Cesario, it is old and plain;
The spinsters and the knitters in the sun,
And the free maids that weave their thread with bones,
Do use to chant it; it is silly sooth,
And dallies with the innocence of love   45
Like the old age.
FESTE Are you ready, sir?
ORSINO Ay, prithee sing.

(Music)
The Song

Come away, come away, death,
And in sad cypress let me be laid.   50
Fie away, fie away, breath,
I am slain by a fair cruel maid;
My shroud of white, stuck all with yew,
O prepare it.
My part of death no one so true   55
Did share it.

39 SD FESTE] *This edn; not in* F   51 Fie...fie] F; Fly...fly *Rowe*   53–6] *As Pope; two lines in* F, *ending...* prepare
it / ...share it

39 **even when** just when.
41 **plain** artless.
42 **spinsters** spinners.
43 **free...bones** i.e. carefree maidens who
make lace by weaving the thread on bone bobbins.
44 **silly sooth** simple truth.
45 **dallies** sports with.
46 **Like...age** As in former (and better) times.
48 SD *The Song* Although the original music is
not known, it was clearly a folk song. Katherine
Garvin (*N&Q* 170 (9 May 1936), 326–8, cited by
Seng, p. 110) speculates that it may refer to the Old
French *chansons de toile* popular in the twelfth
century. Sung by women, the words suggest patient
devotion towards men who treat them badly. To
support her suggestion, she argues that Shakespeare
knew Huguenots in London, many of whom were
lacemakers and clothworkers; he lodged for a time

with a maker of ornamental headdresses (by 1604
but perhaps earlier). Seng records the earliest of
modern settings as one by Thomas Arne (1710–78),
included in *The Shakespeare Vocal Album*, 1864,
p. 90.
49 **Come away** Come hither.
50 **sad cypress** A coffin of cypress wood or a
bier covered with cypress boughs; the tree was
emblematic of mourning.
51 **Fie...fie away** Seng (p. 112) points out that
there is a song in Thomas Ravenscroft's *Melismata*
(1611, sig. C2) which begins 'Fie away, fie away, fie,
fie, fie', thus supporting the wording in F. Following
Rowe, editors usually emend to 'Fly...fly away'.
53 **yew** Like the cypress, a tree associated with
mourning.
55–6 **My part...share it** No one ever died for
love who was so constant as I.

> Not a flower, not a flower sweet,
> On my black coffin let there be strown;
> Not a friend, not a friend greet
> My poor corpse, where my bones shall be thrown: 60
>   A thousand thousand sighs to save,
>   Lay me, O where
>   Sad true lover never find my grave,
>   To weep there.

ORSINO There's for thy pains. [*Gives money*]   65

FESTE No pains, sir, I take pleasure in singing, sir.

ORSINO I'll pay thy pleasure then.

FESTE Truly, sir, and pleasure will be paid, one time or another.

ORSINO Give me now leave to leave thee.

FESTE Now the melancholy god protect thee, and the tailor make thy   70
doublet of changeable taffeta, for thy mind is a very opal. I would
have men of such constancy put to sea, that their business might
be everything and their intent everywhere, for that's it that always
makes a good voyage of nothing. Farewell.   *Exit*

ORSINO Let all the rest give place.

> [*Curio and attendants retire*]

>   Once more, Cesario,   75
> Get thee to yond same sovereign cruelty.
> Tell her my love, more noble than the world,
> Prizes not quantity of dirty lands;
> The parts that fortune hath bestowed upon her
> Tell her I hold as giddily as fortune;   80

61–4] *As Pope; two lines in* F, *ending*...where / ...there   65 SD *Gives money*] *Collier²; not in* F   75 SD *Curio*...*retire*]
Cam.; not in F

68 pleasure...another Feste plays on the proverbial idea that pleasure must be paid for with pain (Tilley P420, with variant forms).

69 Give...thee Orsino dismisses Feste courteously and wittily, employing the rhetorical trick of using the same word in different senses (antaclasis). This is one of Shakespeare's favourite devices: see for example 3.1.1–9, 3.2.39, 42–3.

70 melancholy god Saturn, who determined the melancholy temperament which would vary according to social types. Of these, the melancholy of a lover is a composite, as Jaques explains in *AYLI* 4.1.10–15, and hence the worst. At 109 below, it is described as a 'green and yellow melancholy'.

71 doublet...taffeta jacket of iridescent silk.

71 opal Shakespeare's apt characterisation of this iridescent stone (and his only other reference to it) is in the catalogue in *A Lover's Complaint*: 'The heaven-hu'd sapphire and the opal blend / With objects manifold' (215–16).

73 intent port of call.

73–4 for that's...nothing i.e. that's what makes a so-called 'good' voyage but, in fact, one without profit. Tilley (E194) cites the proverb 'He that is everywhere is nowhere.'

79–80 The parts...as fortune i.e. the social status and wealth that chance to be Olivia's, he evaluates as lightly as fickle fortune herself.

> But 'tis that miracle and queen of gems
> That nature pranks her in attracts my soul.

VIOLA But if she cannot love you, sir?

ORSINO I cannot be so answered.

VIOLA   Sooth, but you must.
> Say that some lady, as perhaps there is,   85
> Hath for your love as great a pang of heart
> As you have for Olivia. You cannot love her.
> You tell her so. Must she not then be answered?

ORSINO There is no woman's sides
> Can bide the beating of so strong a passion   90
> As love doth give my heart; no woman's heart
> So big, to hold so much. They lack retention.
> Alas, their love may be called appetite,
> No motion of the liver, but the palate,
> That suffers surfeit, cloyment, and revolt,   95
> But mine is all as hungry as the sea,
> And can digest as much. Make no compare
> Between that love a woman can bear me,
> And that I owe Olivia.

VIOLA   Ay, but I know –

ORSINO What dost thou know?   100

VIOLA Too well what love women to men may owe.
> In faith, they are as true of heart as we.
> My father had a daughter loved a man
> As it might be perhaps, were I a woman,
> I should your lordship.

ORSINO   And what's her history?   105

VIOLA A blank, my lord. She never told her love,
> But let concealment like a worm i'th'bud

---

84 I] *Hanmer*; It F   95 suffers] *Rowe*; suffer F   99 know –] *Rowe*; know. F

81–2 **that miracle...in** i.e. the inestimable beauty with which nature has decked her, as opposed to the 'dirty lands' which fortune has bestowed on her.

84 *I Hanmer's emendation of F's 'It' is sanctioned by Cesario's use of the second person in reply.

90 **bide** endure.

92 **retention** the power to retain. A medical term following on 'woman's sides' and 'heart' and looking toward 'digest' at 97.

93 **appetite** no more than desire. Like the appetite for music in 1.1.1–3.

94 **No...liver** No impulse (i.e. emotion) in the liver. The liver was considered the throne of the passions, as in 1.1.37–8.

95 **suffers...revolt** experiences satiety and revulsion; 'cloyment' is a nonce usage. Orsino's words here about the quality of women's love provide an ironic comment on his opening speech in Act 1.

97 **compare** comparison.

99 **owe** bear. As also at 101.

107 **concealment...bud** secrecy like a canker worm destroying the budding rose. In *Temp.* 1.2.416, it is 'grief' that is 'beauty's canker'.

Feed on her damask cheek. She pined in thought,
And with a green and yellow melancholy
She sat like Patience on a monument,   110
Smiling at grief. Was not this love indeed?
We men may say more, swear more, but indeed
Our shows are more than will: for still we prove
Much in our vows, but little in our love.

ORSINO But died thy sister of her love, my boy?   115

VIOLA I am all the daughters of my father's house,
And all the brothers, too – and yet I know not.
Sir, shall I to this lady?

ORSINO   Ay, that's the theme.
To her in haste; give her this jewel; say   120
My love can give no place, bide no denay.

                                                    Exeunt

117 too –] *Rowe;* too: F

108 **damask** mingled red and white. Like the '*damask'd*' roses of *Sonnets* 130.5.

109 **green...melancholy** The pallor typical of a melancholic lover, according to Jaques Ferrand's '*Erotomania*, is either a mixture of white and yellow or of white, yellow and green (French edn 1612, trans. 1640, p. 121, quoted in Lawrence Babb, *The Elizabethan Malady*, 1951, p. 136).

111 **Smiling...grief** Most editors assume that 'grief' is a generalised, rather than a personified, abstraction, but the monument is perhaps graced with two figures. 'Patience' and 'Monument' are capitalised in F, but not 'grief'. Capitalisation is of little expressive significance in the *STM* manuscript (Hand D) or in texts believed to have been set from foul papers. That Shakespeare conceived of Patience as smiling is supported by *Per.* 5.1.137–9: 'Yet thou dost look / Like Patience gazing on king's graves, and smiling / Extremity out of act.' For an account of contemporary representations of the figure of Patience, frequently coupled with other virtues such as Fortitude and Hope, see W. S. Heckscher, 'Shakespeare in his relationship to the visual arts', *Research Opportunities in Renaissance Drama* 13–14 (1970–1), 35–56. Alternatively, 'grief' can simply refer to the cause of suffering or sorrow (Onions).

113 **Our...will** Our display is greater than our determination.

113 **still we prove** always we demonstrate.

117 **and yet...not** Though Viola's 'own escape' has allowed her to take hope in a like escape for Sebastian; she is uncertain.

119 **give...jewel** This Viola does not do; instead the emphasis at 3.1 is on the ring Olivia sent 'in chase' of her (2.2).

120 **give...denay** yield no ground, endure no denial.

2.5 *Enter* SIR TOBY, SIR ANDREW, *and* FABIAN

SIR TOBY Come thy ways, Signior Fabian.

FABIAN Nay, I'll come. If I lose a scruple of this sport, let me be boiled
to death with melancholy.

SIR TOBY Wouldst thou not be glad to have the niggardly rascally
sheep-biter come by some notable shame?   5

FABIAN I would exult, man. You know he brought me out o'favour with
my lady about a bear-baiting here.

SIR TOBY To anger him, we'll have the bear again; and we will fool
him black and blue, shall we not, Sir Andrew?

SIR ANDREW And we do not, it is pity of our lives.   10

SIR TOBY Here comes the little villain.

Enter MARIA

How now, my metal of India?

MARIA Get ye all three into the box-tree. Malvolio's coming down this
walk. He has been yonder i'the sun practising behaviour to his own
shadow this half hour. Observe him, for the love of mockery, for   15
I know this letter will make a contemplative idiot of him. Close,
in the name of jesting!

[The men hide]

Act 2, Scene 5   2.5] *Scena Quinta.* F   11 SD] *Dyce; after 10* F   17 SD *The men hide] Capell subst.; not in* F

Act 2, Scene 5
Location Olivia's garden (Pope).
0 SD Fabian, rather than Feste as Maria
originally specified, makes up the trio of observers.
See 2.3.146 n.
1 Come thy ways Come along.
2 Nay i.e. protesting that he needs no urging.
2 scruple Figuratively, 'the least bit'; literally,
a third of a dram.
2–3 boiled...melancholy A jest, in that 'boil'
and (black) 'bile', the cause of the cold and dry
humour of melancholy, were homonyms up
through the eighteenth century and continued so
in dialectal pronunciation.
5 sheep-biter An opprobrious term for a
dissembler. Nashe applies it to merchants turned
usurers (*Works*, II, 98); to a pander (II, 260–1),
leering 'like a sheep-biter', of whom he also says,
'If he be halfe a puritan, and have scripture
continually in his mouth, hee speeds the better';
and directly to a puritan in an anti-Martinist tract
(III, 372), 'What say you [Martin] to that zealous
sheepbyter of your owne edition in Cambridge?'

7 bear-baiting One of the many Sabbath
pastimes to which the puritans objected (along with
plays and interludes).
8–9 fool...blue Figuratively, 'bruise him with
fooling'.
10 it is...lives Proverbial (in the singular) for
'we do not deserve to live' (Dent P368.1).
11 little villain Used as a term of endearment,
as in *Tro.* 3.2.33 – Cressida 'the prettiest villain' –
and to comment again on Maria's diminutive size.
12 metal of India i.e. like pure gold from the
'bountiful' mines of India (*1H4* 3.1.166–7). 'India'
was also used to refer to the East Indies, which had
recently been more fully delineated than ever before
on a new map ('with the augmentation of the
Indies'), to which Maria refers in 3.2.62–3. F's
'mettle' was simply a variant spelling of 'metal'
which, used figuratively (*OED* Metal *sb* 1f), referred
to the character of an individual. Thus for
Shakespeare's period there was no pun involved.
13 box-tree An evergreen shrub.
16 contemplative idiot meditative fool.
16 Close Keep still and out of sight.

Lie thou there [*Drops a letter*]; for here comes the trout that must
be caught with tickling.   *Exit*

Enter MALVOLIO

MALVOLIO 'Tis but fortune; all is fortune. Maria once told me she did   20
affect me, and I have heard herself come thus near, that should she
fancy, it should be one of my complexion. Besides, she uses me with
a more exalted respect than any one else that follows her. What
should I think on't?

SIR TOBY Here's an overweening rogue!   25

FABIAN O peace! Contemplation makes a rare turkey-cock of him; how
he jets under his advanced plumes!

SIR ANDREW 'Slight, I could so beat the rogue!

FABIAN Peace, I say!

MALVOLIO To be Count Malvolio!   30

SIR TOBY Ah, rogue!

SIR ANDREW Pistol him, pistol him!

FABIAN Peace, peace!

MALVOLIO There is example for't: the Lady of the Strachy married
the yeoman of the wardrobe –   35

---

18 SD *Drops a letter*] *Theobald subst.; not in* F   29 SH FABIAN] *NS, conj. Cam.; To.* F   33 SH FABIAN] *NS, conj. Cam.;
To.* F   35 wardrobe –] *This edn;* wardrobe. F

18–19 **trout...tickling** Proverbial (Tilley T537
and, for later entries, Dent) for the use of flattery
to beguile a person just as the fish was caught by
being 'rubbed and clawed' (Thomas Cogan, *The
Haven of Health* (1584), sig. S4).

20 **she** i.e. Olivia.

20–1 **did affect me** was fond of me.

21–2 **should...complexion** should she love, it
would be one of my appearance and temperament.
Temperament was dictated by the mixture of the
four humours; see 2.3.8 n.

23 **follows her** i.e. in her service and as a suitor
(*OED* Follow v 3b). This second meaning provides
the evidence, in Maria's words (3.4.34), of
Malvolio's 'ridiculous boldness'.

26 **Contemplation** Thought. Picking up
Maria's diction in 16.

26 **rare** extraordinary (intensive).

26 **turkey-cock** Symbol of foolish vanity.

27 **jets...advanced plumes** struts under his
raised feathers. In view of Malvolio's social
pretensions, 'advanced' applies both literally and
metaphorically.

28 **'Slight** By God's light. A mild oath
characteristic of Sir Andrew; he uses it again at
3.2.9. By 1633, it was considered an asseveration
and not an oath (Furness).

29 SH *FABIAN Following on a conjecture in

Cam., NS assigns this speech and also 33 to Fabian,
rather than to Sir Toby as F does, since it is Fabian
who tries to quiet the other two in 26, and again at
37, 43, 48 and 53. Such restraint accords with his
character and position as gentleman servitor to the
countess and contrasts with that of her irrepressible
kinsman. F abbreviates the speech headings here as
Fa. or *Fab.* and *To.* (though elsewhere as *Tob.*), and
majuscule T was easily confused in Secretary hand
with other letters. Samuel A. Tannenbaum points
out (*The Handwriting of the Renaissance*, 1930, p.
115) that Thomas Heywood was in the habit of
crossing his T's, thus making them look exactly like
F's.

32 **Pistol him** Shoot him.

34–5 **The Lady...wardrobe** The allusion has
yet to be explained and has occasioned many
attempted emendations. Sisson (1, 188–91) connects
William Strachey, a shareholder in the rival
Blackfriars Theatre, with David Yeomans, a
'tyreman' of that company in 1606, but such a
topical reference would have had to be a late
addition, an unlikely possibility if F's text derived
from a scribal copy of foul papers. See Textual
Analysis, pp. 152–3 below. Others assume that
Strachy is a place-name, and still others (like
Dr Johnson) that it is a reference to 'some old story'.

SIR ANDREW Fie on him, Jezebel!

FABIAN O peace! Now he's deeply in. Look how imagination blows him.

MALVOLIO Having been three months married to her, sitting in my state –

SIR TOBY O for a stone-bow to hit him in the eye!

MALVOLIO Calling my officers about me, in my branched velvet gown,   40
  having come from a day-bed, where I have left Olivia sleeping –

SIR TOBY Fire and brimstone!

FABIAN O peace, peace!

MALVOLIO And then to have the humour of state; and after a demure
  travel of regard – telling them I know my place, as I would they   45
  should do theirs – to ask for my kinsman Toby –

SIR TOBY Bolts and shackles!

FABIAN O peace, peace, peace! Now, now.

MALVOLIO Seven of my people, with an obedient start, make out for
  him. I frown the while, and perchance wind up my watch, or play   50
  with my – some rich jewel. Toby approaches; curtsies there to me –

SIR TOBY Shall this fellow live?

FABIAN Though our silence be drawn from us by th'ears, yet peace!

MALVOLIO I extend my hand to him thus, quenching my familiar smile
  with an austere regard of control –   55

SIR TOBY And does not 'Toby' take you a blow o'the lips then?

---

38 state –] *Pope;* state. F   41 sleeping –] *Cam.;* sleeping. F   45–6 regard – …theirs –] *Capell;* regard: …theirs: F
46 Toby –] *Rowe;* Toby. F   51 my – some] *Collier;* my some F   51 me –] *Cam. subst.;* me. F   53 by th'ears] *Hanmer;*
with cars F   55 control –] *Cam. subst.;* controll. F

36 **Jezebel** The proud widow of Ahab, King of Israel, who was cast down to the street to become the food for dogs (2 Kings 19).

37 **blows** inflates.

38 **state** Canopied chair of state.

39 **stone-bow** A cross-bow that shot stones in place of arrows.

40 **branched** wrought, embroidered with flowers (Linthicum, p. 126).

44 **humour of state** caprice of rank.

44–5 **demure…regard** sober survey (of the officers of the household).

46 **kinsman Toby** Malvolio's dropping the formality of Sir Toby's title here and at 51 elicits a response both vehement and mocking (56).

47 **Bolts** Irons (to fasten the shackles on Malvolio).

49 **with…start** jumping out in obsequious obedience.

49 **make out** go.

50–1 **play with my –** For a moment Malvolio forgets that in his new status he will not be wearing his steward's chain.

51 **curtsies** bows (in deference). A variant of the two-syllable verb 'courtesy'.

53 *****by th'ears** i.e. by what we hear and by force. As in *2H4* 2.4.289–90, where Hal says punningly to Falstaff, 'I come to draw you out by the ears.' Hanmer's emendation of F's 'with cars' is reasonable in terms of a misreading of Secretary hand since 'c' and 'e' are frequently confused, and a malformed 'by' (or 'bi') + 'th' could be read as 'wy' (or 'wi') + 'th'. Editors who retain the F reading, because Shakespeare elsewhere uses 'car' to mean 'chariot', similarly assume the meaning to be 'by force or torment'.

55 **austere…control** severe glance of command. (See illustration 3, p. 14 above.)

56 **take…a blow** Sixteenth-century idiom for 'give…a blow'.

MALVOLIO Saying, 'Cousin Toby, my fortunes having cast me on your
 niece, give me this prerogative of speech – '

SIR TOBY What, what?

MALVOLIO 'You must amend your drunkenness.' 60

SIR TOBY Out, scab!

FABIAN Nay, patience, or we break the sinews of our plot.

MALVOLIO 'Besides, you waste the treasure of your time with a foolish
 knight – '

SIR ANDREW That's me, I warrant you. 65

MALVOLIO 'One Sir Andrew – '

SIR ANDREW I knew 'twas I, for many do call me fool.

MALVOLIO [*Taking up the letter*] What employment have we here?

SIR TOBY Now is the woodcock near the gin.

FABIAN O peace, and the spirit of humours intimate reading aloud to 70
 him!

MALVOLIO By my life, this is my lady's hand: these be her very c's,
 her u's, and her t's, and thus makes she her great P's. It is, in
 contempt of question, her hand.

SIR ANDREW Her c's, her u's, and her t's: why that? 75

MALVOLIO [*Reads*] 'To the unknown beloved, this, and my good
 wishes' – her very phrases! By your leave, wax. Soft! And the
 impressure her Lucrece, with which she uses to seal: 'tis my lady.
 To whom should this be? [*Opens the letter*]

FABIAN This wins him, liver and all. 80

---

58 speech –'] *Cam.*; speech. F   64 knight –'] *Cam.*; knight. F   66 Andrew –'] *Theobald*; *Andrew*. F   68 SD
Taking…letter] *Rowe*; *not in* F   69 SH SIR TOBY] *Conj. NS*; *Fa.* F   70 SH FABIAN] *Conj. NS*; *To.* F   76 SD
Reads] *Capell*; *not in* F   77 wishes' –] *Cam. subst.*; *Wishes*: F   79 SD *Opens the letter*] *NS subst.*; *not in* F

62 **sinews** Used metaphorically to mean
'strength' (Schmidt).

68 **employment** business.

69 **woodcock** Proverbial symbol of stupidity
(Tilley W746). In exorcising Malvolio's devil (4.2),
Feste remarks that even the soul of his grandam
had passed into a woodcock (45–6).

69 **gin** snare or trap. Aphetic form of 'engine'.

*69–71 The speeches of Fabian and Sir Toby
have been redistributed, in accord with 29 n. above.

70–1 **the spirit…him** may a capricious impulse
suggest his reading it aloud.

72–3 **her very c's…t's** A *double entendre*,
incorporating a slang reference to the female
pudenda (Kökeritz, p. 133, n. 1). Other examples
from the drama are cited in NS.

73 **her great P's** Another *double entendre*. It also
indicates that, despite the use of upper case in F,
the other letters should be minuscules.

73–4 **in contempt of** beyond.

77 **By…wax** For a comparable conventional
apology addressed to the seal on a letter, see *Cym.*
3.2.35: 'Good wax, thy leave.'

78 **impressure…Lucrece** The wax is
impressed with the device Olivia has chosen for her
seal; it represents Lucretia, the Roman matron who
committed suicide after she was violated by Sextus
Tarquinius. Shakespeare had told the story at
length in *The Rape of Lucrece* (1594).

80 **liver and all** through and through. Literally,
the liver (the seat of the passions, as at 1.1.37–8) is
affected and everything else too.

MALVOLIO [*Reads*]   Jove knows I love,
                     But who?
                     Lips, do not move:
                     No man must know.
    'No man must know.' What follows? The numbers altered! 'No   85
man must know'! If this should be thee, Malvolio!

SIR TOBY   Marry, hang thee, brock!

MALVOLIO [*Reads*]   I may command where I adore,
                     But silence, like a Lucrece knife,
                     With bloodless stroke my heart doth gore;   90
                     M.O.A.I. doth sway my life.

FABIAN   A fustian riddle!

SIR TOBY   Excellent wench, say I.

MALVOLIO   'M.O.A.I. doth sway my life.' Nay, but first let me see, let
me see, let me see.   95

FABIAN   What dish o'poison has she dressed him!

SIR TOBY   And with what wing the staniel checks at it!

MALVOLIO   'I may command where I adore.' Why, she may command
me: I serve her; she is my lady. Why, this is evident to any formal
capacity. There is no obstruction in this, and the end – what should   100
that alphabetical position portend? If I could make that resemble
something in me – Softly! 'M.O.A.I.' –

SIR TOBY   O ay, make up that! He is now at a cold scent.

FABIAN   Sowter will cry upon't for all this, though it be as rank as a
fox.   105

---

81 SD *Reads*] *Capell; not in* F   81–4] *As verse, Capell; as prose,* F   88 SD *Reads*] *Capell; not in* F   88–91] *As
Hanmer; as two lines* F   96 dish o'] *Dyce;* dish a F   97 staniel] *Hanmer;* stallion F   100 end –] *Cam.;* end. F
101–2 portend? ...me –] *Capell;* portend, ...me? F   102 me – Softly! 'M.O.A.I.' –] *Cam. subst.;* me? Softly,
M.O.A.I. F

85 numbers versification (of 88–91).
87 brock badger. An animal noted for its evil
odour; hence a term of opprobrium.
91 M.O.A.I....life Compare Orlando's verses
(*AYLI* 3.2.1–10) which contain the line 'Thy
huntress' name that my full life doth sway'.
92 fustian affected, pretentious. A figurative
usage, from the fact that the cloth served as a
substitute for silk (Linthicum, pp. 108–9); thus
Pistol (*2H4* 2.4.189) is called a 'fustian rascal' and
Cassio (*Oth.* 2.3.280) describes himself as dis-
coursing 'fustian' in his drunken state.
96 What dish What a dish. The omission of the
article after 'what' in the sense of 'what kind of'
(Abbott 86) is common, as in *JC* 1.3.42: 'Cassius,
what night is this!'
96 dressed prepared (for).
97 wing speed.

97 *staniel kestrel. An inferior kind of hawk.
97 checks is led astray. A figurative usage, from
the ease with which the staniel may be diverted from
its course by a chance bird. The image is used again
at 3.1.54–5.
99–100 any...capacity any normal person. As
in *Err.* 5.1.104–5: 'With wholesome syrups,
drugs, and holy prayers, / To make of him a formal
man again'.
100 obstruction difficult meaning.
101 position arrangement.
103 O ay Echoing letters of the riddle.
103 make up construe, make sense of.
104–5 Sowter...fox Even though the scent (the
clue to the riddle) be as strong as the smell of a fox,
Sowter (literally, 'cobbler') will cry out in triumph
or 'give tongue' to his success.

MALVOLIO 'M' – Malvolio. 'M' – why, that begins my name!

FABIAN Did not I say he would work it out? The cur is excellent at
faults.

MALVOLIO 'M' – but then there is no consonancy in the sequel that
suffers under probation. 'A' should follow, but 'O' does.   110

FABIAN And O shall end, I hope.

SIR TOBY Ay, or I'll cudgel him and make him cry 'O'!

MALVOLIO And then 'I' comes behind.

FABIAN Ay, and you had any eye behind you, you might see more
detraction at your heels than fortunes before you.   115

MALVOLIO 'M.O.A.I.' This simulation is not as the former, and yet,
to crush this a little, it would bow to me, for every one of these
letters are in my name. Soft, here follows prose. [*Reads*] 'If this
fall into thy hand, revolve. In my stars I am above thee, but be not
afraid of greatness. Some are born great, some achieve greatness,   120
and some have greatness thrust upon 'em. Thy fates open their
hands; let thy blood and spirit embrace them, and, to inure thyself
to what thou art like to be, cast thy humble slough and appear fresh.
Be opposite with a kinsman, surly with servants; let thy tongue tang
arguments of state; put thyself into the trick of singularity. She thus   125

---

106 'M' – Malvolio. 'M' –] *Cam. subst.*; *M. Malvolio, M.* F   118 SD *Reads*] *Capell; not in* F   120 born] *Douai
MS., Rowe; become* F   120 achieve] F2; *atcheeues* F

107–8 **excellent at faults** clever at finding the
scent again after the trail is lost. A 'fault' is a break
in the scent. The hunting diction continues here,
but ironically, implying that Malvolio will follow up
a false scent and so be easily duped.

109–10 **no consonancy...probation** no consistency in what follows that will hold up under
examination.

111 **And O...end** And misery shall conclude.
(The verb is intransitive.) 'O' here is a substantive,
as in *Rom.* 3.3.90: 'Why should you fall into so deep
an O?' In the next line, it is an exclamation,
expressing pain or shock. Dr Johnson suggests that
it refers to the hangman's noose.

113–14 **I...Ay...eye** Playing on the sound of
the letter 'I' in the riddle (as on the letter 'O' in
the preceding lines).

114 **eye behind you** Kittredge notes that the
virtue Prudence was characterised as having a third
eye in the back of her head.

115 **fortunes** possessions, wealth. To accord
with his wish to be 'Count Malvolio'.

116 **simulation** surface resemblance (*OED* sv *sb*
2).

117 **crush** force.

117 **bow** yield.

119 **revolve** turn (it) over in your mind. (See
illustration 4, p. 15 above.)

119 **my stars** i.e. the determinants of my wealth
and rank.

120 ***born** Rowe's emendation of F's 'become' is
substantiated by the quotations in 3.4.37 and
5.1.349.

120 **achieve** F2's correction of F's 'atcheeves' is
also substantiated by the quotations at 3.4.39 and
5.1.349.

121–2 **open their hands** offer bounty. As in *H8*
3.2.184: 'my hand has open'd bounty to you'.

122 **blood and spirit** i.e. mettle.

122 **inure** accustom.

123 **like** likely.

123 **cast...slough** abandon your lowly demeanour as a snake sloughs off its old skin.

123 **fresh** new; 'fresh and new' are used as
synonyms in *Wiv.* 4.5.8.

124 **Be opposite** In 3.4.60 Malvolio interprets
this as to 'appear stubborn' to Sir Toby.

124–5 **tang...state** sound forth on the subject
of statecraft.

125 **put...singularity** adopt the habit of
eccentricity.

advises thee that sighs for thee. Remember who commended thy
yellow stockings and wished to see thee ever cross-gartered: I say,
remember. Go to, thou art made if thou desir'st to be so; if not,
let me see thee a steward still, the fellow of servants, and not worthy
to touch Fortune's fingers. Farewell. She that would alter services   130
with thee,
                              The Fortunate-Unhappy.'

Daylight and champain discovers not more! This is open. I will be
proud, I will read politic authors, I will baffle Sir Toby, I will wash
off gross acquaintance, I will be point-device, the very man. I do   135
not now fool myself to let imagination jade me; for every reason
excites to this, that my lady loves me. She did commend my yellow
stockings of late, she did praise my leg being cross-gartered; and
in this she manifests herself to my love, and with a kind of
injunction drives me to these habits of her liking. I thank my stars,   140
I am happy. I will be strange, stout, in yellow stockings, and
cross-gartered, even with the swiftness of putting on. Jove and my

---

131–3 thee, The Fortunate-Unhappy.' Daylight] *Capell subst.; ;* thee; tht fortunate vnhappy daylight F

---

127 **yellow stockings** A symbol here of love;
used frequently elsewhere in the drama to indicate
marriage and jealousy after marriage (Linthicum, p.
48, with many citations from the drama).

127 **cross-gartered** i.e. the garters are placed
below the knee, crossed at the back, brought round
above the knee and tied at the side. They were
fashionable, according to Linthicum (p. 264 and
nn.) from the 1560s until *c.* 1600. For the fashion
in 1562, see illustration 5, p. 18 above; for an
inamorato wearing cross-garters in 1628, see
illustration 6, p. 19. Earlier ('Malvolio's cross-
gartered yellow stockings', *MP* 25 (1927–8), 92 n.),
Linthicum offered the likely suggestion that
cross-gartering may have been taken to indicate a
hopeful as opposed to a despairing lover. This
would be in accord with Malvolio's declaration that
'every reason' impels him to conclude that Olivia
loves him (136–7). Shakespeare certainly makes
clear that the opposite mode of dress was the sign
of an unhappy lover. Valentine is said to have chided
Sir Proteus for going ungartered, the reason being
that, in contrast to the smiling Malvolio, he could
not as a result of tears see to garter his hose (*TGV*
2.1.73, 76–7); Rosalind specifies that the hose of one
suffering the 'quotidian of love' should be
ungartered (*AYLI* 3.2.378), and so Ophelia
describes Hamlet (*Ham.* F 976 (2.1.77)).

128 **thou art made** i.e. you are favoured by
fortune, literally – by the economic status of the

Countess Olivia – and metaphorically – by the
goddess Fortuna.

130–1 **alter services...thee** exchange places,
becoming subservient to his mastery.

133 **champain** open country.

133 **discovers** reveals.

134 **politic authors** i.e. writers from whom he
can learn to 'tang arguments of state' (see
124–5 n.).

134 **baffle** use (him) contemptuously. The literal
meaning is 'deprive Sir Toby of his knighthood',
'degrade him'. The tables are turned in 5.1.348
when Olivia says to him, 'Alas, poor fool, how have
they baffled thee!'

135 **gross** base.

135 **point-device** i.e. precisely as described in
the letter.

136 **jade me** make me ridiculous. Literally, a
'jade' is a vicious or worthless horse.

137 **excites to this** impels this (thought).

140 **habits** Both (1) dress (as in his comment at
3.4.65 on 'the habit of some sir of note') and (2)
deportment.

141 **happy** blessed by fortune.

141 **strange** distant.

141 **stout** proud.

142 **Jove** Editors have taken the use of 'Jove'
here and elsewhere in the play (some nine times) as
suggesting late revision to comply with the 1606
statute of non-profanity on the stage, but as Turner

stars be praised! Here is yet a postscript. [*Reads*] 'Thou canst not choose but know who I am. If thou entertain'st my love, let it appear in thy smiling; thy smiles become thee well. Therefore in my 145 presence still smile, dear my sweet, I prithee.' Jove, I thank thee. I will smile; I will do every thing that thou wilt have me.   *Exit*

FABIAN I will not give my part of this sport for a pension of thousands to be paid from the sophy.

SIR TOBY I could marry this wench for this device –   150

SIR ANDREW So could I, too.

SIR TOBY And ask no other dowry with her but such another jest.

SIR ANDREW Nor I neither.

FABIAN Here comes my noble gull-catcher.

Enter MARIA

SIR TOBY Wilt thou set thy foot o'my neck?   155

SIR ANDREW Or o'mine either?

SIR TOBY Shall I play my freedom at tray-trip and become thy bondslave?

SIR ANDREW I'faith, or I either?

SIR TOBY Why, thou hast put him in such a dream that when the image 160 of it leaves him, he must run mad.

MARIA Nay, but say true, does it work upon him?

SIR TOBY Like acqua-vitae with a midwife.

MARIA If you will then see the fruits of the sport, mark his first approach before my lady. He will come to her in yellow stockings, and 'tis 165 a colour she abhors, and cross-gartered, a fashion she detests; and he will smile upon her, which will now be so unsuitable to her

---

143 SD *Reads*] Collier; *not in* F   146 dear] F2 (deere); deero F   154 SD *Enter Maria*] Capell; *after 152* F

has pointed out ('The text of *Twelfth Night*'), the use of 'God' sixteen times (as well as four instances of the contracted forms – 'slight, 'slid and 'odds) scarcely supports that notion. It would indeed be unthinkable, as he notes, for God to be invoked at 3.1.38.

149 **sophy** Title of the Shah of Persia, deriving from the surname of the dynastic rulers from *c*. 1500 to 1736. Together with the second reference to the sophy (3.4.236), this has been taken to reflect current interest in the accounts (published 1600 and 1601) of Sir Anthony Sherley's adventures when serving as an ambassador for the shah.

153 **Nor I neither** For examples of double (and triple) negatives, see 3.1.144 n.

154 **gull-catcher** One who preys on the credulity of others; as Maria with Malvolio, so Sir Toby with Sir Andrew.

157 **play** wager.

157 **tray-trip** A dice game in which the winner threw a three (a 'tray' or, as in *LLL* F 2137 (5.2.232), a 'trey').

163 **acqua-vitae** A 'hot infusion', in Autolycus's words (*WT* 4.4.786–7); it is elsewhere specified as favoured by an Irishman (*Wiv.* 2.2.303–4) and by Juliet's nurse (*Rom.* 3.2.88) but not by a midwife.

165–6 **yellow...detests** Olivia's antipathy to yellow stockings and cross-garters is, of course, pointedly at odds with Malvolio's notion (137–8) that she had commended them.

disposition, being addicted to a melancholy as she is, that it cannot
but turn him into a notable contempt. If you will see it, follow me.

SIR TOBY To the gates of Tartar, thou most excellent devil of wit!   170
SIR ANDREW I'll make one, too.

Exeunt

3.1 *Enter* VIOLA *and* CLOWN [FESTE, *playing on a pipe and tabor*]

VIOLA Save thee, friend, and thy music! Dost thou live by thy tabor?
FESTE No, sir, I live by the church.
VIOLA Art thou a churchman?
FESTE No such matter, sir. I do live by the church; for I do live at my
house, and my house doth stand by the church.   5
VIOLA So thou mayst say the king lies by a beggar, if a beggar dwell
near him; or the church stands by thy tabor if thy tabor stand by
the church.
FESTE You have said, sir. To see this age! A sentence is but a cheveril
glove to a good wit – how quickly the wrong side may be turned   10
outward!
VIOLA Nay, that's certain: they that dally nicely with words may
quickly make them wanton.

---

171 SD *Exeunt*] Exeunt. / *Finis Actus secundus* F   Act 3, Scene 1 3.1] *Actus Tertius, Scæna prima.* F
0 SD FESTE, *playing...tabor*] Collier²; *not in* F   6 king] F2; kings F

---

170 **Tartar** Tartarus, equivalent to the Christian
hell.

Act 3, Scene 1
    Location Olivia's garden (Capell).
    0 SD A pipe and tabor (small drum) were
traditional stage properties of the clown, and Viola's
first words indicate that he enters playing. See
illustration 2, p. 11 above.
    1 **Save thee** May God preserve thee.
    1 **live by** make your living by. A question that
induces Feste's quibbling in the next line where he
uses 'by' to mean 'beside'.
    3 **churchman** ecclesiastic. A mocking retort in
view of the dress the fool was probably wearing; see
1.5.21 and 46 nn.
    4 **No such matter** Nothing of the kind.
Dent lists this idiomatic phrase as proverbial
(M754.1).
    6 **the king...beggar** Viola perhaps here
assumes Feste's musical knowledge to include the
ballad of the 'illustrate King Cophetua' and the

'pernicious and indubitate beggar Zenelophon'
(*LLL* 4.1.65–6).
    6 **lies by** Quibbling on (1) lies near and (2) lies
with.
    7 **stands by...stand by** Quibbling on the
literal meaning ('is placed near') and the figurative
('is maintained by').
    9 **You have said** 'You are right.' Dent (s118.1)
records this as proverbial.
    9 **sentence** (1) opinion, (2) judgement, or even
(3) axiom.
    9 **cheveril** kidskin. A soft and pliable kind of
leather, aptly used in reference both to 'wit' (as here
and in *Rom.* 2.4.83) and to 'conscience' (as in *H8*
2.3.32 and Tilley c608). Pronounced *chevril*.
    10–11 **wrong side...outward** Dent (s431.1)
records this as proverbial.
    12 **dally nicely** play curiously.
    13 **wanton** wayward. Viola's diction, beginning
in 6, carries sexual overtones which Feste then
exploits. Compare *Venus and Adonis* 105–6, 'And
for my sake [Mars] hath learn'd... / To toy, to
wanton, dally, smile and jest.'

FESTE I would therefore my sister had had no name, sir.

VIOLA Why, man?   15

FESTE Why, sir, her name's a word, and to dally with that word might
make my sister wanton; but, indeed, words are very rascals, since
bonds disgraced them.

VIOLA Thy reason, man?

FESTE Truth, sir, I can yield you none without words, and words are   20
grown so false, I am loath to prove reason with them.

VIOLA I warrant thou art a merry fellow and car'st for nothing.

FESTE Not so, sir, I do care for something; but in my conscience, sir,
I do not care for you: if that be to care for nothing, I would it would
make you invisible.   25

VIOLA Art not thou the Lady Olivia's fool?

FESTE No, indeed, sir. The Lady Olivia has no folly. She will keep no
fool, sir, till she be married, and fools are as like husbands as
pilchards are to herrings – the husband's the bigger. I am indeed
not her fool but her corrupter of words.   30

VIOLA I saw thee late at the Count Orsino's.

FESTE Foolery, sir, does walk about the orb like the sun; it shines
everywhere. I would be sorry, sir, but the fool should be as oft
with your master as with my mistress: I think I saw your wisdom
there.   35

VIOLA Nay, and thou pass upon me, I'll no more with thee. Hold,
there's expenses for thee. [*Gives a coin*]

FESTE Now Jove, in his next commodity of hair, send thee a beard!

---

29 pilchards] *Capell*, Pilchers F   37 SD *Gives...coin*] *Hanmer subst.; not in* F

17–18 words...disgraced them words are
untrustworthy in that promises (bonds) are no
longer to be relied on. Julia (*TGV* 2.7.75) says of
Proteus: 'His words are bonds.'
  20 none no explanation.
  21 reason with them anything rational by them.
  23–5 I do care...invisible Asserting that he
does care for something, Feste excludes Viola; if
that is to care 'for nothing', as she has just said, then
he wishes that as a 'no-thing' she should also not
be visible.
  23 in my conscience in truth.
  28–9 fools are...the bigger Feste establishes
his disparaging comment by a familiar comparison:
Nashe terms pilchards 'counterfets to the red
Herring, as Copper to Golde, or Ockamie [a
silver-coloured alloy] to silver' (*Works*, III, 192).
  31 late lately.
  32 orb The earth, the centre of the universe in
the Ptolemaic system.

32–3 sun...everywhere Compare the proverb
(Tilley s985), 'The sun shines upon all alike.'
  33–4 I would be...mistress I should be sorry
unless a fool (i.e. Viola) would be as often with your
master as (one is) with my mistress. 'Would' is used
for 'should' just as 'should' is for 'would'; see
Abbott (120, 331), though he interprets the generic
'fool' as Feste's reference to himself, thus missing
the mockery of the next line.
  34 your wisdom A mocking title to point up
Viola's role as her master's fool.
  36 pass (1) give sentence, (2) thrust (a fencing
term, here used of Feste's barbs). Compare Jonson's
Every Man in His Humour (1601), 1.3.207 ff.
(modernised):
  Matheo How mean you 'pass upon me'?
  Bobadill Why, thus, sir, make a thrust at me – come in
    upon my time; control your point, and make a full
    career [lunge] at the body.
  38 commodity consignment.

VIOLA By my troth, I'll tell thee, I am almost sick for one – [*Aside*]
   though I would not have it grow on my chin. Is thy lady within?   40
FESTE Would not a pair of these have bred, sir?
VIOLA Yes, being kept together and put to use.
FESTE I would play Lord Pandarus of Phrygia, sir, to bring a Cressida
   to this Troilus.
VIOLA I understand you sir; 'tis well begged. [*Gives another coin*]
FESTE The matter, I hope, is not great, sir – begging but a beggar:
   Cressida was a beggar. My lady is within, sir. I will conster to them
   whence you come. Who you are, and what you would are out of
   my welkin – I might say 'element', but the word is overworn.

                                                        Exit

VIOLA This fellow is wise enough to play the fool,   50
   And to do that well craves a kind of wit;
   He must observe their mood on whom he jests,
   The quality of persons, and the time;

39 SD *Aside*] Cam.; *not in* F   45 SD *Gives…coin*] Collier² *subst.; not in* F

39 **sick for one** (1) lovesick for one who has a
beard, (2) longing to be able to grow a beard.
   41 **bred** produced more. The double meaning is
that the coin would multiply (1) if there was another
coin to mate with, (2) if the coin was put out to
interest. Viola acknowledges both meanings in the
next line; 'use' is interest paid on borrowed money,
but it also refers to sexual activity. Compare the
Lord Chief Justice's charge against Falstaff (*2H4*
2.1.114–16): 'You have…practic'd upon the
easy-yielding spirit of this woman, and made her
serve your uses both in purse and in person.'
   43 **Pandarus** Cressida's uncle, who acted as a
pander in order to bring his niece and Troilus
together, as set forth in Chaucer's great love poem
Troilus and Criseyde. Close to the time when he was
writing *TN*, Shakespeare turned this Chaucerian
material into dramatic form but giving it a dark and
cynical tone. Here Feste is applying the names of
the lovers to the coin he has received and the one
he hopes to receive, but the implicit suggestion is
that he will bring Olivia and Cesario together.
   46 **The matter…beggar** Having been re-
warded a second time for his willingness to bring this
Troilus (literally, the coin and, figuratively,
Troilus's surrogate, Cesario) to a Cressida, Feste
says it is no great thing for him to beg for a beggar
like Cressida, thus denying Viola's 'well-begged' of
the previous line. According to the *Testament of
Cresseid*, Robert Henryson's fifteenth-century con-
tinuation of the story, she became a leper and was
forced to beg for her living.

47 **conster** Though simply a variant of
'construe', F's spelling is retained for the sake of
euphony; from early on up to the nineteenth
century, the stress was on the first syllable.
   49 **welkin** sky. Most often in poetical use.
   49 **element** Referring to one of the four
elements, each of which was regarded as the natural
habitat for particular sorts of creatures – the air for
birds, and so on; but since 'element' could also refer
to the sky (as in 1.1.26), Feste is punning as well
as remarking on his incapacity to say 'who' Cesario
is or 'what' it is he wants.
   49 **overworn** It seems that Feste is referring to
'element' as one of Malvolio's special words: note
his supercilious remark to Sir Toby, Maria and
Fabian at 3.4.106. For another example of a special
word, see 4.2.73 and n. Editors have often accepted
that Shakespeare is glancing here at the frequent use
of the word by the character representing Jonson in
Satiromastix (1601), Dekker's contribution to the
current 'war of the theatres'. But throughout *TN*
Shakespeare comments on affectations of diction by
means of Orsino's stilted language, Viola's variability, Sir Toby's waywardness, Sir Andrew's
inadequacy and Feste's nice dallying.
   50 Playing on the proverbial statement 'No man
can play the fool so well as the wise man' (Tilley
M321) and perhaps also 'He is not wise who cannot
play the fool' (Tilley M428).
   53 **quality** (1) nature, (2) rank.

Not, like the haggard, check at every feather
That comes before his eye. This is a practice,   55
As full of labour as a wise man's art:
For folly that he wisely shows is fit;
But wise men, folly-fall'n, quite taint their wit.

Enter SIR TOBY *and* [SIR] ANDREW

SIR TOBY Save you, gentleman.

VIOLA And you, sir.   60

SIR ANDREW *Dieu vous garde, monsieur.*

VIOLA *Et vous aussi; votre serviteur.*

SIR ANDREW I hope, sir, you are, and I am yours.

SIR TOBY Will you encounter the house? My niece is desirous you
should enter, if your trade be to her.   65

VIOLA I am bound to your niece, sir; I mean, she is the list of my voyage.

SIR TOBY Taste your legs, sir; put them to motion.

VIOLA My legs do better understand me, sir, than I understand what
you mean by bidding me taste my legs.

SIR TOBY I mean, to go, sir, to enter.   70

VIOLA I will answer you with gait and entrance – but we are prevented.

Enter OLIVIA *and* GENTLEWOMAN [MARIA]

Most excellent accomplished lady, the heavens rain odours on you!

54 Not] *Rann, conj. Johnson;* And F   58 wise men, ...fall'n] *Capell;* wisemens folly falne F   58 SD SIR ANDREW]
Rowe; Andrew. F   71 SD MARIA] *Rowe; Gentlewoman.* F

54 *Not Rann's emendation of F's 'And',
conjectured by Dr Johnson, is required in order to
make Cesario's point about Feste's judicious wit
(57).
54 like the haggard...feather like the wild
hawk, seize on every prey.
55 practice professional exercise.
57 wisely shows judiciously reveals.
57 is fit suits the purpose.
58 *folly-fall'n having stooped to folly.
58 quite taint completely infect.
61–2 *Dieu...serviteur* 'God keep you, sir.' 'And
you too. At your service.' Sir Andrew here both
understands and responds (in his way) to the
conventional French salutations; as Sir Toby says
(1.3.22), he can speak 'three or four languages word
for word' (though at 1.3.77 he could not grasp the
meaning of *pourquoi*).
64 encounter i.e. go to meet. Another of Sir
Toby's verbal affectations.
65 trade business (of any kind). It also suggests

a commercial venture, which is the meaning Viola
picks up in the next line.
66 bound to (1) intending to go to, (2) confined
to.
66 list boundary. As in *1H4* 4.1.51–2: 'The very
list, the very utmost bound / Of all our fortunes'.
But also, affectedly, 'goal' or 'destination'
(Schmidt).
67 Taste Try. Used in the same sense at 3.4.207:
'to taste their valour'.
68–9 My legs...mean A Launce-like quibble,
as in *TGV* 2.5.32: 'Why, stand-under and
under-stand is all one.'
71 I...entrance I will respond by going and
entering. With a quibble on 'gate' (the spelling in
F) and 'entrance'.
71 prevented anticipated.
72 the heavens...you For Shakespeare's use
of the optative subjunctive with the omission of
'may', see Abbott 365, where he observes that this
usage gives 'great vigour' to a line.

SIR ANDREW That youth's a rare courtier – 'rain odours' – well.

VIOLA My matter hath no voice, lady, but to your own most pregnant
    and vouchsafed ear.   75

SIR ANDREW 'Odours', 'pregnant', and 'vouchsafed': I'll get 'em all
    three all ready.

OLIVIA Let the garden door be shut, and leave me to my hearing.
             [Exeunt Sir Toby, Sir Andrew, and Maria]
    Give me your hand, sir.

VIOLA My duty, madam, and most humble service.   80

OLIVIA What is your name?

VIOLA Cesario is your servant's name, fair princess.

OLIVIA My servant, sir? 'Twas never merry world
    Since lowly feigning was called compliment.
    Y'are servant to the Count Orsino, youth.   85

VIOLA And he is yours, and his must needs be yours:
    Your servant's servant is your servant, madam.

OLIVIA For him, I think not on him; for his thoughts,
    Would they were blanks, rather than filled with me!

VIOLA Madam, I come to whet your gentle thoughts   90
    On his behalf.

OLIVIA   O by your leave, I pray you!
    I bade you never speak again of him;
    But would you undertake another suit
    I had rather hear you to solicit that,
    Than music from the spheres.

VIOLA   Dear lady –   95

---

73 courtier – 'rain odours' –] *NS;* Courtier, raine odours, F   77 all ready] *Malone;* already F   78 SD *Exeunt...Maria*]
Rowe; not in F   95 lady –] *Theobald subst.;* Lady. F

---

73 **'rain odours' – well** Sir Andrew's 'well'
may suggest that he is commenting (1) admiringly
(as 76–7 would indicate) or (2) adversely on
Cesario's wrenched metaphor (catachresis). For
another example of wrenching, compare Falstaff's
'Let the sky rain potatoes' (*Wiv.* 5.5.18–19).

74 **pregnant** ready. As at 2.2.25.

75 **vouchsafed** proffered.

76–7 **get...ready** keep them in mind for ready
use. Perhaps he writes in his 'tables' or commonplace book.

78 **hearing** audience. Compare the mocking
response to similar inflated diction in *Wiv.* 2.2.40–3:

Quickly. Shall I vouchsafe your worship a word or two?
Falstaff. Two thousand,...and I'll vouchsafe thee the
hearing.

83–4 **'Twas never...Since** A proverbial
expression used to introduce a variety of

conclusions – since there were so many puritans,
since there was so much preaching, etc. (Dent
w878.1).

84 **lowly feigning** pretended humility.

86 **he is yours** he is your servant. Used here to
mean 'suitor'; Viola then immediately reverts to its
complimentary use.

88 **For** As regards.

89 **blanks** empty (like sheets of paper). Compare
Sonnets 77.9–10: 'Look what thy memory cannot
contain / Commit to these waste blanks'; though
'blanks' in this instance is Theobald's conjecture
for 'blacks', it is a satisfactory one since n:c were
easily confused in Secretary hand.

95 **music...spheres** In their rotations, the
crystalline spheres containing the planets and the
fixed stars were held to create a ravishing harmony
inaudible to mortal ears.

OLIVIA Give me leave, beseech you. I did send,
        After the last enchantment you did here,
        A ring in chase of you. So did I abuse
        Myself, my servant, and, I fear me, you.
        Under your hard construction must I sit,   100
        To force that on you in a shameful cunning
        Which you knew none of yours. What might you think?
        Have you not set mine honour at the stake,
        And baited it with all th'unmuzzled thoughts
        That tyrannous heart can think? To one of your receiving   105
        Enough is shown; a cypress, not a bosom,
        Hides my heart: so, let me hear you speak.
VIOLA I pity you.
OLIVIA   That's a degree to love.
VIOLA No, not a grise; for 'tis a vulgar proof
        That very oft we pity enemies.   110
OLIVIA Why then, methinks 'tis time to smile again.
        O world, how apt the poor are to be proud!
        If one should be a prey, how much the better

97 here] *Warburton, conj. Thirlby;* heare F   105–9 think...receiving / ...bosom, / ...speak. / ...proof] F; ...think /
...shown / ...heart / ...grise / ...proof / *NS*   107 my] F; my poore F2

96 **Give me...beseech you** In moving from
courteous formula (91) to entreaty, Olivia betrays
her intensity both by the abrupt grammatical shift
from second to first person and by omission of the
subject for the second verb (beseech).
98 **abuse** (1) deceive, (2) disgrace. Both senses
are probably intended.
99 **I fear me** i.e. I am afraid. This old form of
reflexive is common in Elizabethan English.
100 **hard construction** harsh interpretation;
'construction' is used in the same sense at 2.3.147.
Elsewhere Shakespeare has 'illegitimate construction' (*Ado* 3.4.50); 'merciful construction' (*H8*
Epilogue 10); and 'good construction' (*Cor.* 5.6.20).
101 **that** the ring.
101 **in...cunning** by means of a disgraceful
trick.
102 **knew none** knew was none. The verb is
understood.
103–5 **Have you...think** The image is of
bear-baiting, with Olivia tied to the stake and set
on by all the unrestrained thoughts, like unmuzzled
dogs, that a cruel heart (like Cesario's) can conceive.
105–9 *The lineation of F, retained here, has
occasioned much editorial rearranging; that of NS,
with lines ending '...think / ...shown / ...heart

/ ...grise / ...proof' has a good deal to commend
it, in that making 105 short ('That...can think')
suggests a break in Olivia's delivery.
105 **receiving** understanding.
106 **cypress** A light transparent material
resembling cobweb lawn or crape. Olivia's revealing
her feelings here parallels the situation at their first
meeting when she metaphorically drew 'the
curtain' and unveiled herself to Viola.
108 **degree** step. In the next line, 'grise' has the
same meaning.
109 **vulgar proof** common experience.
111 Ironic in that she has at least the 'pity' of
an enemy.
112 **how...proud** how ready the deprived are to
be full of self-esteem. Again, ironic.
113–14 **If...wolf** This seems to mean that if one
must be a victim, how much better it would be to
succumb to the lion (i.e. the duke) rather than the
wolf (i.e. Cesario, a professed enemy). The name
Orsino means 'little bear' but this point need not
have occurred to Shakespeare here. Compare the
proverb 'The lion spares the suppliant' (Tilley
L316). Mahood takes 'lion' to refer to Cesario as a
king of men, 'wolf' (since she does not equate it with
anyone) apparently to the species of animal.

To fall before the lion than the wolf!
(*Clock strikes*)
The clock upbraids me with the waste of time.   115
Be not afraid, good youth; I will not have you –
And yet when wit and youth is come to harvest,
Your wife is like to reap a proper man.
There lies your way, due west.

VIOLA   Then westward ho!
Grace and good disposition attend your ladyship!   120
You'll nothing, madam, to my lord by me?

OLIVIA Stay!
I prithee tell me what thou think'st of me.

VIOLA That you do think you are not what you are.

OLIVIA If I think so, I think the same of you.   125

VIOLA Then think you right: I am not what I am.

OLIVIA I would you were as I would have you be.

VIOLA Would it be better, madam, than I am?
I wish it might, for now I am your fool.

OLIVIA [*Aside*] O what a deal of scorn looks beautiful   130
In the contempt and anger of his lip!
A murd'rous guilt shows not itself more soon,
Than love that would seem hid. Love's night is noon.
Cesario, by the roses of the spring,
By maidhood, honour, truth, and everything,   135
I love thee so that, maugre all thy pride,
Nor wit nor reason can my passion hide.

122–3 Stay! / ...me] *Capell subst.; one line in* F   130 SD *Aside*] *Staunton; not in* F

118 **proper** handsome, fine.

119 **westward ho** The cry of the Thames watermen for passengers going to Westminster.

120 **Grace...disposition** The favour of heaven and a happy frame of mind (Kittredge).

121 **You'll nothing** i.e. send no message.

124 Three layers of meaning: (1) you do not consider that you are a noblewoman; (2) you do not imagine you are in love with a woman, and therefore (3) you do not believe you are out of your mind. In each, the negative is transferred to the main verb.

125 Understanding Viola-Cesario to intend only the third meaning, Olivia retorts in kind.

126 Viola takes the retort literally, fully concurring that she is not what she seems to be.

131 **contempt...his lip** i.e. characterised by a drooping lip, as in *WT* 1.2.371–3: 'when he, / Wafting his eyes to th'contrary and falling / A lip of much contempt'.

132 Compare the proverbial 'Murder will out' (Tilley M1315).

133 **Love's...noon** i.e. as clear or evident as midday: as the proverb has it, 'Love cannot be hid' (Tilley L500 and L490). Dent adds Olivia's aphoristic statement to Tilley's N167, 'Dark night is Cupid's day', but the implication here is utterly at odds with the salacious use of that proverb.

136 **maugre...pride** in spite of all your unkindness. In this line Olivia shifts to the familiar second-person singular.

Do not extort thy reasons from this clause,
For that I woo, thou therefore hast no cause;
But rather reason thus with reason fetter: 140
Love sought is good, but giv'n unsought is better.

VIOLA   By innocence I swear, and by my youth,
I have one heart, one bosom, and one truth,
And that no woman has; nor never none
Shall mistress be of it, save I alone.   145
And so, adieu, good madam; never more
Will I my master's tears to you deplore.

OLIVIA   Yet come again: for thou perhaps mayst move
That heart which now abhors to like his love.

Exeunt

3.2   *Enter* SIR TOBY, SIR ANDREW, *and* FABIAN

SIR ANDREW   No, faith, I'll not stay a jot longer!

SIR TOBY   Thy reason, dear venom, give thy reason.

FABIAN   You must needs yield your reason, Sir Andrew.

SIR ANDREW   Marry, I saw your niece do more favours to the count's
servingman than ever she bestowed upon me. I saw't i'th'orchard.   5

SIR TOBY   Did she see thee the while, old boy? Tell me that.

SIR ANDREW   As plain as I see you now.

FABIAN   This was a great argument of love in her toward you.

SIR ANDREW   'Slight! Will you make an ass o'me?

FABIAN   I will prove it legitimate, sir, upon the oaths of judgement and   10
reason.

Act 3, Scene 2   3.2] *Scæna Secunda.* F   6 thee the] F3; the F

138–41 Do not...better Do not forcibly extract
your argument from the proposition that because I
woo you, you have no motive or reason (to love);
rather, thus shackle one reason to another, which is,
that love sought is good but given unsought is
better; 'clause' as 'proposition' is a nonce usage.

144 nor...none See 2.5.153 for an example of
a double negative and *AYLI* 1.2.27–8 for another
instance of a triple one.

Act 3, Scene 2
Location Olivia's house (Rowe).

2 **dear venom** Sir Toby responds with this
vocative to the virulence of Sir Andrew's statement
(metonymy – here, a substitution of the cause for
the effect).

5 **orchard** A walled or enclosed garden, as in
3.1.78.

8 **argument** proof.

9 **'Slight** See 2.5.28 n.

9 **Will you...me** Dent (A379.1) lists this as
proverbial.

10 **legitimate** logically admissible (Schmidt,
Onions). Curiously the earliest example given in the
OED is from the eighteenth century.

10–11 **oaths...reason** sworn testimony of
judgement and reason. Fabian here and Sir Toby
in the next line are trying to muddle Sir Andrew
by mixing (1) logical and legal and (2) abstract and
concrete terms.

SIR TOBY And they have been grand-jurymen since before Noah was
a sailor.

FABIAN She did show favour to the youth in your sight only to
exasperate you, to awake your dormouse valour, to put fire in your   15
heart, and brimstone in your liver. You should then have accosted
her, and with some excellent jests, fire-new from the mint, you
should have banged the youth into dumbness. This was looked for
at your hand, and this was balked. The double gilt of this
opportunity you let time wash off, and you are now sailed into the   20
north of my lady's opinion, where you will hang like an icicle on
a Dutchman's beard unless you do redeem it by some laudable
attempt, either of valour or policy.

SIR ANDREW And't be any way, it must be with valour, for policy I
hate. I had as lief be a Brownist as a politician.   25

SIR TOBY Why then, build me thy fortunes upon the basis of valour.
Challenge me the count's youth to fight with him, hurt him in eleven
places – my niece shall take note of it – and assure thyself, there
is no love-broker in the world can more prevail in man's commen-
dation with woman than report of valour.   30

FABIAN There is no way but this, Sir Andrew.

SIR ANDREW Will either of you bear me a challenge to him?

SIR TOBY Go, write it in a martial hand, be curst and brief; it is no
matter how witty, so it be eloquent, and full of invention. Taunt
him with the licence of ink. If thou 'thou'st' him some thrice, it   35

15 **to awake...valour** The dormouse sleeps
throughout the winter.

16 **accosted** A well-selected word on Fabian's
part since its meaning had been spelled out to Sir
Andrew at 1.3.46–7.

18 **banged** Figuratively, 'struck'.

19 **balked** neglected.

19 **double gilt** Gilt plate twice washed with gold
(NS).

20–2 **sailed...beard** Editors agree that this is
a topical reference to the arctic voyage made by the
Dutchman William Barents in 1596–7; an English
translation of the account by Gerrit de Veer,
detailing the harsh suffering of the crew, had been
entered in the *SR* in June 1598, making the allusion
timely. See also 62–3 n.

23 **policy** strategy. In the next lines Sir Andrew
takes this in its derogatory sense of 'scheming', as
with 'politicians' (2.3.66).

25 **Brownist** A member of the extreme separatist
sect established by Robert Browne, notorious in this
period for his writing of controversial tracts.

26, 27 **me** Sir Toby's use of the ethical dative
here and again at 3.4.148 is intended to convey his
sympathetic concern.

27 **to fight** i.e. by offering to fight.

29 **love-broker** go-between. The only instance
in Shakespeare.

29–30 **in man's...woman** in commending a
man to a woman.

33 **curst** harsh. As in *2H6* 3.2.311–15: 'terms /
As curst, as harsh, and horrible to hear... / As
lean-fac'd Envy in her loathsome cave'.

34 **invention** untruth. Compare *AWW*
3.6.97–8: 'but return with an invention, and clap
upon you two or three probable [plausible] lies'.

35 **licence of ink** the freedom that the distance
of a written taunt confers.

35 **If thou 'thou'st'** i.e. if you use the familiar
form employed in addressing intimates and
servants. To use it with a stranger would be
offensive.

shall not be amiss, and as many lies as will lie in thy sheet of paper,
although the sheet were big enough for the bed of Ware in England,
set 'em down. Go, about it! Let there be gall enough in thy ink;
though thou write with a goose-pen, no matter. About it!

SIR ANDREW Where shall I find you?   40

SIR TOBY We'll call thee at the cubiculo. Go!

Exit Sir Andrew

FABIAN This is a dear manikin to you, Sir Toby.

SIR TOBY I have been dear to him, lad, some two thousand strong, or
so.

FABIAN We shall have a rare letter from him, but you'll not deliver't?   45

SIR TOBY Never trust me then, and by all means stir on the youth to
an answer. I think oxen and wainropes cannot hale them together.
For Andrew, if he were opened and you find so much blood in his
liver as will clog the foot of a flea, I'll eat the rest of th'anatomy.

FABIAN And his opposite, the youth, bears in his visage no great presage   50
of cruelty.

Enter MARIA

SIR TOBY Look where the youngest wren of mine comes –

MARIA If you desire the spleen, and will laugh yourselves into stitches,
follow me. Yond gull Malvolio is turned heathen, a very renegado;

---

45 deliver't?] *Dyce*; deliver't. F   52 mine] F; nine *Theobald*

---

37 bed of Ware This carved bed, famous among
the Elizabethans, was ten-feet square and could
accommodate a dozen people.

38 gall Punning on (1) the figurative meaning,
'venom', and (2) the literal, the growth on oak trees
used in making ink.

39 goose-pen A pen made from the quill of a
goose and, here, used by a goose.

41 call...cubiculo call for you at the bedcham-
ber. Sir Toby is affecting either the ablative form
of Latin *cubiculum* or the Italian *cubiculo*.

42 dear...you little plaything dear to you. In the
next line Sir Toby plays on the second meaning by
stressing how 'costly' he has been to Sir Andrew.

45 rare extraordinary.

46 Never...then Have no fear. But on learning
how 'excellently ignorant' the written challenge is,
Sir Toby determines (at 3.4.158–9) to deliver it in
his own words.

47 wainropes wagon ropes.

47 hale drag.

48 opened dissected.

48–9 blood...liver A liver lacking in blood –

that is, white and pale – was, according to Falstaff
(*2H4* 4.3.104–6), 'the badge of pusillanimity and
cowardice'.

49 anatomy skeleton. Here it means the rest of
the body as well but suggests that it is only skin and
bones (*OED sv sb* 6); compare the description of
Pinch in *Err.* 5.1.238–9: 'a hungry lean-fac'd villain
/ A mere anatomy'.

50 opposite adversary.

52 of mine Used to indicate affection, as with
'my Ariel' (*Temp.* 1.2.188), 'my Oberon' (*MND*
4.1.76) and 'my eyas-musket [young hawk]' *Wiv.*
3.3.22). Since the wren is a diminutive bird, Sir
Toby again remarks on Maria's small stature. Most
editors follow Theobald and emend to 'of nine' and
explain that the last of nine eggs to be hatched would
be the smallest specimen, though not explaining the
significance of 'nine' as against ten or any other
number of eggs, as Furness notes.

53 spleen a fit of laughter. The spleen was
believed to be the seat of laughter.

54 renegado apostate.

for there is no Christian that means to be saved by believing rightly   55
can ever believe such impossible passages of grossness. He's in
yellow stockings.

SIR TOBY And cross-gartered?

MARIA Most villainously. Like a pedant that keeps a school i'th'church.
I have dogged him like his murderer. He does obey every point of   60
the letter that I dropped to betray him. He does smile his face into
more lines than is in the new map with the augmentation of the
Indies; you have not seen such a thing as 'tis. I can hardly forbear
hurling things at him; I know my lady will strike him. If she do,
he'll smile and take't for a great favour.   65

SIR TOBY Come bring us, bring us where he is.

                                                                Exeunt

3.3 *Enter* SEBASTIAN *and* ANTONIO

SEBASTIAN I would not by my will have troubled you,
                    But since you make your pleasure of your pains,
                    I will no further chide you.

ANTONIO I could not stay behind you. My desire,
                    More sharp than filèd steel, did spur me forth;   5
                    And not all love to see you (though so much
                    As might have drawn one to a longer voyage),
                    But jealousy what might befall your travel,
                    Being skilless in these parts which to a stranger,

---

66 SD] *Exeunt omnes* F   Act 3, Scene 3   3.3] *Scæna Tertia* F

56 such...grossness such grossly unbelievable statements (as those in Maria's letter). The implication is that Malvolio has adopted them as his creed.

59 pedant...church i.e. ostentatious (like a pedantic schoolmaster). For cross-gartering, see 2.5.127 n. NS suggests that teaching in a church rather than in a schoolhouse proper was becoming obsolete at this date and such a 'pedant' might seem something of an oddity.

62–3 more lines...Indies This is accepted as a reference to a new map based on the Mercator principles of projection, prepared by Edward Wright and others and printed in 1600. It shows the East Indies more fully than in earlier maps, gives a slight suggestion of the unknown continent of Australia, and also, for the first time in English maps, Novaya Zemlya, this last as a result of Barents's arctic voyage in 1596–7 (see 20–2 n). A facsimile of it is included in the second volume of *Voyages and Works of John Davis*, ed. A. H. Markham, 1880, Hakluyt Society, vol. 59, and there is a note on the 'new map' by C. H. Coote in the first volume. The rhumb lines form a veritable network, prompting Maria's image.

Act 3, Scene 3
  Location The street (Rowe).
  6 all only.
  6 so much enough (love).
  8 jealousy apprehension.
  9 skilless in ignorant of.

Unguided, and unfriended, often prove   10
Rough and unhospitable. My willing love,
The rather by these arguments of fear,
Set forth in your pursuit.

SEBASTIAN   My kind Antonio,
I can no other answer make but thanks,
And thanks, and ever thanks; and oft good turns   15
Are shuffled off with such uncurrent pay;
But were my worth, as is my conscience, firm,
You should find better dealing. What's to do?
Shall we go see the relics of this town?

ANTONIO Tomorrow, sir; best first go see your lodging.   20

SEBASTIAN I am not weary, and 'tis long to night.
I pray you, let us satisfy our eyes
With the memorials and the things of fame
That do renown this city.

ANTONIO   Would you'd pardon me.
I do not without danger walk these streets.   25
Once in a sea-fight 'gainst the count his galleys
I did some service, of such note indeed
That were I tane here, it would scarce be answered.

SEBASTIAN Belike you slew great number of his people?

ANTONIO Th'offence is not of such a bloody nature,   30
Albeit the quality of the time and quarrel
Might well have given us bloody argument.
It might have since been answered in repaying

---

15 And thanks, and ever thanks; and oft] *Theobald*; And thankes: and ever oft F   29 people?] *Dyce*; people. F

9–11 **to a stranger...unhospitable** Illyria was noted for its pirates, as in *2H6* 4.1.108, 'Bargulus, the strong Illyrian pirate'; in *MM* 4.3.71, the Ragusan 'Ragozine, a most notorious pirate'; and here in 5.1.58 (Hotson, pp. 151–2). This view of what Illyria is like contrasts markedly with the sentimental–romantic milieu of the two noble households.

12 **The rather** The more quickly. Comparative form of the obsolete adverb 'rathe'.

15 *thanks...oft This line, defective in F (and hence omitted in the later Folios), has occasioned many emendations, all of them closely related. Theobald's, adopted here, acknowledges either scribal or compositorial error in the omission of two words ('thanks', 'and') which have already appeared in the line.

16 **uncurrent pay** coins no longer in circulation. By extension, 'valueless rewards'.

17 **worth** wealth.

17 **conscience** sense of being indebted.

18 **dealing** treatment.

19 **relics** i.e. 'memorials' and 'things of fame', as in 23.

26 **count his** i.e. count's (an old genitive form).

28 **scarce** hardly.

28 **answered** (1) accounted for, (2) atoned for (by 'repaying', as in 33).

29 **Belike** I suppose.

31–2 **Albeit...argument** Although the nature of the occasion and the dispute might well have given us cause for shedding blood. Antonio's statement here does not concur with what Orsino says of that 'scathful grapple' at 5.1.45–8.

What we took from them, which for traffic's sake
Most of our city did. Only myself stood out,   35
For which if I be lapsèd in this place
I shall pay dear.

SEBASTIAN   Do not then walk too open.

ANTONIO It doth not fit me. Hold, sir, here's my purse.
In the south suburbs at the Elephant
Is best to lodge; I will bespeak our diet,   40
Whiles you beguile the time, and feed your knowledge
With viewing of the town; there shall you have me.

SEBASTIAN Why I your purse?

ANTONIO Haply your eye shall light upon some toy
You have desire to purchase; and your store,   45
I think, is not for idle markets, sir.

SEBASTIAN I'll be your purse-bearer and leave you for
An hour.

ANTONIO   To th'Elephant.

SEBASTIAN   I do remember.

                                                        Exeunt

3.4 *Enter* OLIVIA *and* MARIA *[following]*

OLIVIA *[Aside]* I have sent after him; he says he'll come –
How shall I feast him? What bestow of him?

Act 3, Scene 4 3.4 *Scæna Quarta.* F   o SD *following*] *This edn; not in* F   1 SD *Aside*] *Staunton; not in* F

34 **traffic's sake** the sake of trading.
35 **stood out** i.e. refused to pay.
36 **lapsèd** apprehended. Perhaps associated with 'fall into the laps of' (Onions).
38 **fit** conform to my situation.
39 **Elephant** Shakespeare is recalling the Oliphant (a common Elizabethan spelling), an inn located on the Bankside in Elephant Alley. Next to it was the Horseshoe Inn, with a way leading from Horseshoe Yard to the Globe. Formerly the Red Hart, the inn (called the Oliphant in 1598) dates from the early part of the fourteenth century and in 1507 was acquired by the Tallow Chandlers' Company, which continued to retain the property (M. F. Monier-Williams, *Records of the Worshipful Company of Tallow Chandlers*, 1897, pp. 113–14, and [W. W. Braines], *The Site of the Globe Playhouse, Southwark*, 1921, rev. edn 1924, p. 80). Robin Hood has called my attention to an eighteenth-century engraving of an original painting of the time of Edward VI's coronation, 1547, which

shows the inn seventh from the left from the top of Goat Stairs.
40 **bespeak our diet** order our meals. Meanwhile Sebastian (in the next line) 'feeds' his knowledge by sightseeing.
41 **beguile** pass. Literally, 'deceive', as in *MND* 5.1.40–1: 'How shall we beguile / The lazy time, if not with some delight?'
44 **Haply** Perhaps.
45–6 **your store...markets** your supply of money does not extend to unnecessary purchases.

Act 3, Scene 4
Location Olivia's garden (Capell).
1 **he says** It is necessary to understand an introductory 'if', the broken sequence indicating that Olivia is musing to herself; not until 51–2 does she ascertain that Cesario has returned, even if reluctantly.
2 **of him** The use of 'of' for 'on' is frequent (Abbott 175); for another example, see 5.1.297.

For youth is bought more oft than begged or borrowed.
I speak too loud –
Where's Malvolio? He is sad and civil,   5
And suits well for a servant with my fortunes.
Where is Malvolio?

MARIA He's coming, madam, but in very strange manner. He is sure
possessed, madam.

OLIVIA Why, what's the matter? Does he rave?   10

MARIA No, madam, he does nothing but smile. Your ladyship were best
to have some guard about you, if he come, for sure the man is
tainted in's wits.

OLIVIA Go call him hither.

[Exit Maria]

I am as mad as he
If sad and merry madness equal be.   15

Enter [MARIA *with*] MALVOLIO

How now, Malvolio?

MALVOLIO Sweet lady, ho, ho!

OLIVIA Smil'st thou? I sent for thee upon a sad occasion.

MALVOLIO Sad, lady? I could be sad. This does make some obstruction
in the blood, this cross-gartering, but what of that? If it please the   20
eye of one, it is with me as the very true sonnet is: 'Please one,
and please all.'

OLIVIA Why, how dost thou, man? What is the matter with thee?

4–5] *As two lines, Pope; as one* F   8–9 He's...madam.] *As prose, Pope; as verse,* F (He's...Madame:/ But...Madam.)
14 Go...he] *As Capell; two lines,* F (Go...hither. / Enter Maluolio. / I...hee,)   14 SD *Exit Maria*] *Dyce; not in* F
15 SD *Maria with*] *Dyce subst.; not in* F   19–22 Sad...all] *As prose, Pope; as verse,* F (Sad...sad: / ...blood: / .. that?
/ ...true / ...all.)   23 SH OLIVIA] F2 (*Ol.*); *Mal.* F   23] *As prose, Pope; as verse,* F (man? / What...thee?)

3 Olivia's rather cynical observation combines
the proverbial 'better to buy than to borrow' (Tilley
B783) with 'beg' meaning (1) to ask alms and (2)
to petition the Court of Wards for the custody of
a (wealthy) minor.
5 **sad and civil** grave (as again in 18) and
circumspect.
9 **possessed** (1) taken over by the devil or (2)
mad. Feste (as Sir Topas) acknowledges both
meanings in 4.2.
13 **tainted** diseased. As in 3.1.58, where Viola
aptly observes that wise men who have fallen into
folly 'quite taint their wit'.
15 i.e. if a melancholic disorder is equated with
a smiling one.
19 **I...sad** I could be melancholic. The result of
'this cross-gartering', as he explains in the next line.

21 **sonnet** song.
21–2 **Please one...all** From 'A prettie newe
Ballad intytuled: The Crowe sits upon the Wall /
Please one and please all' entered in the *SR* in
January 1592, and attributed to the player Richard
Tarlton in the new *STC*. Stanza 10, of its seventeen
(not nineteen as Furness has it), gives an indication
that Malvolio, if he remembers more than the
refrain, could find justification for 'such impossible
passages of grossness' (3.2.56) as Maria ordered
in her letter:

    Let her have her own will,
    Thus the crow pypeth still,
    Whatever she command
    See that you do it out of hand.

23 SH *OLIVIA F's *Mal.* is another instance of
misassigning; corrected in F2.

MALVOLIO Not black in my mind, though yellow in my legs. It did
  come to his hands, and commands shall be executed. I think we   25
  do know the sweet Roman hand.

OLIVIA Wilt thou go to bed, Malvolio?

MALVOLIO To bed? Ay, sweetheart, and I'll come to thee.

OLIVIA God comfort thee! Why dost thou smile so and kiss thy hand
  so oft?   30

MARIA How do you, Malvolio?

MALVOLIO At your request!
  Yes, nightingales answer daws!

MARIA Why appear you with this ridiculous boldness before my lady?

MALVOLIO 'Be not afraid of greatness': 'twas well writ.   35

OLIVIA What mean'st thou by that, Malvolio?

MALVOLIO 'Some are born great – '

OLIVIA Ha?

MALVOLIO 'Some achieve greatness – '

OLIVIA What say'st thou?   40

MALVOLIO 'And some have greatness thrust upon them.'

OLIVIA Heaven restore thee!

MALVOLIO 'Remember who commended thy yellow stockings – '

OLIVIA Thy yellow stockings?

MALVOLIO 'And wished to see thee cross-gartered.'   45

OLIVIA Cross-gartered?

MALVOLIO 'Go to, thou art made, if thou desir'st to be so – '

OLIVIA Am I made?

---

24 Not black...in my legs i.e. not a
melancholic (from an excess of black bile). Nashe
refers to wearing the two colours in a song (in
Summers Last Will and Testament, Works, III, 239),
and a popular ballad tune was called 'Black and
Yellow'; the music is reproduced in Edward
Rimbault, *Musical Illustrations of Bishop Percy's
Reliques of Antient English Poetry*, 1850, p. 11
(Linthicum, p. 50).

24–6 It...Roman hand 'It' is Maria's letter; in
the first clause Malvolio answers to what he takes
as Olivia's opening words in the letter, 'If this fall
into thy hand' (2.5.118–19). His pronouns in this
speech modulate crazily from 'my' to 'it' to an
impersonal 'his' to an (?) intimate or (?) regal 'we'.

26 sweet Roman hand A fashionable Italian
style of handwriting rather than the native English
(Secretary) hand.

28 Ay...to thee Apparently a line from a
popular ballad; on 1 August 1586, a ballad called

'An answere to "goo to bed swete harte"' was
entered to Edward White (*SR*, II, 209). By singing
his response, Malvolio could tone down his
forwardness.

32 At your request At the request of one like
you (now subordinate to me). A response in accord
with the directive in Maria's letter (2.5.124) to be
'surly with servants'.

33 The lineation follows F and perhaps suggests
the pacing for delivery (R. Flatter, *Shakespeare's
Producing Hand*, 1948, pp. 150–1). There was no
reason for the compositor to set the lines so except
that he was following copy.

33 daws jackdaws. Thought to be stupid birds.

43 thy Olivia is startled by the familiar forms
used by her servant here and at 45 and 47 ('thee'
and 'thou'). This accounts for her amazed echoing
of Malvolio's words. Some editors emend 'thy' (44)
to 'my' on the grounds that Olivia is taking his
words as if directed to her, as she surely does in 48.

MALVOLIO 'If not, let me see thee a servant still.'

OLIVIA Why, this is very midsummer madness.   50

Enter SERVANT

SERVANT Madam, the young gentleman of the Count Orsino's is
returned; I could hardly entreat him back. He attends your
ladyship's pleasure.

OLIVIA I'll come to him.

                                                        [*Exit Servant*]

Good Maria, let this fellow be looked to. Where's my cousin Toby?   55
Let some of my people have a special care of him; I would not have
him miscarry for the half of my dowry.

                                                [*Exeunt Olivia and Maria*]

MALVOLIO O ho, do you come near me now? No worse man than Sir
Toby to look to me! This concurs directly with the letter: she sends
him on purpose that I may appear stubborn to him; for she incites   60
me to that in the letter. 'Cast thy humble slough', says she; 'be
opposite with a kinsman, surly with servants, let thy tongue tang
with arguments of state, put thyself into the trick of singularity',
and consequently sets down the manner how: as a sad face, a
reverend carriage, a slow tongue, in the habit of some sir of note,   65
and so forth. I have limed her, but it is Jove's doing, and Jove make
me thankful! And when she went away now, 'Let this fellow be
looked to' – 'Fellow'! Not 'Malvolio', nor after my degree, but

---

54 SD *Exit Servant*] Capell; *not in* F   57 SD *Exeunt...Maria*] Capell; *exit* F   62 tang] F2; langer F

---

50 midsummer Proverbial season for madness. Compare 'dog days' and Tilley M1117, 'It is midsummer moon [i.e. lunacy] with you', but here perhaps an allusion to the projected season of the play's action. See pp. 3–4 above.

57 miscarry come to harm.

58 come near touch closely, affect (Onions, sv near). As in *Oth.* 4.1.198–9: 'for if it touch not you, it comes near nobody', and *1H4* 1.2.13: 'Indeed you come near me now, Hal.' Dent (N56.1) dates this idiomatic expression from *c.* 1585. Malvolio takes Olivia's last words to mean that up to this point she has been dissembling her real feelings in front of Maria.

62 *tang F2's correction of 'langer' is accounted for by the earlier use (2.5.124) of the word which Malvolio is recalling. The compositor may have read a final tick or finishing stroke as a superscript 'er' – a very common breviograph. Some editors

delete the following preposition though there is no real reason to do so.

64 consequently accordingly.

66 limed i.e. caught her like a bird entangled by lime, a glutinous substance. Thus Ursula says of Beatrice, 'She's limed, I warrant you' (*Ado* 3.1.104).

66–7 Jove's doing...thankful Luce refers this to Ps. 118.23: 'This was the Lord's doing, and it is marvelous in our eyes.' Should the audience detect the Biblical allusion, it would be one more comic foible on Malvolio's part.

68 Fellow Malvolio conveniently forgets the phrasing of Maria's letter – 'the fellow [companion] of servants' – taking it now only in reference to Olivia.

68 after my degree according to my rank in the hierarchy of servants.

'fellow'. Why, everything adheres together, that no dram of a
scruple, no scruple of a scruple, no obstacle, no incredulous or   70
unsafe circumstance – what can be said? Nothing that can be can
come between me and the full prospect of my hopes. Well, Jove,
not I, is the doer of this, and he is to be thanked!

Enter [SIR] TOBY, FABIAN, *and* MARIA

SIR TOBY Which way is he, in the name of sanctity? If all the devils
of hell be drawn in little, and Legion himself possessed him, yet   75
I'll speak to him.

FABIAN Here he is, here he is. How is't with you, sir?

SIR TOBY How is't with you, man?

MALVOLIO Go off, I discard you. Let me enjoy my private. Go off!

MARIA Lo, how hollow the fiend speaks within him! Did not I tell you?   80
Sir Toby, my lady prays you to have a care of him.

MALVOLIO Ah ha! Does she so?

SIR TOBY Go to, go to; peace, peace! We must deal gently with him.
Let me alone. How do you, Malvolio? How is't with you? What,
man, defy the devil! Consider, he's an enemy to mankind.   85

MALVOLIO Do you know what you say?

MARIA La you, and you speak ill of the devil, how he takes it at heart!
Pray God he be not bewitched!

---

73 SD SIR] *Capell subst.; not in* F   **78** SH SIR TOBY] *NS, anon. conj. Cam.; not in* F, *which treats the line as part of Fabian's
speech at 77*

---

69 adheres accords.

69–70 dram of a scruple a third of a scruple.
Scruple refers to an apothecary's measure and used
figuratively means 'a small amount' (as in 2.5.2) as
well as 'doubt' or 'hesitation'. Falstaff (*2H4*
1.2.130–1) also plays on these meanings: 'the wise
may make some dram of a scruple, or indeed a
scruple itself'.

70 incredulous incredible. Not pre-
Shakespearean (Onions).

71 unsafe circumstance unreliable evidence (of
the facts).

74 sanctity Sir Toby invokes 'sanctity' before
encountering the possessed Malvolio, as Hamlet
(*Ham.* F 623 (1.4.39)) does before encountering
the ghost: 'Angels and ministers of grace defend
us' (NS).

75 drawn in little (1) portrayed in miniature (as
'his picture in little', *Ham.* F 1412 (2.2.366)); (2)
contracted into one body.

75 Legion A reference to the unclean spirit in

Mark 5.8–9, who when asked his name answered,
'My name is Legion: for we are manie'; the gloss
reads 'above 6000 in nombre'.

78 *How…man Assigned to Fabian in F, but
the use of 'man' here, as opposed to Fabian's earlier
'sir', accords with Sir Toby's habit of familiar
address at 85, 98, 100. Compositorial confusion
between *Tob.* and *Fab.* (or *To.* and *Fa.*) seems to
have occurred earlier at 2.5.29, 33, 70–1; here, as
NS notes, the two questions are printed on separate
lines.

79 private privacy. Not pre-Shakespearean
(Onions).

80 hollow falsely. A figurative use (see *OED* sv
adv 1) but perhaps with an overtone of 'sepulchral'.

84 Let me alone Leave him to me.

85 defy renounce. As in *Lear* 3.4.97–8: 'defy the
foul fiend'.

87 La you Look you (Onions).

88 bewitched Different from demoniac possession and needing different treatment.

FABIAN Carry his water to th'wise woman.

MARIA Marry, and it shall be done tomorrow morning if I live. My lady   90
would not lose him for more than I'll say.

MALVOLIO How now, mistress?

MARIA O Lord!

SIR TOBY Prithee, hold thy peace; this is not the way. Do you not see
you move him? Let me alone with him.   95

FABIAN No way but gentleness; gently, gently: the fiend is rough, and
will not be roughly used.

SIR TOBY Why, how now, my bawcock? How dost thou, chuck?

MALVOLIO Sir!

SIR TOBY Ay, biddy, come with me. What, man, 'tis not for gravity   100
to play at cherry-pit with Satan. Hang him, foul collier!

MARIA Get him to say his prayers, good Sir Toby, get him to pray.

MALVOLIO My prayers, minx!

MARIA No, I warrant you, he will not hear of godliness.

MALVOLIO Go hang yourselves all! You are idle, shallow things; I am   105
not of your element. You shall know more hereafter.   *Exit*

SIR TOBY Is't possible?

FABIAN If this were played upon a stage now, I could condemn it as
an improbable fiction.

SIR TOBY His very genius hath taken the infection of the device, man.   110

MARIA Nay, pursue him now, lest the device take air and taint.

---

89 i.e. for inspecting his urine for a medical diagnosis; 'wise women' were those skilled in occult arts such as fortune-telling and palmistry and, according to Thomas Heywood in the *Wise Woman of Hogsden* (1638), 'casting of Waters' (cited in Furness); the term is equivalent to a harmless or 'good' witch.

95 move excite.

95 Let me alone As in 84 above.

96 rough violent.

98 bawcock...chuck Terms of endearment; 'bawcock' (*beau coq*) is masculine (as in *WT* 1.2.121) and 'chuck' (= chick, like 'biddy' in Sir Toby's next speech) usually feminine (as in *Mac.* 3.2.45). Such language, as Kittredge notes, enrages Mavolio even more.

100 gravity i.e. a grave person.

101 play at cherry-pit be on familiar terms with. From the child's game of tossing cherry pits into a hole.

101 foul collier i.e. 'the fiend' of 96, from the proverb (Tilley L287) 'Like will to like, quoth the devil to the collier.' As a dealer in pit-coal, a collier was assumed to be like the devil, black in heart as

well as in appearance. An interlude dating from 1568 by Ulpian Fulwell uses this proverb as its title; *ODEP* dates it from *c.* 1559.

105 idle foolish.

105–6 I am...element I am out of your sphere. Shakespeare is again having sport with the word 'element' and its 'overworn' use, either as Malvolio's special word or, perhaps, Jonson's. (See 3.1.49 and n.)

108–9 If...fiction Like 1.3.48, the line is guaranteed to evoke audience-response, but it is also a typically Shakespearean comment on the unreality of theatrical illusion.

110 genius nature. In this period 'genius' was more frequently used to refer to the tutelary spirit (or angel) guarding an individual.

110 device stratagem.

111 take air (1) become infectious, (2) become known. The first meaning accords with Sir Toby's medical image; compare *Lear* 2.4.163–4: 'Strike her young bones, / You taking airs, with lameness!'

111 taint be spoiled. Continues the disease image.

FABIAN Why, we shall make him mad indeed.

MARIA The house will be the quieter.

SIR TOBY Come, we'll have him in a dark room and bound. My niece
is already in the belief that he's mad. We may carry it thus for our   115
pleasure, and his penance, till our very pastime, tired out of breath,
prompt us to have mercy on him; at which time we will bring the
device to the bar and crown thee for a finder of madmen. But see,
but see!

Enter SIR ANDREW

FABIAN More matter for a May morning!   120

SIR ANDREW Here's the challenge; read it. I warrant there's vinegar
and pepper in't.

FABIAN Is't so saucy?

SIR ANDREW Ay, is't. I warrant him; do but read.

SIR TOBY Give me. [*Reads*] 'Youth, whatsoever thou art, thou art but   125
a scurvy fellow.'

FABIAN Good, and valiant.

SIR TOBY [*Reads*] 'Wonder not, nor admire not in thy mind, why I do
call thee so, for I will show thee no reason for't.'

FABIAN A good note! That keeps you from the blow of the law.   130

SIR TOBY [*Reads*] 'Thou com'st to the Lady Olivia, and in my sight
she uses thee kindly. But thou liest in thy throat. That is not the
matter I challenge thee for.'

FABIAN Very brief, and to exceeding good sense [*Aside*] – less.

SIR TOBY [*Reads*] 'I will waylay thee going home, where if it be thy   135
chance to kill me –'

FABIAN Good.

125, 128, 131, 135, 138, 140 SD *Reads*] Capell; not in F   134 sense [*Aside*] – less] NS *subst.;* sence-less F

---

114 we'll...bound The usual treatment for
madness. Compare *Err.* 4.4.92–4: 'Mistress, both
man and master is possess'd: / ...They must be
bound and laid in some dark room.'

115 carry manage.

118 bar i.e. to be judged.

118 a finder of madmen Like those acting
under the writ *De lunatico inquirendo* which 'found'
(i.e. declared) an individual mad.

120 matter...morning i.e. fit for May-day
plays or games. Also perhaps an allusion to the
season which the play seems intended to represent.
See pp. 3–4 above.

123 saucy (1) salty, (2) impertinent. The first
meaning carries the sense 'bitter'; compare 'salt
scorn' (*Tro.* 1.3.370).

124 I warrant him I can assure him (i.e.
Cesario). Used as an asseveration.

125 thou This is in accord with Sir Toby's
advice at 3.2.35–6.

128 admire marvel.

130 blow of the law legal punishment (for
breach of the peace). All Sir Andrew's taunts, as NS
notes, are carefully hedged.

132 liest...throat Proverbial charge of menda-
city (Tilley T268).

SIR TOBY [*Reads*] 'Thou kill'st me like a rogue and a villain.'

FABIAN Still you keep o'th'windy side of the law. Good.

SIR TOBY [*Reads*] 'Fare thee well, and God have mercy upon one of   140
our souls! He may have mercy upon mine, but my hope is better,
and so look to thyself. Thy friend, as thou usest him, and thy sworn
enemy,

                                        Andrew Aguecheek.'

If this letter move him not, his legs cannot. I'll give't him.   145

MARIA You may have very fit occasion for't; he is now in some
commerce with my lady and will by and by depart.

SIR TOBY Go, Sir Andrew, scout me for him at the corner of the orchard
like a bumbaily. So soon as ever thou seest him, draw, and as thou
draw'st, swear horrible; for it comes to pass oft that a terrible oath,   150
with a swaggering accent sharply twanged off, gives manhood more
approbation than ever proof itself would have earned him. Away!

SIR ANDREW Nay, let me alone for swearing.   *Exit*

SIR TOBY Now will not I deliver his letter; for the behaviour of the
young gentleman gives him out to be of good capacity and breeding;   155
his employment between his lord and my niece confirms no less.
Therefore this letter, being so excellently ignorant, will breed no
terror in the youth; he will find it comes from a clodpole. But, sir,
I will deliver his challenge by word of mouth, set upon Aguecheek
a notable report of valour, and drive the gentleman (as I know his   160
youth will aptly receive it) into a most hideous opinion of his rage,
skill, fury, and impetuosity. This will so fright them both that they
will kill one another by the look, like cockatrices.

138 **rogue and a villain** In Sir Andrew's ambiguous style, the terms could refer equally well to 'thou' or to 'me'.

139 **windy...law** The seaman sails towards the wind to avoid being driven on to rocks on the leeside; hence the 'windy side' is the 'safe side'; compare *Ado* 2.1.314–15 where the merry heart of Beatrice keeps on 'the windy side of care'.

141 **but my...better** but I hope for something better (than God's mercy on my soul), i.e. to be allowed to win.

142 **as thou usest him** in so far as you treat him (like a friend).

145 **If this letter...cannot** Sir Toby plays on 'move' as (1) incite and (2) propel.

146–7 **in...commerce** in some transaction.

147 **by and by** very soon.

148 **me** Another example of Sir Toby's use of the ethical dative, as in 3.2.26, 27.

149 **bumbaily** A bailiff who attempts to apprehend a debtor from behind. The only instance in Shakespeare, and the earliest cited in *OED*.

151–2 **gives...approbation** gives more credit to manliness.

153 **Indeed, as for swearing, leave it to me.** As in *Shr.* 4.2.71: 'Take [in] your love, and then let me alone.' Up to this point, Sir Andrew's skill has been limited to the imprecation ''Slight' (2.5.28, 3.2.9).

158 **clodpole** blockhead.

160–1 **his youth...it** because of his inexperience he will readily believe it.

163 **cockatrices** Also called 'basilisks'. The belief that these fabulous serpents possessed a 'death-[darting] eye' (*Rom.* 3.2.47) had become proverbial (Tilley C495, Dent C496.2 and B99.1).

FABIAN Here he comes with your niece; give them way till he take leave
and presently after him.   165

Enter OLIVIA *and* VIOLA

SIR TOBY I will meditate the while upon some horrid message for a
challenge.
[*Exeunt Sir Toby, Fabian, and Maria*]
OLIVIA I have said too much unto a heart of stone,
    And laid mine honour too unchary on't;
    There's something in me that reproves my fault,   170
    But such a headstrong potent fault it is,
    That it but mocks reproof.
VIOLA With the same 'haviour that your passion bears
    Goes on my master's griefs.
OLIVIA Here, wear this jewel for me; 'tis my picture.   175
    Refuse it not; it hath no tongue to vex you.
    And, I beseech you, come again tomorrow.
    What shall you ask of me that I'll deny,
    That honour, saved, may upon asking give?
VIOLA Nothing but this – your true love for my master.   180
OLIVIA How with mine honour may I give him that
    Which I have given to you?
VIOLA   I will acquit you.
OLIVIA Well, come again tomorrow. Fare thee well.
    A friend like thee might bear my soul to hell.   [*Exit*]

Enter SIR TOBY *and* FABIAN

SIR TOBY Gentleman, God save thee.   185
VIOLA And you, sir.
SIR TOBY That defence thou hast, betake thee to't. Of what nature the

---

165 SD *Enter...* VIOLA] *This edn; after 163* F   167 SD *Exeunt...Maria*] *Capell; Exeunt.* F2; *not in* F   169 on't] F; *out*
Theobald   184 SD *Exit*] F2; *not in* F

164 **give them way** keep out of their way.
165 **presently** immediately. As at 5.1.161.
166 **horrid** Literally, 'bristling'.
168 **a heart of stone** Then proverbial (Tilley
H311), if now a cliché.
169 **And placed** (or staked) my reputation too
heedlessly on (that heart of stone). Following
Theobald, many editors emend 'on't' to 'out',
justifying the change on the grounds of an easy
compositorial error.
174 **Goes...griefs** The use of a singular verb

ending in *s* preceding a plural noun is common, as
in *TGV* 2.4.71–2: '(for far behind his worth /
Comes all the praises that I now bestow)...'
175 Olivia's gift of a jewelled miniature recalls the
earlier situation of her unveiling the 'picture' of
herself to Cesario.
182 **acquit you** release you (from that gift).
184 **like thee** in your likeness.
187 **That defence thou hast** Whatever skill in
fencing you have.

wrongs are thou hast done him, I know not; but thy intercepter, full
of despite, bloody as the hunter, attends thee at the orchard-end.
Dismount thy tuck, be yare in thy preparation, for thy assailant is   190
quick, skilful, and deadly.

VIOLA You mistake, sir. I am sure no man hath any quarrel to me. My
remembrance is very free and clear from any image of offence done
to any man.

SIR TOBY You'll find it otherwise, I assure you. Therefore, if you hold   195
your life at any price, betake you to your guard; for your opposite
hath in him what youth, strength, skill, and wrath can furnish man
withal.

VIOLA I pray you, sir, what is he?

SIR TOBY He is knight, dubbed with unhatched rapier, and on carpet   200
consideration, but he is a devil in private brawl. Souls and bodies
hath he divorced three, and his incensement at this moment is so
implacable that satisfaction can be none but by pangs of death and
sepulchre. Hob nob is his word: give't or take't.

VIOLA I will return again into the house and desire some conduct of   205
the lady. I am no fighter. I have heard of some kind of men that
put quarrels purposely on others to taste their valour; belike this
is a man of that quirk.

SIR TOBY Sir, no. His indignation derives itself out of a very competent
injury; therefore get you on and give him his desire. Back you shall   210
not to the house, unless you undertake that with me which with
as much safety you might answer him; therefore on, or strip your

---

192 sir. I am sure no] *NS;* sir, I am sure, no F   209 competent] F4; computent F

---

189 **despite** ill will.

189 **bloody . . . hunter** bloodthirsty like a hunting
dog after its prey.

190 **Dismount thy tuck** i.e. unsheathe your
(small) rapier. 'Dismount' is properly used of a
cannon; Sir Toby's inflated diction is a further
means of intimidation.

190 **yare** prompt.

192 **to** with. The same idiomatic use of the
preposition appears in *Ado* 2.1.236–7: 'The Lady
Beatrice hath a quarrel to you.'

196 **opposite** opponent.

199 **what is he** i.e. of what quality and rank. As
at 1.2.35 and 1.5.104. This contrasts with 'what
manner of man is he' at 223.

200 **unhatched** Either 'unhacked' or 'never
drawn from its scabbard'.

200–1 **on carpet consideration** dubbed for

domestic (rather than military) service and perhaps
in return for payment. Nashe (*Works*, I, 353)
describes 'carpet knights' as being 'the basest
cowards under heaven, covering an apes hart with
a lion's case, and making false alarums when they
mean nothing but a May-game' (compare 120
above). See also Benedict's reference to 'quondam
carpetmongers' in *Ado* 5.2.32–3, specifying the
inadequacy of such famous lovers as Leander and
Troilus.

204 **Hob . . . word** 'Have it or have it not' is his
motto. Tilley (H479) dates its earliest use to 1530.

205 **conduct** escort.

207 **put** foist.

207 **taste** try.

209 ***competent** sufficient.

211 **undertake that** i.e. fight a duel.

212–13 **strip . . . naked** fully unsheathe your sword.

sword stark naked; for meddle you must, that's certain, or forswear
to wear iron about you.

VIOLA This is as uncivil as strange. I beseech you, do me this courteous   215
office as to know of the knight what my offence to him is. It is
something of my negligence, nothing of my purpose.

SIR TOBY I will do so. Signior Fabian, stay you by this gentleman till
my return.   *Exit [Sir] Toby*

VIOLA Pray you, sir, do you know of this matter?   220

FABIAN I know the knight is incensed against you, even to a mortal
arbitrement, but nothing of the circumstance more.

VIOLA I beseech you, what manner of man is he?

FABIAN Nothing of that wonderful promise, to read him by his form,
as you are like to find him in the proof of his valour. He is indeed,   225
sir, the most skilful, bloody, and fatal opposite that you could
possibly have found in any part of Illyria. Will you walk towards
him? I will make your peace with him if I can.

VIOLA I shall be much bound to you for't. I am one that had rather
go with sir priest than sir knight. I care not who knows so much   230
of my mettle.

                                                      Exeunt

            Enter [SIR] TOBY *and* [SIR] ANDREW

SIR TOBY Why, man, he's a very devil. I have not seen such a firago.
I had a pass with him, rapier, scabbard, and all, and he gives me

---

219 SD *Sir*] *Capell; not in* F   231 SD.2 SIR…SIR] *Capell; not in* F

---

213 **meddle** become involved.
215 **uncivil** discourteous.
216 **know of** enquire from.
217 **something…purpose** the result of some oversight, nothing intentional.
221–2 **mortal arbitrement** settlement to the death.
224 **to read** to judge.
230 **sir priest** The designation of one who has taken a Bachelor of Arts degree and by courtesy extended to a clergyman lacking the degree. Thus 'Sir Topas the curate' in 4.2.
231 SD F's unnecessary *Exeunt*, occasioning the re-entry of Viola and Fabian at 246, poses something of a problem, since their departure clears the stage as if it were the end of the scene, which it is not. Moreover, Sir Toby has directed Fabian (218–19) to stay with Viola until his return; he then alarms Sir Andrew by declaring that Fabian is scarcely able to hold Cesario 'yonder' (238–9), a

suggestion of some stage business within view of the audience. Capell solved the problem by deleting the directives for exiting and re-entry, a procedure that is frequently adopted in modern texts and productions. On an Elizabethan stage, presumably Viola and Fabian could still be seen ('yonder') through the doorway through which they exit. Sir Toby and Sir Andrew then enter through the second door and proceed down stage so that when Fabian and Viola re-enter, they are positioned diagonally, permitting Sir Toby, as well as Fabian, to accost each in turn and to incite each of them with the same words, 'There's no remedy' (251, 258). The duellists would thus be at centre stage when Antonio enters. See illustration 1*b*, p. 3.
232 **firago** virago. For comic effect Sir Toby applies a term applicable to a woman to one whom he supposes to be a man (Kittredge).
233 **pass** bout. Its more usual meaning is 'lunge' or 'thrust'.

the stuck-in with such a mortal motion that it is inevitable; and on
the answer, he pays you as surely as your feet hits the ground they   235
step on. They say he has been fencer to the sophy.

SIR ANDREW Pox on't. I'll not meddle with him.

SIR TOBY Ay, but he will not now be pacified. Fabian can scarce hold
him yonder.

SIR ANDREW Plague on't, and I thought he had been valiant, and so   240
cunning in fence, I'd have seen him damned ere I'd have challenged
him. Let him let the matter slip, and I'll give him my horse, Grey
Capilet.

SIR TOBY I'll make the motion. Stand here, make a good show on't.
This shall end without the perdition of souls. [*Aside*] Marry, I'll   245
ride your horse as well as I ride you.

Enter FABIAN *and* VIOLA

[*To Fabian*] I have his horse to take up the quarrel. I have
persuaded him the youth's a devil.

FABIAN He is as horribly conceited of him and pants and looks pale,
as if a bear were at his heels.   250

SIR TOBY [*To Viola*] There's no remedy, sir. He will fight with you
for's oath sake. Marry, he hath better bethought him of his quarrel,
and he finds that now scarce to be worth talking of. Therefore, draw
for the supportance of his vow. He protests he will not hurt you.

---

235 hits] F; hit *Rowe*   238–9 Ay...yonder] *As prose, Capell; as verse,* F   245 SD *Aside*] *Theobald; not in* F
247 SD *To Fabian*] *Rowe; not in* F   251 SD *To Viola*] *Capell; not in* F

---

234 **stuck-in** thrust. Sir Toby's form of Italian
stoccata. Compare *Ham.* 3152 (4.7.161): 'If he by
chance escape your venom'd stuck' and *Wiv.*
2.1.225–6: 'your passes, stoccadoes, and I know not
what'.

234 **inevitable** unavoidable. As in *Ant.*
4.14.64–7: 'when I should see... / Th'inevitable
prosecution of / Disgrace and horror... / Thou
then wouldst kill me'.

234–5 **on the answer...surely** on the return he
pays you home (with a mortal hit). Compare Falstaff
(*1H4* 2.4.192–3): 'Two I am sure I have paid, two
rogues in buckrom suits.'

235 **hits** Sir Toby's use of the singular here is
either a colloquial touch (since it is retained in the
three later Folios) or a misprint (with a final flourish
read as *s*); many editors, following Rowe, correct to
the plural form.

236 **fencer to the sophy** Accepted as a topical
reference to a second Sherley, this time Sir Robert,
who was serving in the shah's military organisation;
see 2.5.149 n. for the reference to Sir Anthony.

242–3 **Grey Capilet** The Elizabethans typically
used a characterising word when naming horses; the
queen, for example, owned 'Grey Markham', called
after a standard bearer of the royal guard of
Gentlemen Pensioners; 'Roan Barbary' was Richard
II's favourite mount, and 'Bay Curtal' was a prized
possession of Lafew's (*AWW* 2.3.59).

244 **motion** offer.

245 **perdition** loss. But in accord with Sir Toby's
inflated diction, it probably carries an overtone of
'damnation'.

246 **ride you** Figuratively, 'make a fool of', with
an obvious quibble.

247 **I have...quarrel** I have the promise of his
horse to settle the quarrel. See 274–5.

249 **He...conceited of him** He is possessed of
as fearsome an idea of him.

252 **oath sake** oath's sake.

252 **quarrel** grounds for challenging.

254 **supportance** upholding.

VIOLA [*Aside*] Pray God defend me! A little thing would make me tell   255
   them how much I lack of a man.
FABIAN Give ground if you see him furious.
SIR TOBY Come, Sir Andrew, there's no remedy: the gentleman will
   for his honour's sake have one bout with you; he cannot by the
   duello avoid it, but he has promised me, as he is a gentleman and   260
   a soldier, he will not hurt you. Come on, to't.
SIR ANDREW Pray God he keep his oath!
VIOLA I do assure you, 'tis against my will.

                         [*They draw*]

                     Enter ANTONIO

ANTONIO [*Drawing*] Put up your sword! If this young gentleman
   Have done offence, I take the fault on me;   265
   If you offend him, I for him defy you.
SIR TOBY You, sir? Why, what are you?
ANTONIO One, sir, that for his love dares yet do more
   Than you have heard him brag to you he will.
SIR TOBY Nay, if you be an undertaker, I am for you. [*Draws*]   270

                     Enter OFFICERS

FABIAN O good Sir Toby, hold! Here comes the officers.
SIR TOBY [*To Antonio*] I'll be with you anon.
VIOLA [*To Sir Andrew*] Pray, sir, put your sword up, if you please.
SIR ANDREW Marry, will I, sir; and for that I promised you, I'll be
   as good as my word. He will bear you easily and reins well.   275
I OFFICER This is the man; do thy office.
2 OFFICER Antonio, I arrest thee at the suit

---

255 SD *Aside*] Malone; *not in* F   263 SD.1 *They draw*] Rowe; *not in* F   263 SD.2 *Enter* ANTONIO] Dyce, Cam.; *after*
262 *in* F   264 SD *Drawing*] Rowe (*after* 266); *not in* F   270 SD.1 *Draws*] Rowe; *not in* F   272 SD *To Antonio*] Capell;
not in F   273 SD *To Sir Andrew*] Rowe; *not in* F

259 **one bout** one thrust and parry.
259–60 **by the duello** by the code and conduct proper to duelling.
263 SD The earlier directive to Sir Andrew to be on the lookout for Cesario at the 'corner of the orchard' (148) and the information that he is waiting for his opponent at the 'orchard-end' (189) presumably mean that Antonio and the Officers come on to the duelling scene as if from the street.
270 **undertaker** (1) one who takes on responsibility for something (as in *Oth.* 4.1.211); (2) one who takes on a fight (as in *Cym.* 2.1.26–7); and,

particularly here, (3) one who meddles in another's business.
270 **I am for you** I am ready for you. Compare *Shr.* 4.3.151: 'I am for thee straight.'
272 **I'll...anon** I'll have a bout with you soon. In the presence of the Officers, Sir Toby must sheathe his sword and probably stands out of the way.
274–5 **be as...word** i.e. surrender Grey Capilet, about which Viola knows nothing. Dent (W773.1) gives other Shakespearean examples of this idiom from the plays written around this date and earlier.

Of Count Orsino.

ANTONIO   You do mistake me, sir.

1 OFFICER No, sir, no jot. I know your favour well,
                Though now you have no sea-cap on your head.   280
                Take him away; he knows I know him well.

ANTONIO I must obey. [*To Viola*] This comes with seeking you.
                But there's no remedy; I shall answer it.
                What will you do, now my necessity
                Makes me to ask you for my purse? It grieves me   285
                Much more for what I cannot do for you
                Than what befalls myself. You stand amazed,
                But be of comfort.

2 OFFICER Come, sir, away.

ANTONIO I must entreat of you some of that money.   290

VIOLA What money, sir?
                For the fair kindness you have showed me here,
                And part being prompted by your present trouble,
                Out of my lean and low ability
                I'll lend you something. My having is not much;   295
                I'll make division of my present with you.
                Hold, there's half my coffer.

ANTONIO Will you deny me now?
                Is't possible that my deserts to you
                Can lack persuasion? Do not tempt my misery,   300
                Lest that it make me so unsound a man
                As to upbraid you with those kindnesses
                That I have done for you.

VIOLA   I know of none,
                Nor know I you by voice or any feature.
                I hate ingratitude more in a man   305

---

282 SD *To Viola*] Collier; *not in* F

279 **favour** features. As again at 332.

283 **answer** Either (1) atone for it by repaying (as at 3.3.28, 33), or (2) attempt a defence.

287 **amazed** bewildered. (A strong word.)

293 **part** partly.

295 **My having** What I have.

296 **present** present store of money.

297 **coffer** money-chest. Such hyperbole in referring to the purse or small money-bag Cesario carries is a comic touch.

300 **lack persuasion** fail to move you.

300 **tempt** try too sorely.

301 **unsound** unorthodox (in not conforming

to the doctrine of manliness). Compare *H8* 5.2.115–16: 'Do not I know you for a favorer / Of this new sect? Ye are not sound.' Note the religious diction in 312–14.

304 **feature** shape or form. As again at 317. The sense 'lineaments of the face' is not in Shakespeare (Onions).

305 **ingratitude** The idea that ingratitude is an inhuman quality is frequent in Shakespeare; it is characterised as 'monstrous' in *Cor.* 2.3.9 and a 'monster' in *Lear* 1.5.39–40; in *Tro.* 3.3.145–7 Time is called 'A great-siz'd monster of ingratitudes'.

Than lying, vainness, babbling drunkenness,
Or any taint of vice whose strong corruption
Inhabits our frail blood.
ANTONIO   O heavens themselves!
2 OFFICER Come, sir, I pray you go.
ANTONIO Let me speak a little. This youth that you see here,   310
I snatched one-half out of the jaws of death,
Relieved him with such sanctity of love;
And to his image, which methought did promise
Most venerable worth, did I devotion.
1 OFFICER What's that to us? The time goes by. Away!   315
ANTONIO But O how vile an idol proves this god!
Thou hast, Sebastian, done good feature shame.
In nature there's no blemish but the mind:
None can be called deformed but the unkind.
Virtue is beauty, but the beauteous-evil   320
Are empty trunks, o'er-flourished by the devil.
1 OFFICER The man grows mad. Away with him! Come, come, sir.
ANTONIO Lead me on.
                                          Exit [with Officers]

---

320 beauteous-evil] *Malone; not hyphenated in* F   322] *As Dyce; two lines in* F (him: / ...sir) 323 SD *with Officers*]
Theobald; not in F

306 vainness boasting. Compare 1 Tim. 6.20: 'avoide profane & vaine bablings' (repeated 2 Tim. 2.16). Editors frequently alter the punctuation in F (which is followed here) to make two units with their modifiers or to make a series of four sorts of 'vice' though 'babbling' (without a modifier) scarcely seems to qualify as one.

308 blood nature.

311 one-half...death i.e. half-dead.

312 such sanctity of love such holiness of love (as is directed to a religious object). The religious diction continues with 'image' (= (1) appearance, (2) statue), 'venerable worth' (= worthy of veneration), 'devotion' and in Antonio's next speech with 'idol', 'god' (316) and 'devil' (321). In F the first letter of 'love' looks like a damaged capital 'I' (Ioue), though the later Folios read 'love' (Ard.).

317 done...shame disgraced your goodly exterior by the nature of your response. For earlier and later allusions to this motif, see 1.2.50–1 and 5.1.120; 'feature' is used here in the same sense as at 304.

318–21 Antonio's shift to sententious rhyming couplets elicits Sir Toby's mocking reference at 328–9. Dramatically, the verse (as a 'higher' medium than prose) serves to dignify Antonio's philosophic reflections (though they seem only 'sage saws' to Sir Toby).

319 unkind (1) cruel, (2) unnatural. In *AYLI* (2.7.174–6) man's ingratitude is said to be more 'unkind' than the cruel winter wind.

320–1 beauteous-evil...devil i.e. individuals who are beautiful but morally bad are only vacant bodies that have been lavishly, perhaps over, embellished or, perhaps, embellished 'all over' by the hand of Satan. As *OED* points out, the force of 'over' in combination with verbs is extremely difficult to pin down (*OED* Over-*prep* and *adv* 25, 8 and 27). In spite of the consistency of idea and image in these lines many editors take 'trunks' to refer to carved chests holding household furnishings, but for the same use of 'trunk', see 4.2.40 n.; for Shakespeare's frequent contrast between an inner beauty and the outward show, see 317 n.

VIOLA Methinks his words do from such passion fly
        That he believes himself; so do not I.   325
        Prove true, imagination, O prove true,
        That I, dear brother, be now tane for you!

SIR TOBY Come hither, knight, come hither, Fabian. We'll whisper o'er
        a couplet or two of most sage saws.

VIOLA He named Sebastian. I my brother know   330
        Yet living in my glass; even such and so
        In favour was my brother, and he went
        Still in this fashion, colour, ornament,
        For him I imitate. O if it prove,
        Tempests are kind, and salt waves fresh in love.   [*Exit*]   335

SIR TOBY A very dishonest paltry boy, and more a coward than a hare;
        his dishonesty appears in leaving his friend here in necessity, and
        denying him; and for his cowardship, ask Fabian.

FABIAN A coward, a most devout coward, religious in it.

SIR ANDREW 'Slid, I'll after him again and beat him.   340

SIR TOBY Do, cuff him soundly, but never draw thy sword.

SIR ANDREW And I do not –   [*Exit*]

FABIAN Come, let's see the event.

SIR TOBY I dare lay any money, 'twill be nothing yet.

                                                                   Exeunt

4.1 *Enter* SEBASTIAN *and* CLOWN [FESTE]

FESTE Will you make me believe that I am not sent for you?

SEBASTIAN Go to, go to, thou art a foolish fellow.
        Let me be clear of thee.

---

335 SD *Exit*] F2; *not in* F   **342** not –] *Theobald*; not. F   **342** SD *Exit*] *Theobald*; *not in* F   **344** SD *Exeunt*] *Rowe*; *Exit* F
Act 4, Scene 1   **4.1**] *Actus Quartus, Scæna prima.* F

---

324 passion vehement feeling.

325 That he believes himself That he himself believes (that I am Sebastian).

330–1 I my brother...glass Whenever I look in my mirror, I see my brother's image to the life (Kittredge).

332 favour features. As before, 279.

334 if it prove if my hope prove true.

336 dishonest dishonourable.

336 more a coward...hare A proverbial instance of cowardice, as the Bastard in *John* (2.1.137–8) notes: 'You are the hare of whom the proverb goes, / Where valor plucks dead lions by the beard.' See Tilley H165.

338 denying disavowing.

339 religious in it devoted to it (i.e. to the concept of 'cowardship').

340 'Slid By God's eyelid.

343 event outcome.

344 yet after all.

Act 4, Scene 1

Location Before Olivia's house (Capell subst.).

1 Feste's opening words indicate that this exchange about Sebastian's identity has been going on for some time, as does his 'Well held out' – i.e. well kept up (4).

FESTE Well held out, i'faith! No, I do not know you, nor I am not sent
to you by my lady to bid you come speak with her; nor your name   5
is not Master Cesario; nor this is not my nose neither. Nothing that
is so is so.

SEBASTIAN I prithee, vent thy folly somewhere else.
Thou know'st not me.

FESTE Vent my folly! He has heard that word of some great man and   10
now applies it to a fool. Vent my folly! I am afraid this great lubber
the world will prove a cockney. I prithee now, ungird thy
strangeness and tell me what I shall vent to my lady. Shall I vent
to her that thou art coming?

SEBASTIAN I prithee, foolish Greek, depart from me.   15
There's money for thee. If you tarry longer,
I shall give worse payment.

FESTE By my troth, thou hast an open hand. These wise men that give
fools money get themselves a good report – after fourteen years'
purchase.   20

Enter [SIR] ANDREW, [SIR] TOBY, *and* FABIAN

SIR ANDREW Now, sir, have I met you again? There's for you!
[*Strikes Sebastian*]

8–9] *As verse, Capell; as prose* F   15–17] *As verse, Capell; as prose* F   20 SD SIR...SIR] *Capell; not in* F   21 SD *Strikes Sebastian*] *Douai MS., Rowe subst.; not in* F

6 nor this...neither For a similar ironic use
of this comparison, see *TGV* 2.1.135–6: 'O jest
unseen, inscrutable; invisible, / As a nose on a
man's face, or a weathercock on a steeple'; for the
triple negative, see 3.1.144 n.

8–20 This exchange, with its emphasis on (1) a
matter of diction and (2) a gift of money, 'twins'
with Feste's encounter with Viola at 3.1.1–49.

8 vent get rid of. As in *Cor.* 1.1.225–6: 'then we
shall ha'means to vent / Our musty superfluity'.
Feste then goes on to pick up (13) the more common
Shakespearean meaning 'utter' (as also in *Cor.*
1.1.209: 'They vented their complainings.').

10–11 He...fool i.e. he has appropriated
'vent' – diction proper to some great man – and
makes use of it in addressing a fool. Feste's
'damnable iteration' then travesties the term.

11 lubber booby.

12 cockney i.e. one guilty of affectations.

12–13 ungird thy strangeness i.e. stop being
outlandish. Literally, 'divest yourself of acting (1)

like a foreigner, (2) aloof and (3) unfamiliar' (the
several senses of 'strange').

15 foolish Greek (1) talker of nonsense or (2)
merrygreek. (1) = 'unintelligible', as in the proverbial phrase (Tilley G439), 'It is Greek to me.'
(2) is a term for a buffoon derived from a character
of that name in Nicholas Udall's *Ralph Roister
Doister* (*SR*, 1566); in *Tro.* 1.2.109, it is used of
Helen both literally and metaphorically.

18 open liberal. This, following the two rewards
earlier received (3.1.36–7, 45), confirms Feste's
identification of Sebastian with Viola.

19 report reputation.

19–20 after...purchase Either 'after a long
time' or 'for a price'. The market value of land was
the sum of the yearly rent for a fixed number of
years, as twelve, fourteen, etc.

21 There's for you Sir Andrew's actions should
accord with Sir Toby's instructions (3.4.341), 'cuff
him soundly but never draw thy sword'.

SEBASTIAN Why, there's for thee, and there, and there!
                    [*Beats Sir Andrew*]
          Are all the people mad?
SIR TOBY Hold, sir, or I'll throw your dagger o'er the house.
FESTE This will I tell my lady straight; I would not be in some of your   25
          coats for twopence.   [*Exit*]
SIR TOBY Come on, sir, hold!
SIR ANDREW Nay, let him alone. I'll go another way to work with him;
          I'll have an action of battery against him, if there be any law in
          Illyria. Though I struck him first, yet it's no matter for that.   30
SEBASTIAN Let go thy hand!
SIR TOBY Come, sir, I will not let you go. Come, my young soldier,
          put up your iron. You are well fleshed. Come on!
SEBASTIAN I will be free from thee. [*Draws his sword*] What wouldst
          thou now?
          If thou dar'st tempt me further, draw thy sword.   35
SIR TOBY What, what! Nay, then, I must have an ounce or two of this
          malapert blood from you. [*Draws*]

                    Enter OLIVIA

OLIVIA Hold, Toby! On thy life I charge thee hold!
SIR TOBY Madam –
OLIVIA Will it be ever thus? Ungracious wretch,   40
          Fit for the mountains and the barbarous caves,
          Where manners ne'er were preached! Out of my sight!
          Be not offended, dear Cesario.
          Rudesby, be gone!
                    [*Exeunt Sir Toby, Sir Andrew, and Fabian*]
          I prithee, gentle friend,

22 SD *Beats Sir Andrew*] Rowe subst.; not in F   26 SD *Exit*] Rowe; not in F   30 struck] F4; stroke F   34 SD *Draws his sword*] Capell subst.; not in F   37 SD *Draws*] Capell subst.; not in F   39 Madam –] Collier; Madam. F   44 SD Exeunt...Fabian] Capell; not in F

22 **Why...there** Sebastian's words (followed by those of Sir Toby) indicate that he has drawn his dagger and uses the hilt to beat Sir Andrew; Kittredge cites *Rom.* 4.5.117–18 for this use of a dagger: 'Then will I lay the serving-creature's dagger on your pate.'
24 **I'll...house** Sir Toby's threatening hyperbole, as Ard. notes, establishes the location of the scene.
25 **straight** at once.
28 **I'll go...to work** Proverbial for adopting a different tactic (Tilley W150).

29 **action of battery** lawsuit for assault and battery.
33 **well fleshed** eager for combat. Used originally of a hawk or hound that has been fed only on flesh (Onions). Following earlier commentators, NS takes this speech as ironically directed to Sir Andrew.
35 **tempt me** try me. There is a double sense: (1) make trial of me and (2) provoke.
37 **malapert** impudent.
44 **Rudesby** Ruffian. Used only here and in *Shr.* 3.2.10: 'a mad-brain rudesby full of spleen'.

Let thy fair wisdom, not thy passion, sway   45
In this uncivil and unjust extent
Against thy peace. Go with me to my house
And hear thou there how many fruitless pranks
This ruffian hath botched up, that thou thereby
Mayst smile at this. Thou shalt not choose but go.   50
Do not deny. Beshrew his soul for me,
He started one poor heart of mine, in thee.

SEBASTIAN What relish is in this? How runs the stream?
Or I am mad, or else this is a dream.
Let fancy still my sense in Lethe steep;   55
If it be thus to dream, still let me sleep!

OLIVIA Nay, come, I prithee; would thou'dst be ruled by me!

SEBASTIAN Madam, I will.

OLIVIA   O say so, and so be!

Exeunt

4.2 *Enter* MARIA *and* CLOWN [FESTE]

MARIA Nay, I prithee put on this gown and this beard; make him
believe thou art Sir Topas the curate. Do it quickly. I'll call Sir
Toby the whilst.   [*Exit*]

Act 4, Scene 2 4.2] *Scæna Secunda.* F 0 SD FESTE] *This edn; not in* F 3 Exit] *Theobald; not in* F

45 **fair** equitable.
46 **uncivil** Here (and perhaps at 5.1.101)
'uncivil' means 'uncivilised' and thus fit for
dwellers in 'barbarous caves' (41). Elsewhere
(2.3.104, 3.4.215) it is somewhat less emphatic.
46 **unjust extent** unjustified assault.
48 **pranks** mischiefs.
49 **botched up** patched up. For Feste's use of
'botcher', see 1.5.38.
51 **deny** refuse.
51 **Beshrew his soul** Literally, 'curse his soul',
a stronger sense than at 2.3.70.
52 **started** (1) roused and (2) startled. The first
sense (which is used of a hare in *1H4* 1.3.198)
initiates a pun on 'hart' and 'heart' (as at
1.1.17–18). For the second sense, compare *AWW*
5.3.232: 'every feather starts you'.
52 **in thee** In accord with the doctrine that lovers
exchange hearts.
53 **relish** taste. Used figuratively: 'What is the
meaning of this?'
54 **Or...or** Either...or.

55 **fancy** imagination. Many editors take it to
mean 'love', which is one meaning of 'fancy' but
surely not a relevant one here.
55 **still** ever.
55 **Lethe** The river of forgetfulness in the
classical underworld.

Act 4, Scene 2
Location Olivia's house (Rowe).
2 **Sir Topas the curate** See 3.4.230 n. for the
complimentary use of 'sir'. Though Shakespeare
probably derives the name from the burlesque
knight in Chaucer's 'Tale of Sir Topas', the topaz,
according to Reginald Scot, 'healeth the lunatic
person of his passion of lunacie' (quoted by
Furness); Batman upon Bartholome (*De Proprieta-
tibus Rerum* (1582), sig. 2z4) also records that since
the topaz follows the course of the moon, it helps
against the 'Lunatik' passion, and he cites
Dioscorides as saying it aids against 'evill thoughts
and phrensie'.
3 **the whilst** in the meantime.

FESTE Well, I'll put it on, and I will dissemble myself in't, and I would
I were the first that ever dissembled in such a gown. I am not tall   5
enough to become the function well, nor lean enough to be thought
a good student; but to be said an honest man and a good
housekeeper goes as fairly as to say a careful man and a great
scholar. The competitors enter.

Enter [SIR] TOBY [*and* MARIA]

SIR TOBY Jove bless thee, Master Parson.   10
FESTE *Bonos dies*, Sir Toby. For as the old hermit of Prague, that never
saw pen and ink, very wittily said to a niece of King Gorboduc,
'That that is, is', so I, being Master Parson, am Master Parson;
for what is 'that' but 'that' and 'is' but 'is'?
SIR TOBY To him, Sir Topas.   15
FESTE What ho, I say! Peace in this prison!
SIR TOBY The knave counterfeits well. A good knave.

---

9 SD SIR...*and* MARIA] *Theobald; not in* F   12 Gorboduc] Gorbodacke F, *Capell*

---

4 dissemble (1) disguise and (2) conceal one's
true nature. This is the only example of (1) in
Shakespeare (Onions). Both meanings permit a
satiric glance in the next line to 'dissembling'
puritan members of the clergy who concealed the
Genevan black gown under the traditional white
surplice. See Roger Warren, *N&Q* 218 (1973),
136–8.

5 tall Probably 'stout' or 'sturdy' to contrast
with 'lean' in the next line.

6 function office.

6–7 nor lean...student Like Chaucer's Clerk of
Oxenford; 'student' here means 'scholar'. Though
F's form 'studient' is (like 'dexteriously' (1.5.49) and
'jealious' (4.3.27 n.)) an Elizabethan variant, both
forms (with and without the *i*) appear in the early
texts. NS notes, somewhat questionably, that it may
reflect Shakespeare's own practice, since the same
form appears in *Ham.* 1.2.177 (Q1 but not F) and
Wiv. 3.1.38 (F but not Q1).

7 said called.

7 honest honourable. (The primary meaning in
OED.)

7–8 good housekeeper one keeping open
hospitality (and therefore prosperous). In calling up
a jury by which to be tried, Sir John Harington in
his mock-encomium *The Metamorphosis of Ajax*,
ed. E. S. Donno, 1962, pp. 223 ff., specifies that he
will have none but those who are great and good
housekeepers, i.e. wealthy owners of great houses.
Given the fact that Feste has been warned about

being turned away (1.5.14–15), it is fitting he should
commend the dispensing of hospitality in great
houses.

8 goes as fairly sounds as honourable. Compare
MV 1.1.127–30: 'my chief care / Is to come fairly
off from the great debts / Wherein my time
something too prodigal / Hath left me gag'd'.

8 careful careworn from studies (Onions). In
view of the antitheses posed (an honourable as
against a careworn man, a prosperous householder
as against a poor scholar), this sense of the word
seems altogether right. Onions prints it with a
query.

9 The competitors My partners.

11 *Bonos dies* Good day. Correctly *bonus dies*. It
is fitting that Feste as clown (and curate) should use
bad Latin.

11–12 old hermit...Gorboduc Like Quinapalus (1.5.29) and Pigrogromitus and the Vapians
(2.3.20), this is an example of Feste's mock learning;
Gorboduc, from the name of a legendary British
king, is the title of the first English tragedy in
blank verse, written by Thomas Norton and
Thomas Sackville and published in 1565.

13 That...is Compare Feste's ironic observation
at 4.1.6–7. Both statements can be true, at least in
Illyria; see p. 12 above.

17 knave Literally, 'boy', but often a term of
affection, as with Lear addressing the Fool (1.4.96):
'How now, my pretty knave, how dost thou?'

MALVOLIO (*Within*) Who calls there?

FESTE Sir Topas the curate, who comes to visit Malvolio the lunatic.

MALVOLIO Sir Topas, Sir Topas, good Sir Topas, go to my lady.   20

FESTE Out, hyperbolical fiend! How vexest thou this man! Talk'st thou nothing but of ladies?

SIR TOBY Well said, Master Parson.

MALVOLIO Sir Topas, never was man thus wronged. Good Sir Topas, do not think I am mad. They have laid me here in hideous darkness.   25

FESTE Fie, thou dishonest Satan! I call thee by the most modest terms, for I am one of those gentle ones that will use the devil himself with courtesy. Say'st thou that the house is dark?

MALVOLIO As hell, Sir Topas.

FESTE Why, it hath bay windows transparent as barricadoes, and the   30
clerestories toward the south-north are as lustrous as ebony; and yet complain'st thou of obstruction?

MALVOLIO I am not mad, Sir Topas; I say to you this house is dark.

FESTE Madman, thou errest. I say there is no darkness but ignorance, in which thou art more puzzled than the Egyptians in their fog.   35

MALVOLIO I say this house is as dark as ignorance, though ignorance were as dark as hell; and I say there was never man thus abused. I am no more mad than you are. Make the trial of it in any constant question.

FESTE What is the opinion of Pythagoras concerning wildfowl?   40

MALVOLIO That the soul of our grandam might haply inhabit a bird.

FESTE What think'st thou of his opinion?

---

18 SH, SD] SD *precedes* SH *in* F   28 the] *Anon. conj., Cam.; not in* F   31 clerestories] *Conj. Blakeway (in Var. 1821)*; cleere stores F

---

21 **hyperbolical** overreaching, raging. Hyperbole is the rhetorical technique of using exaggerated or extravagant language; as an English name for the Greek term, George Puttenham (*The Arte of English Poesie*, ed. G. D. Willcock and A. Walker, 1936, p. 191) gives 'over-reacher' or 'lowd lyar'.

26 **modest** moderate. As in 1.3.6.

29 **as hell** A proverbial comparison (Tilley H397).

30 **barricadoes** fortifications. From the fact that the first barricades in Paris in the sixteenth century were made of casks (from French *barrique* or Spanish *barrica*) filled with earth and stones.

31 **clerestories** Windows in the upper part of a wall, particularly in large churches or cathedrals.

32 **of obstruction** of the light being shut out.

35 **puzzled** bewildered.

35 **Egyptians...fog** From Exod. 10.21–3, recounting the 'blacke darkenesse' which the Egyptians endured for three days.

38–9 **constant question** formally conducted discussion (Onions).

40 **Pythagoras** The Greek philosopher who held, as Gratiano puts it (*MV* 4.1.132–3), 'That souls of animals infuse themselves / Into the trunks of men'.

41 **haply** perchance. Onions notes that in Shakespeare's early printed texts, the spelling 'haply' occurs about twice as frequently as 'happily', the form that appears here in F.

MALVOLIO I think nobly of the soul, and no way approve his opinion.

FESTE Fare thee well. Remain thou still in darkness. Thou shalt hold
th'opinion of Pythagoras ere I will allow of thy wits, and fear to   45
kill a woodcock lest thou dispossess the soul of thy grandam. Fare
thee well.

MALVOLIO Sir Topas, Sir Topas!

SIR TOBY My most exquisite Sir Topas!

FESTE Nay, I am for all waters.   50

MARIA Thou mightst have done this without thy beard and gown; he
sees thee not.

SIR TOBY To him in thine own voice, and bring me word how thou
find'st him. I would we were well rid of this knavery. If he may
be conveniently delivered, I would he were, for I am now so far   55
in offence with my niece that I cannot pursue with any safety this
sport to the upshot. [*To Maria*] Come by and by to my chamber.

Exit [*with Maria*]

FESTE [*Sings*]   Hey Robin, jolly Robin,
                         Tell me how thy lady does.

MALVOLIO Fool!   60

---

57 sport to the] *Rowe;* sport the F   57 SD *To Maria*] *This edn; not in* F   57 SD *with Maria*] *Theobald; not in* F
58, 61, 63, 65 SD *Sings*] *Rowe subst.; not in* F   58–9] *As verse, Capell; as prose* F

---

45 **allow...wits** certify your sanity.
46 **woodcock** The proverbially stupid bird. Used
of Malvolio earlier (2.5.69).
50 Indeed, I can turn my hand to anything
(Malone). The literal meaning is much debated;
Furness gives several interpretations, and Dent
adds examples to Tilley C421 ('To have a cloak for
all waters').
51–2 **Thou mightst...not** Maria's speech
serves as a cue to staging, indicating that Sir Topas
has spoken to Malvolio from outside a curtain or
some kind of enclosure representing the 'dark
room'. Such staging also allows the actor (originally,
it seems, Robert Armin) to reveal his skill in
impersonating by quick shifts of voice at 80–2 and
84–6, where he speaks as Feste and Sir Topas by
turns. For the earliest known picture of Malvolio in
a 'dark room' and Feste in a curate's gown (1709),
see illustration 7 (p. 21 above); for a later example
by Fuseli (1805), see illustration 8, p. 22.
55 **conveniently delivered** without incon-
venience set free.
57 **to the upshot** to its conclusion. A term from
archery, indicating the final shot; the term appears
again only in *Ham.* F 3879 (5.2.384).
57 SD* At 5.1 we learn that 'in recompense' for

Maria's device, Sir Toby 'hath married her'; his
words here would thus seem most appropriately
addressed to her (see p. 9 above). Also, having no
further lines to speak, she would naturally exit at
this point.
58–65 **Hey Robin...another** Feste makes
himself known to Malvolio by singing part of a
dialogue song (thus representing two voices),
attributed to Sir Thomas Wyatt but perhaps
developed from an earlier version. The following
two stanzas are from Wyatt's *Collected Poems*, ed.
Kenneth Muir and Patricia Thomson, 1969, pp.
41–2: (1) 'A Robyn / Joly Robyn / Tell me how
thy leman [sweetheart] doeth / And thou shall
knowe of myn.' (2) 'My lady is unkynd, perde!' /
'Alack, whi is she so?' / 'She loveth an othre better
than me, / And yet she will say no.' The music is
by Wyatt's courtly contemporary William Cornyshe,
and there are scholarly editions of it by Gustave
Reese (*Music in the Renaissance*, 1954, p. 770) and
John Stevens (*Music at the Court of Henry VIII*,
1962, pp. 38 ff.). For a full account, including
manuscript sources, see Seng, pp. 116–19; he notes
that the song of a forsaken lover is a further means
to gull Malvolio.

FESTE [*Sings*]   My lady is unkind, perdy.

MALVOLIO Fool!

FESTE [*Sings*]   Alas, why is she so?

MALVOLIO Fool, I say!

FESTE [*Sings*]   She loves another –   65
                        Who calls, ha?

MALVOLIO Good fool, as ever thou wilt deserve well at my hand, help
me to a candle and pen, ink, and paper. As I am a gentleman, I
will live to be thankful to thee for't.

FESTE Master Malvolio?   .   70

MALVOLIO Ay, good fool.

FESTE Alas, sir, how fell you besides your five wits?

MALVOLIO Fool, there was never man so notoriously abused. I am as
well in my wits, fool, as thou art.

FESTE But as well? Then you are mad indeed, if you be no better in   75
your wits than a fool.

MALVOLIO They have here propertied me: keep me in darkness, send
ministers to me, asses, and do all they can to face me out of my
wits.

FESTE Advise you what you say. The minister is here. [*As Sir Topas*]   80
Malvolio, Malvolio, thy wits the heavens restore. Endeavour thyself
to sleep and leave thy vain bibble babble.

MALVOLIO Sir Topas!

FESTE [*As Sir Topas*] Maintain no words with him, good fellow. [*As
himself*] Who, I, sir? Not I, sir. God b'w'you, good Sir Topas.   85
[*As Sir Topas*] Marry, amen. [*As himself*] I will, sir, I will.

80, 84, 84–5, 86 SD *As Sir Topas...As Sir Topas...As himself...As Sir Topas...As himself*] Hanmer subst.; not in F
85 God b'w'] *Pope;* God buy F

61 perdy A corruption of the oath *par Dieu*.

72 besides out of. As in *Sonnets* 23.1–2: 'As an
unperfect actor on the stage, / Who with his fear
is put besides his part'.

72 five wits i.e. mental faculties. Specifically, the
common wit, imagination, fantasy, estimation and
memory.

73 notoriously abused egregiously maltreated;
'notoriously' is apparently another of Malvolio's
special words. The only two adverbial instances in
Shakespeare occur here and at 5.1.356; taken
together with the two adjectival uses (5.1.308,
322), the word nicely conveys Malvolio's own sense
of wounded dignity.

75 But Only.

77 propertied made a movable object. Perhaps
with the suggestion of a piece of stage property in
the comic interlude that is being performed; at

5.1.350 Feste refers to the deception practised on
Malvolio as an 'interlude'.

78–9 face me...wits i.e. brazenly (and falsely)
insisting that I am mad. For a similar usage of 'face
me out', see 5.1.77.

80 Advise you Consider.

82 bibble babble idle talk. The only instance in
Shakespeare, apart from Fluellen's Welsh version,
'pibble babble' (*H5* 4.1.71).

85 God b'w'you God be with you. Equivalent
to modern 'good-bye'. F contracts the form to 'God
buy you', perhaps more difficult for a modern
reader to grasp than Pope's form adopted here.

86 Marry, amen Though used elsewhere as a
mild expletive (e.g. 1.3.56, 1.5.104, 3.4.90, 3.4.274),
perhaps here it is intended to carry something of the
original sense of invoking the Virgin.

MALVOLIO Fool, fool, fool, I say!

FESTE Alas, sir, be patient. What say you, sir? I am shent for speaking
to you.

MALVOLIO Good fool, help me to some light and some paper; I tell 90
thee, I am as well in my wits as any man in Illyria.

FESTE Well-a-day, that you were, sir!

MALVOLIO By this hand, I am! Good fool, some ink, paper and light,
and convey what I will set down to my lady. It shall advantage thee
more than ever the bearing of letter did. 95

FESTE I will help you to't. But tell me true, are you not mad indeed
or do you but counterfeit?

MALVOLIO Believe me, I am not. I tell thee true.

FESTE Nay, I'll ne'er believe a madman till I see his brains. I will fetch
you light and paper and ink. 100

MALVOLIO Fool, I'll requite it in the highest degree. I prithee be gone.

FESTE [*Sings*]   I am gone, sir,
    And anon, sir,
      I'll be with you again,
    In a trice 105
    Like to the old Vice,
      Your need to sustain;
    Who, with dagger of lath,
    In his rage and his wrath,
      Cries, 'Ah ha' to the devil, 110
    Like a mad lad,
    'Pare thy nails, dad?'
    Adieu, goodman devil.   *Exit*

102 SD *Sings*] Rowe subst.; *not in* F   102–13] *As Capell; lines end*...sir, / ...againe: / ...vice, / ...sustaine. / ...wrath,
/ ...diuell: / ...dad, / ...diuell. / F   113 goodman] *Capell;* good man F

88 shent scolded.

92 Well-a-day Alas. An exclamation, aptly
picking up Malvolio's 'well' of the previous line.

93 By this hand A conventional oath. On the
Elizabethan stage Malvolio perhaps thrusts forth
his hand from behind an arras or 'within' (18 SD)
a curtained area; for non-Elizabethan staging, see
illustrations 7 and 8, pp. 21–2 above.

94 advantage profit.

97 counterfeit pretend. Compare the passage
in *AYLI* (4.3.165–82) where Rosalind-Ganymede
insists that her swooning was but 'counterfeit'.

102–13 I am gone...devil No music has been
found for these lines, but, given Feste's vocal skills,
it seems likely they were intended to be sung.

F. W. Sternfeld (*Music in Shakespearean Tragedy*,
1963, p. 113) describes the situation here as that of
a 'musical jester goading an anti-musical puritan'.

106 old Vice A character in the morality plays
who carried a harmless dagger of lath; a predecessor
of the Elizabethan fool.

112 Pare thy nails, dad Tilley (N12) dates its
earliest appearance as 1548, and Ard. notes that in
the undated play *Lusty Juventus* (?1565) the Vice is
the devil's son. Slightly earlier than *TN*, Shakespeare
combined several of the elements of the song to
characterise Pistol as 'this roaring devil i'th'old
play, that everyone may pare his nails with a wooden
dagger' (*H5* 4.4.71–2).

113 Adieu...devil Serving as Feste's (perhaps

4.3 *Enter* SEBASTIAN

SEBASTIAN This is the air, that is the glorious sun,
        This pearl she gave me, I do feel't and see't,
        And though 'tis wonder that enwraps me thus,
        Yet 'tis not madness. Where's Antonio then?
        I could not find him at the Elephant,   5
        Yet there he was, and there I found this credit,
        That he did range the town to seek me out.
        His counsel now might do me golden service,
        For though my soul disputes well with my sense
        That this may be some error, but no madness,   10
        Yet doth this accident and flood of fortune
        So far exceed all instance, all discourse,
        That I am ready to distrust mine eyes,
        And wrangle with my reason that persuades me
        To any other trust but that I am mad,   15
        Or else the lady's mad; yet if 'twere so,
        She could not sway her house, command her followers,
        Take and give back affairs and them dispatch,
        With such a smooth, discreet, and stable bearing
        As I perceive she does. There's something in't   20
        That is deceivable. But here the lady comes.

Act 4, Scene 3   4.3] *Scæna Tertia.* F   18 them] *Conj. Dyce²;* their F

dancing) exit line, this is probably addressed to Malvolio, although it could be conceived as part of the Vice's speech to the devil. Shakespeare uses the term 'goodman' in several ways, of which two are particularly apt here: (1) prefixed to a designation of occupation, as the address to the grave-digger, 'goodman delver', *Ham.* F 3203 (5.1.14), and (2) jocularly and ironically (Onions) as here and in Prince Hal's speech (*1H4* 2.4.92–4): 'I am now of all humors that have show'd themselves humors since the old days of goodman Adam.' The latter also picks up Adam's occupation as a farmer, as in the well-known medieval rhyme 'When Adam delved and Eve span / Who was then the gentleman?'

Act 4, Scene 3
Location Olivia's garden (Capell).
6 was had been.
6 credit report. This meaning of the word is peculiar to Shakespeare (Onions).
9 my soul...sense i.e. my reason argues soundly in accord with the evidence of my senses.
11 this accident...fortune this unexpected event and (this) abundant (good) fortune. The

literal 'accident and flood' is now, appropriately, used metaphorically.
12 instance example, precedent.
12 discourse reason. As in Hamlet's well-known soliloquy (Q2): 'Sure He that made us with such large discourse,...gave us not / That capability and godlike reason / To fust in us unus'd' (4.4.36–9).
15 trust conviction.
17 sway rule or manage.
18 *Take...dispatch i.e. take in hand her (household) affairs and promptly settle them; 'dispatch' carries the sense of (1) finishing a business and (2) doing it with speed. F's reading 'their', emended here to 'them' following Dyce's suggestion, represents an easy graphic error. Commentators who retain 'their' explain that 'take' governs 'affairs' and 'give back' governs 'dispatch', but even so the line remains an anacoluthon, lacking in grammatical sequence. Sebastian's observation on Olivia's household management, suggesting a passage of time, serves to make the succeeding action seem somewhat less precipitate.
19 stable steady.
21 deceivable misleading.

Enter OLIVIA *and* PRIEST

OLIVIA Blame not this haste of mine. If you mean well,
　　　　Now go with me, and with this holy man
　　　　Into the chantry by; there before him,
　　　　And underneath that consecrated roof,   25
　　　　Plight me the full assurance of your faith,
　　　　That my most jealous and too doubtful soul
　　　　May live at peace. He shall conceal it
　　　　Whiles you are willing it shall come to note;
　　　　What time we will our celebration keep   30
　　　　According to my birth. What do you say?
SEBASTIAN I'll follow this good man, and go with you,
　　　　And having sworn truth, ever will be true.
OLIVIA Then lead the way, good father, and heavens so shine,
　　　　That they may fairly note this act of mine!   35

　　　　　　　　　　　　　　　　　　　　　　　　　　　Exeunt

5.1 *Enter* CLOWN [FESTE] *and* FABIAN

FABIAN Now, as thou lov'st me, let me see his letter.
FESTE Good Master Fabian, grant me another request.
FABIAN Anything.
FESTE Do not desire to see this letter.
FABIAN This is to give a dog and in recompense desire my dog again.   5

---

35 SD *Exeunt*] Exeunt. / *Finis Actus Quartus.* F　　Act 5, Scene 1　5.1] *Actus Quintus. Scena Prima.* F

24 **chantry** A private endowed chapel where a priest (or priests) sang masses for the souls of specified individuals.

24 **by** near by.

26 i.e. pledge that you accept me as your spouse. Such a pledge or contract (known as *sponsalia per verbi de praesenti*) was legally binding; the priest describes the ceremony at 5.1.145–52.

27 **jealous** F reads 'jealious', which is an Elizabethan variant, but the modern spelling is the more frequent in Shakespeare's texts.

27 **doubtful** apprehensive.

29 **Whiles** Until.

29 **come to note** become known.

30 **What time** At which time.

31 **According...birth** In a fashion that accords with my social rank.

32–5 The couplets here (in contrast with those at 3.4.318–21) accord with Shakespeare's general practice of giving verse to highborn and romantic characters and using rhyme to signal the end of an act.

35 **fairly note** look with favour on.

Act 5, Scene 1

Location Before Olivia's house (Capell).

5 **This...again** Apparently an allusion to the clever response of the queen's kinsman Dr Bullein when she asked him for a dog on which he doted, assuring him that he could have whatever he desired in recompense; having surrendered it, he followed up with his counter-request, 'I pray you give me my dog againe' (from the *Diary* of John Manningham, who also records a Middle Temple performance of *TN*; see p. 1 above).

Enter DUKE [ORSINO], VIOLA, CURIO, *and Lords*

ORSINO Belong you to the Lady Olivia, friends?

FESTE Ay, sir, we are some of her trappings.

ORSINO I know thee well. How dost thou, my good fellow?

FESTE Truly, sir, the better for my foes, and the worse for my friends.

ORSINO Just the contrary: the better for thy friends.   10

FESTE No, sir, the worse.

ORSINO How can that be?

FESTE Marry, sir, they praise me, and make an ass of me. Now my foes
tell me plainly I am an ass, so that by my foes, sir, I profit in the
knowledge of myself, and by my friends I am abused; so that,   15
conclusions to be as kisses, if your four negatives make your two
affirmatives, why then, the worse for my friends and the better for
my foes.

ORSINO Why, this is excellent.

FESTE By my troth, sir, no, though it please you to be one of my friends.   20

ORSINO Thou shalt not be the worse for me; there's gold.

FESTE But that it would be double-dealing, sir, I would you could make
it another.

ORSINO O you give me ill counsel.

7 trappings Figuratively, 'superficial decora-
tion'; literally a caparison for a horse, usually gaily
ornamented.

13 Marry...foes Feste's paradoxical argument derives from his applying the Latin grammatical rule that two negatives make an affirmative
to an English construction, and from the multiple
senses his words convey. The Latin rule was well
known from the authorised *Grammar* of William
Lily, which was frequently alluded to in popular
writing.

13 make...of me thus I become an ass.

14 plainly (1) openly and (2) honestly.

14–15 profit...myself (1) benefit in the
knowledge of myself (i.e. the knowledge that I am
an ass), and (2) improve. The first meaning accords
with the Socratic doctrine 'Know thyself' (proverbial from 1481 on, Tilley K175). For the second,
compare *MM* 3.2.32–3: 'Correction and instruction
must both work / Ere this rude beast will profit.'

15 abused (1) deceived, (2) disgraced, (3)
insulted, (4) maltreated. This fourth meaning
appears also at 4.2.73.

15–17 so...affirmatives provided that propo-

sitions be like kisses, where 'no, no, no, no' may
mean 'yes, yes'. Richard Farmer pointed out a
parallel in *Lust's Dominion*, now generally assigned
to Dekker, Haughton and Day (written *c.* 1600,
printed 1657): '"No, no", says "aye", and twice
"away" says "stay"' as well as with a Sidney sonnet
which is keyed to the grammatical rule 'That in one
speech, two negatives affirm' (*Astrophil and Stella*,
63.14, cited in Furness).

16 your Used indefinitely to mean 'that you
know of' (*OED* Your 5b). Compare *Ant.* 2.7.26–7.

17–18 the worse...foes i.e. with respect to my
friends, I am (1) worse off and (2) the less (as in *Lear*
1.4.40–1: 'If I like thee no worse after dinner');
with respect to my foes, I am (1) better off and (2)
the greater (as in *AYLI* 3.1.2: 'But were I not the
better part made mercy').

20 By...no For Feste's oath, see 1.3.3 and n.,
and for a similar self-disparagement with Viola, see
3.1.46.

20 though even though.

22 But...double-dealing Except that it would
be (1) duplicity and (2) double-giving.

FESTE Put your grace in your pocket, sir, for this once, and let your   25
flesh and blood obey it.

ORSINO Well, I will be so much a sinner to be a double-dealer; there's
another.

FESTE *Primo, secundo, tertio* is a good play, and the old saying is 'The
third pays for all'; the triplex, sir, is a good tripping measure; or   30
the bells of St Bennet, sir, may put you in mind – one, two, three.

ORSINO You can fool no more money out of me at this throw. If you
will let your lady know I am here to speak with her, and bring her
along with you, it may awake my bounty further.

FESTE Marry, sir, lullaby to your bounty till I come again. I go, sir,   35
but I would not have you to think that my desire of having is the
sin of covetousness; but, as you say, sir, let your bounty take a nap.
I will awake it anon.   *Exit*

Enter ANTONIO *and* OFFICERS

VIOLA Here comes the man, sir, that did rescue me.

ORSINO That face of his I do remember well;   40
Yet when I saw it last, it was besmeared
As black as Vulcan, in the smoke of war.

---

25 Put...pocket Pay no attention to your honour. This is intended both literally and metaphorically, with a play on 'grace' as (1) favour and (2) the address proper to a duke. (The second meaning could support the idea that Shakespeare originally intended Orsino to be a duke; see 1.1.0 SD n.) Compare the same verbal play in *MM* 4.3.134–5: 'and you shall have.../ Grace of the Duke...'

25–6 let...it i.e. let your human frailty (as opposed to your assumed honour) follow that 'ill counsel'.

27 so much...to be See 2.2.7 for a similar omission of 'as'.

29 *Primo*...play In his request for a third favour, Feste ingeniously resorts to Latin ordinals, with perhaps an allusion to an intricate mathematical game, purportedly invented by Pythagoras, called the 'Philosopher's Game' or the 'battell of numbers'. Played on a double chessboard, odd and even numbers, each under a king, attempt to capture opponents by various mathematical schemes; one form of capture occurs when two numbers find one of their 'enemies' equalling the addition of the two, as 1 and 2 capturing 3. A manual by Ralph Lever and William Fulwood, published in 1563 and dedicated to the Earl of Leicester, refers to French and Latin versions; utilising elaborate

mathematical diagrams, the game was surely not for children as Reginald Scot, cited in NS, implies in likening it to 'children's plaie'.

29–30 the old saying...all Tilley T319 ('The third time pays for all'), with variations. Referring to this idea, Falstaff (*Wiv.* 5.1.3–4) notes that 'They say there is divinity in odd numbers, either in nativity, chance, or death.'

30 triplex Triple time in music.

31 St Bennet St Benedict. Of the several churches in London dedicated to the saint, Halliwell suggests that Feste is referring to St Bennet's at Paul's Wharf, located across from the Globe Theatre (cited in Furness).

32 can fool (1) by jesting and (2) by making a fool of me.

32 at this throw on this occasion. With a quibble on 'a cast of the dice', continuing the diction of gambling from 'good play' (29). In place of a wished-for 'tray-trip', a three, Feste has 'thrown' only an 'ames-ace', two aces, the lowest possible throw (Onions).

35 lullaby farewell. Diction prompted by Orsino's use of 'awake' and carried on in the speech with 'take a nap' and 'will awake'. The only other instance in Shakespeare is in *The Passionate Pilgrim* 15.15.

42 Vulcan Blacksmith in the Roman pantheon.

A baubling vessel was he captain of,
For shallow draught and bulk unprizable,
With which, such scathful grapple did he make   45
With the most noble bottom of our fleet,
That very envy, and the tongue of loss,
Cried fame and honour on him. What's the matter?

1 OFFICER Orsino, this is that Antonio
That took the Phoenix and her fraught from Candy,   50
And this is he that did the Tiger board,
When your young nephew Titus lost his leg.
Here in the streets, desp'rate of shame and state,
In private brabble did we apprehend him.

VIOLA He did me kindness, sir, drew on my side,   55
But in conclusion put strange speech upon me,
I know not what 'twas, but distraction.

ORSINO Notable pirate! Thou salt-water thief!
What foolish boldness brought thee to their mercies,
Whom thou, in terms so bloody and so dear,   60
Hast made thine enemies?

ANTONIO   Orsino, noble sir,
Be pleased that I shake off these names you give me.
Antonio never yet was thief or pirate,
Though I confess, on base and ground enough,
Orsino's enemy. A witchcraft drew me hither.   65
That most ungrateful boy there by your side,
From the rude sea's enraged and foamy mouth
Did I redeem; a wrack past hope he was.

43 baubling contemptible. In *Tro.* 1.3.35, Nestor refers disparagingly to 'shallow bauble boats'.

44 unprizable i.e. not worth being captured as booty ('prize').

45 scathful grapple destructive close fighting.

46 bottom ship.

47 very...loss even (our) mortification and (our) voices as losers.

48 Cried Called out. As in *2H4* 4.1.134–5: 'For all the country in a general voice / Cried hate upon him.'

50 fraught cargo.

50 Candy Used here, correctly, for the capital of Crete, though the Elizabethans frequently used it in reference to the island itself (E. H. Sugden, *A Topographical Dictionary*, 1925, p. 96).

53 desp'rate...state regardless of disgrace and danger (to himself).

54 private brabble personal quarrel.

55 on my side in my defence.

56 put...upon me spoke to me in a singular fashion.

57 but distraction unless (it were) madness.

58 Notable Notorious.

60 in terms...dear in a manner so bloodthirsty and so grievous.

62 shake off deny.

64 on base...enough on sufficient foundation.

65 witchcraft A twin effect: as Viola-Cesario has enchanted Olivia (3.1.97), so Sebastian here is said to have bewitched Antonio.

68 a wrack wreckage. See *OED* Wrack *sb²* 1b. In Shakespeare's period 'wrack' was not orthographically distinguished from 'wreck'.

His life I gave him, and did thereto add
My love without retention, or restraint,   70
All his in dedication. For his sake,
Did I expose myself, pure for his love,
Into the danger of this adverse town,
Drew to defend him when he was beset;
Where being apprehended, his false cunning   75
(Not meaning to partake with me in danger)
Taught him to face me out of his acquaintance,
And grew a twenty-years' removèd thing
While one would wink; denied me mine own purse,
Which I had recommended to his use   80
Not half an hour before.

VIOLA   How can this be?

ORSINO When came he to this town?

ANTONIO Today, my lord, and for three months before,
No int'rim, not a minute's vacancy,
Both day and night did we keep company.   85

Enter OLIVIA *and Attendants*

ORSINO Here comes the countess; now heaven walks on earth.
But for thee, fellow – Fellow, thy words are madness.
Three months this youth hath tended upon me,
But more of that anon. Take him aside.

OLIVIA What would my lord, but that he may not have,   90
Wherein Olivia may seem serviceable?
Cesario, you do not keep promise with me.

VIOLA Madam!

ORSINO Gracious Olivia –

OLIVIA What do you say, Cesario? Good my lord –   95

87 fellow – Fellow] *Dyce subst.;* fellow, fellow F   94 Olivia –] *Theobald subst.;* Olivia. F   95 lord –] *Rowe subst.;* Lord. F

69 **thereto** besides.
70 **retention** reservation.
71 **All...dedication** i.e. dedicated (my love) wholly to him.
72 **pure** only. (An adverbial use.)
73 **adverse** hostile.
77 **to face...acquaintance** brazenly to deny he knew me. (As at 4.2.78–9.)
78 **removèd** distant.
79 **wink** blink (an eye).

80 **recommended** committed.
83 **three months before** For the double-time scheme, see p. 9 above, n. 2.
84 **int'rim** F's elision; NS notes the same spelling for metrical reasons in *Sonnets* 56.9.
87 **for thee** as for thee.
90 **but that...have** except that which he may not have (i.e. Olivia's love).
92 **keep promise** i.e. 'ever' to be true (4.3.33). Cesario is manifestly now in attendance on Orsino.

VIOLA My lord would speak; my duty hushes me.

OLIVIA If it be aught to the old tune, my lord,
          It is as fat and fulsome to mine ear
          As howling after music.

ORSINO   Still so cruel?

OLIVIA Still so constant, lord.   100

ORSINO What, to perverseness? You uncivil lady,
          To whose ingrate and unauspicious altars
          My soul the faithfull'st off'rings have breathed out
          That e'er devotion tendered! What shall I do?

OLIVIA Even what it please my lord that shall become him.   105

ORSINO Why should I not – had I the heart to do it –
          Like to th'Egyptian thief at point of death
          Kill what I love – a savage jealousy
          That sometimes savours nobly? But hear me this.
          Since you to non-regardance cast my faith,   110
          And that I partly know the instrument
          That screws me from my true place in your favour,
          Live you the marble-breasted tyrant still.
          But this your minion, whom I know you love,
          And whom, by heaven I swear, I tender dearly,   115

---

103 have] F; hath *Capell;* has *Pope*

---

96 **duty** sense of respect, obedience.

98 **fat and fulsome** distasteful and disgusting.

101 **uncivil** uncivilised. See 4.1.46 n.

102 **ingrate and unauspicious** thankless and unpropitious. The latter form is used only this once in Shakespeare.

103 **off'rings** F's elision; found elsewhere for the sake of the metre, as in *Tro.* 3216 (5.3.17) and *Mac.* 2.1.52.

103 **have breathed** Pope and even recent editors correct the 'faulty' plural auxiliary, which probably results from the immediately preceding plural object.

105 **become** suit. But also with an overtone of 'grace', as in *Cor.* 2.1.123: 'The wounds become him.'

106–9 This (short-lived) vehemence on Orsino's part, suggesting some degree of violence, is to be compared with his posture as the moody lover in the opening scene of the play. It is also to be contrasted with the actual violence of Sir Toby's and Sir Andrew's fray with Sebastian which is reported at 161 ff.

107 **Like to th'Egyptian thief** A reference to an episode in the Greek romance *Ethiopica* by Heliodorus (translated in 1569 by Thomas Underdowne) where an Egyptian bandit intends, but fails, to slay a beloved captive when he despairs of his own life. NS quotes Heliodorus's comment: 'If the barbarous people be once in despair of their own safety, they have a custom to kill all those by whom they set much, and whose company they desire after death.'

109 **savours nobly** Figuratively, 'exudes or is redolent of nobility'.

110 **to non-regardance** into disregard. Used only by Shakespeare (Onions).

111 **that** since.

111 **instrument** Figuratively, 'agent'; literally, 'tool' – here suggesting torture.

112 **screws** wrests.

113 **marble-breasted** Metonymy. Compare Lear's 'marble-hearted fiend' (1.4.259). Ironically, Olivia has earlier accused Cesario (3.4.168) of being 'a heart of stone'.

114 **minion** favourite. From French *mignon*, pet, darling. Frequently used by Shakespeare in a contemptuous sense.

115 **tender** regard.

Him will I tear out of that cruel eye
Where he sits crownèd in his master's spite.
Come, boy, with me; my thoughts are ripe in mischief.
I'll sacrifice the lamb that I do love,
To spite a raven's heart within a dove. [*Leaving*]   120

VIOLA And I most jocund, apt, and willingly,
To do you rest, a thousand deaths would die. [*Following*]

OLIVIA Where goes Cesario?

VIOLA   After him I love
More than I love these eyes, more than my life,
More, by all mores, than e'er I shall love wife.   125
If I do feign, you witnesses above
Punish my life for tainting of my love!

OLIVIA Ay me, detested! How am I beguiled!

VIOLA Who does beguile you? Who does do you wrong?

OLIVIA Hast thou forgot thyself? Is it so long?   130
Call forth the holy father.

                                         [*Exit an Attendant*]

ORSINO   Come, away!

OLIVIA Whither, my lord? Cesario, husband, stay!

ORSINO Husband?

OLIVIA   Ay, husband. Can he that deny?

ORSINO Her husband, sirrah?

VIOLA   No, my lord, not I.

OLIVIA Alas, it is the baseness of thy fear   135
That makes thee strangle thy propriety.

---

120 SD *Leaving*] *Theobald subst.; not in* F   122 SD *Following*] *Theobald; not in* F   131 SD *Exit an Attendant*] *Capell; not in* F

117 **crownèd** See 1.1.38–9 for Orsino's earlier projection of himself as the 'one selfsame king' of Olivia's affections.

117 **in…spite** i.e. spiting his master (by thwarting his desires).

120 **a raven's…dove** An analogy Shakespeare uses in contrasting the inward nature of a person with his outward appearance, as in *2H6* 3.1.75: 'Seems he a dove? his feathers are but borrowed', and *Rom.* 3.2.76: 'Dove-feather'd raven!' See also 3.4.317 n.

121 **apt** ready. The adjectival form is frequently used for the adverbial.

122 **do you rest** give you repose.

125 **by all mores** by all comparatives.

127 **tainting of** discrediting.

128 **detested** 'abhorred', but also 'denounced'. The logical corollary to Cesario's oath at 126–7.

130 **thou** Olivia continues to use the familiar second-person singular in spite of Cesario's rejection of her.

134 **sirrah** The usual form of address to an inferior, as again at 267, 281; in Shakespeare, except for one occasion (*Ant.* 5.2.229), it is an address to a male.

135 **baseness** meanness. It has both a moral and a social sense, the latter contrasted with the high rank of 139.

136 **strangle thy propriety** i.e. disavow yourself as my husband; 'propriety' is used again by Shakespeare only in *Oth.* 2.3.176, and in a different sense.

Fear not, Cesario, take thy fortunes up;
Be that thou know'st thou art, and then thou art
As great as that thou fear'st.

Enter PRIEST

                    O welcome, father!
Father, I charge thee by thy reverence   140
Here to unfold – though lately we intended
To keep in darkness what occasion now
Reveals before 'tis ripe – what thou dost know
Hath newly passed between this youth and me.

PRIEST A contract of eternal bond of love,   145
Confirmed by mutual joinder of your hands,
Attested by the holy close of lips,
Strengthened by th'interchangement of your rings,
And all the ceremony of this compact
Sealed in my function, by my testimony;   150
Since when, my watch hath told me, toward my grave
I have travelled but two hours.

ORSINO [*To Viola*] O thou dissembling cub! What wilt thou be
When time hath sowed a grizzle on thy case?
Or will not else thy craft so quickly grow   155
That thine own trip shall be thine overthrow?

153 SD *To Viola*] *This edn; not in* F

137 take...up i.e. accept your (prosperous) state
and (happy) lot as the husband of a countess.
139 As great as that Of as high rank as he
whom. Again, an illustration of Shakespeare's fluc-
tuating intention of casting Orsino as duke or
count.
140 by thy reverence in keeping with the regard
due to you.
142 To keep in darkness As determined at
4.3.28–9.
142 occasion necessity.
146 joinder joining. Not pre-Shakespearean in
the general sense, though its legal meaning was the
'coupling of two, in an action against another'
(Onions).
147 close union.
149 compact Accented on the final syllable.
150 function office. As at 4.2.6.
153 dissembling Compare Feste's comments at
4.2.4 and n. Dissembling and disguise are, of course,
major motifs running throughout the play and make

for effects both comic in the sub-plot and serious
in the main plot.
154 sowed a grizzle scattered grey hairs.
154 case Either (1) 'body', as in *Ant.* 4.15.89:
'This case of that huge spirit now is cold', or (2)
'skin', as in *WT* 4.4.814–15, where the Clown
(punningly) says 'though my case be a pitiful one,
I hope I shall not be flay'd out of it'. There is the
additional suggestion, according to the references
cited in Furness, that it alludes particularly to the
skin of a fox, thus picking up the vocative
'dissembling cub'.
155 Or, on the contrary, will not your cunning
so rapidly increase?
156 The line offers both literal and figurative
meanings; 'trip' = 'stumble' in both a physical and
moral sense; it is also the name of a technical trick
in wrestling which causes an opponent to 'fall', i.e.
be thrown over on his back, thus bringing about his
defeat. See *Shakespeare's England*, 2 vols., 1916, II,
455–6.

Farewell, and take her, but direct thy feet
Where thou and I henceforth may never meet.

VIOLA My lord, I do protest –

OLIVIA   O do not swear!
Hold little faith, though thou hast too much fear.   160

Enter SIR ANDREW [*his head bleeding*]

SIR ANDREW For the love of God, a surgeon! Send one presently to
Sir Toby.

OLIVIA What's the matter?

SIR ANDREW H'as broke my head across, and has given Sir Toby a
bloody coxcomb, too. For the love of God, your help! I had rather   165
than forty pound I were at home.

OLIVIA Who has done this, Sir Andrew?

SIR ANDREW The count's gentleman, one Cesario. We took him for a
coward, but he's the very devil incardinate.

ORSINO My gentleman Cesario?   170

SIR ANDREW 'Od's lifelings, here he is! You broke my head for nothing,
and that that I did, I was set on to do't by Sir Toby.

VIOLA Why do you speak to me? I never hurt you.
You drew your sword upon me without cause,
But I bespake you fair, and hurt you not.   175

Enter [SIR] TOBY *and* CLOWN [FESTE]

SIR ANDREW If a bloody coxcomb be a hurt, you have hurt me; I think
you set nothing by a bloody coxcomb. Here comes Sir Toby
halting – you shall hear more; but if he had not been in drink, he
would have tickled you othergates than he did.

---

159 protest –] *Rowe;* protest. F   160 SD *his...bleeding*] *Rowe subst.; not in* F   175 SD SIR, FESTE] *This edn; not in* F

160 Hold little faith Keep to *some* part of your plighted word. See Abbott 86 for omission of the indefinite article.

160 SD As NS notes, the appearance of Sir Andrew with his bleeding head points to a second fray which Shakespeare has not bothered to account for; it is not likely that Sir Andrew would return to active brawling after his threat of 'an action at battery' (4.1.29), nor would Sir Toby be likely to act in defiance of Olivia's words in 4.1.40–2.

164 broke...across cut my head open from side to side.

165 coxcomb head. As in *H5* 5.1.54–5: 'the skin [of the leek] is good for your broken coxcomb'.

169 incardinate in the flesh. Sir Andrew's rendering of 'incarnate'.

171 'Od's lifelings By God's little lives. Compare the equally diminutive ''Od's heartlings' (*Wiv.* 3.4.57), which, as NS points out, shows that Sir Andrew and Slender even swear alike. For the suggestion that John Sincler (or Sincklo) may have played both roles, see 2.3.18 n.

175 fair kindly. (Adverbial form.)

175 SD F's somewhat early SD can emphasise Sir Toby's slow 'halting' entrance; otherwise, it should perhaps come at 177–8.

177 set nothing by think nothing of.

178 halting limping.

179 othergates in another way. An expression surviving in the north and in Warwickshire (Onions).

ORSINO How now, gentleman? How is't with you?   180

SIR TOBY That's all one. H'as hurt me, and there's th'end on't. Sot, didst see Dick Surgeon, sot?

FESTE O he's drunk, Sir Toby, an hour agone; his eyes were set at eight i'th'morning.

SIR TOBY Then he's a rogue, and a passy-measures pavin. I hate a   185 drunken rogue.

OLIVIA Away with him! Who hath made this havoc with them?

SIR ANDREW I'll help you, Sir Toby, because we'll be dressed together.

SIR TOBY Will you help – an ass-head, and a coxcomb, and a knave,   190 a thin-faced knave, a gull?

OLIVIA Get him to bed, and let his hurt be looked to.

       [*Exeunt Feste, Fabian, Sir Toby, and Sir Andrew*]

        Enter SEBASTIAN

SEBASTIAN I am sorry, madam, I have hurt your kinsman.
    But had it been the brother of my blood,
    I must have done no less with wit and safety.   195
    You throw a strange regard upon me, and by that

---

181 H'as] *Rowe;* has F   185 pavin] F2, *Rann;* panyn F   192 SD *Exeunt...Andrew*] *Dyce; not in* F

---

181 That's all one No matter. See p. 5 above, and compare 351 and 384 below.

181 there's th'end that's that. Dent (E113.1) gives it as proverbial and occurring frequently in the early plays.

181 Sot Sir Toby earlier (1.5.100) had addressed Feste in the same fashion when he was also 'half drunk', so its double meaning applies here as well.

183 set Variously explained; Shakespeare's other instances permit of three possible interpretations: (1) 'sunk out of sight', as in *Temp.* 3.2.8–9: 'Drink, servant-monster, when I bid thee. / Thy eyes are almost set in thy head'; (2) 'fixed', as in *The Rape of Lucrece* 1662: 'with sad set eyes', and *Temp.* 2.1.229: 'The setting [fixed look] of thine eye'; and (3) 'closed', as in *John* 5.7.51: 'O cousin, thou art come to set [close] mine eye.' Ard. suggests an image of the setting sun to contrast with 'eight i'th' morning'; the numerical figure, in any case, seems to prompt Sir Toby's response; see next note.

185 passy-measures pavin A 'passing measure pavin' (Italian *passamezzo antico*), a slow stately dance in duple time, in contrast with the more animated galliard in triple time, which is what Sir Toby prefers at 1.3.97, 108. The strains of a pavin or pavan were organised in eights and fours

(F. W. Sternfeld, *Music in Shakespearean Tragedy*, 1963, pp. 250–2). The emendation of F's 'panyn' is readily accounted for by foul case – n for u.

187 made...them brought them so low. As in *Ado* 4.1.195: 'Nor fortune made such havoc of my means'. The second, much stronger meaning of 'havoc' in Shakespeare (adding a comical overtone here) is 'indiscriminate slaughter', as in *1H4* 5.1.81–2: 'Nor moody beggars, starving for a time / Of pell-mell havoc and confusion'.

188 be dressed have our wounds attended to.

190–1 an ass-head...gull Compare a similar run of epithets in *H5* 4.1.77–9 (Fluellen to Gower): 'If the enemy is an ass and a fool, and a prating coxcomb, is it meet, think you, that we should also, look you, be an ass and a fool, and a prating coxcomb...?' For Sir Toby's emphasis on Sir Andrew's thinness, see 1.3.35 and 2.3.18 nn.; for his gulling him, see 2.3.156, and 2.5.154 and 3.2.42 nn.

194 brother of my blood my own brother.

195 with...safety with sensible regard for (my own) safety.

196 throw...regard look (upon me) strangely.

I do perceive it hath offended you.
Pardon me, sweet one, even for the vows
We made each other but so late ago.

ORSINO One face, one voice, one habit, and two persons –   200
A natural perspective, that is and is not!

SEBASTIAN Antonio! O my dear Antonio,
How have the hours racked and tortured me,
Since I have lost thee!

ANTONIO Sebastian are you?

SEBASTIAN   Fear'st thou that, Antonio?   205

ANTONIO How have you made division of yourself?
An apple cleft in two is not more twin
Than these two creatures. Which is Sebastian?

OLIVIA Most wonderful!

SEBASTIAN Do I stand there? I never had a brother;   210
Nor can there be that deity in my nature
Of here and everywhere. I had a sister,
Whom the blind waves and surges have devoured.
Of charity, what kin are you to me?
What countryman? What name? What parentage?   215

VIOLA Of Messaline. Sebastian was my father;
Such a Sebastian was my brother, too;
So went he suited to his wat'ry tomb.
If spirits can assume both form and suit,
You come to fright us.

SEBASTIAN   A spirit I am indeed,   220
But am in that dimension grossly clad

---

200 persons –] *This edn;* persons, F

200 **One** The same. ´
200 **habit** costume. At 3.4.332–4, Viola remarked
that she imitated Sebastian in 'fashion, colour,
ornament'.
201 **A natural perspective** A deception or
illusion produced by nature, in contrast to that
produced by an optical device called a 'perspective
glass' (referred to in 249 below). There were
many kinds; Reginald Scot, for example, names
sixteen, the intent of each being to deceive the
eye (*The Discovery of Witchcraft*, ed. Montague
Summers, 1930, p. 179). 'Perspective' is invariably accented on the antepenultimate syllable in
Shakespeare.
205 **Fear'st thou that?** Do you doubt that?
211 **deity** godhead.
212 **Of here and everywhere** Of being

omnipresent. Compare Hamlet's question to the
ghost (*Ham.* F 853 (1.5.156)): '*Hic et ubique?*'
213 **blind** Figuratively, 'undiscerning'.
214 **Of charity** Out of the goodness of your
heart (tell me).
215 **What countryman?** A man of what
country? The same generalised form of query is used
in *Shr.* 1.2.189.
218 **So...suited** Dressed...like you (and like
herself).
219 **spirits** ghosts.
219 **form and suit** physical appearance and
dress.
220 **spirit** soul. The 'better part' of an individual
as *Sonnets* 74.8 has it.
221 **am in that...clad** (I) am wearing that
corporeal form.

Which from the womb I did participate.
Were you a woman – as the rest goes even –
I should my tears let fall upon your cheek,
And say, 'Thrice welcome, drownèd Viola.'   225
VIOLA My father had a mole upon his brow.
SEBASTIAN And so had mine.
VIOLA And died that day when Viola from her birth
Had numbered thirteen years.
SEBASTIAN O that record is lively in my soul!   230
He finishèd indeed his mortal act
That day that made my sister thirteen years.
VIOLA If nothing lets to make us happy both,
But this my masculine usurped attire,
Do not embrace me, till each circumstance,   235
Of place, time, fortune, do cohere and jump
That I am Viola, which to confirm
I'll bring you to a captain in this town,
Where lie my maiden weeds; by whose gentle help
I was preserved – to serve this noble count.   240
All the occurrence of my fortune since
Hath been between this lady and this lord.
SEBASTIAN [*To Olivia*] So comes it, lady, you have been mistook.
But nature to her bias drew in that.

240 preserved] F; preferr'd *Theobald*   243 SD *To Olivia*] *Rowe; not in* F

222 **participate** have in common with others.

223 **as...even** since all other circumstances accord. See 249 below for another example of this use of 'as'.

228–9 **And died...years** In this recognition scene, Ard. suggests that Shakespeare seems to have forgotten that Viola and Sebastian are twins! It is further suggested there that Viola's speech is possibly a 'deliberate attempt' on Shakespeare's part to suggest that Sebastian is not younger than Olivia. But neither a reading nor a viewing audience would necessarily conclude that the voyage on which the twins were shipwrecked followed pat upon the death of their father, so that Viola's specifying her age at the time of his death is simply to provide another token of identification. For a summary of Shakespeare's spelling out of the ages of the protagonists, see p. 9 above.

230 **record** recollection. As in *Ant.* 5.2.118–20: 'The record of what injuries you did us, / Though written in our flesh, we shall remember / As things but done by chance.' Here the accent falls on the second syllable.

233 **lets** hinders.

236 **cohere and jump** concur and agree.

239 **weeds** garments. As at 257.

240 **preserved – to serve** An example of repetition of the stem of a word which is then used in a different form (paregmenon or polyptoton, a rhetorical device much favoured in the 1590s and following). Some editors from Theobald on have emended 'preserved' to 'preferred' just because of that repetition of sound. However, the device serves to call attention both to Viola's happy reunion with Sebastian and to her devotion to Orsino. Observing that the use of this figure is to delight the ear by the derived sound and to stir the mind by the concord of the matter, Henry Peacham (*The Garden of Eloquence* (1593), Scholars' Facsimiles & Reprints, 1954, p. 55) gives an example from Isaiah, 'the wisdom of the wise'. For another instance, see 264–5 below.

244 **nature...in that** nature made you follow your own bent in being attracted to a disguised form of myself. The metaphor is from the game of bowls.

You would have been contracted to a maid;   245
Nor are you therein, by my life, deceived;
You are betrothed both to a maid and man.

ORSINO Be not amazed, right noble is his blood.
If this be so — as yet the glass seems true —
I shall have share in this most happy wreck.   250
[*To Viola*] Boy, thou hast said to me a thousand times
Thou never shouldst love woman like to me.

VIOLA And all those sayings will I overswear,
And all those swearings keep as true in soul
As doth that orbèd continent the fire   255
That severs day from night.

ORSINO   Give me thy hand.
And let me see thee in thy woman's weeds.

VIOLA The captain that did bring me first on shore
Hath my maid's garments; he upon some action
Is now in durance, at Malvolio's suit,   260
A gentleman and follower of my lady's.

OLIVIA He shall enlarge him; fetch Malvolio hither.
And yet, alas, now I remember me,
They say, poor gentleman, he's much distract.

Enter CLOWN [FESTE], *with a letter, and* FABIAN

A most extracting frenzy of mine own   265

---

249 so — as…true –] *This edn;* so, as…true, F   250 wreck] *Rowe;* wracke F   251 SD *To Viola*] *Rowe; not in* F
255 orbèd continent the fire] *Rowe³;* Orbed Continent, the fire, F   265 extracting] F; exacting F2; distracting *Hanmer*

---

247 a maid and man a virgin youth (Schmidt).

249 as yet…true since now the natural perspective (of 201) appears to be a real (not a deceptive) image.

250 most happy wreck i.e. the shipwreck of 213 with its (now) happy outcome (oxymoron). F's 'wrack' is frequently not distinguished in meaning from 'wreck'.

252 like to me as (you do) me.

253 overswear swear over again.

254 swearings oaths. The only other instance in Shakespeare is in *Wiv.* 5.5.160.

254 keep…soul cherish and preserve in my soul. As in *R3* 2.2.119: 'Must gently be preserv'd, cherish'd, and kept'.

255 As that spherical container (i.e. the sun) doth (keep, preserve, and cherish) its fire. This is a much debated passage: 'orbèd continent' has been taken to refer to (1) the sun, (2) the Ptolemaic sphere and (3) the firmament; 'fire' has been thought to refer

to (1) the element of the sun and (2) the sun itself. F's punctuation puts 'fire' in apposition with 'orbèd continent', making for a difficult but possible reading, particularly since Shakespeare frequently identifies the sun with fire: *Cor.* 5.4.45: 'As certain as I know the sun is fire'; *Lear* 2.2.107: 'like the wreath of radiant fire / On [flick'ring] Phoebus' front'; *Ant.* 1.3.68–9: 'By the fire / That quickens Nilus' slime'; *Tim.* 4.3.184: 'Hyperion's quick'ning fire doth shine' and again 437–8: 'the moon's an errant thief / And her pale fire she snatches from the sun'.

256 Give me thy hand i.e. in a symbolic gesture of marriage.

259 action legal charge.

260 in durance imprisoned.

262 enlarge free.

264 much distract mad.

265 most…own my own most mind-withdrawing madness. For the rhetorical trick of

From my remembrance clearly banished his.
How does he, sirrah?

FESTE Truly, madam, he holds Belzebub at the stave's end as well as
a man in his case may do; h'as here writ a letter to you; I should
have given't you today morning. But as a madman's epistles are no   270
gospels, so it skills not much when they are delivered.

OLIVIA Open't and read it.

FESTE Look then to be well edified when the fool delivers the madman.
[*Reads madly*] 'By the Lord, madam –'

OLIVIA How now, art thou mad?   275

FESTE No, madam, I do but read madness; and your ladyship will have
it as it ought to be, you must allow *vox*.

OLIVIA Prithee read i'thy right wits.

FESTE So I do, madonna; but to read his right wits is to read thus.
Therefore, perpend, my princess, and give ear.   280

OLIVIA [*To Fabian*] Read it you, sirrah.

FABIAN [*Reads*] 'By the Lord, madam, you wrong me, and the world
shall know it. Though you have put me into darkness, and given
your drunken cousin rule over me, yet have I the benefit of my
senses as well as your ladyship. I have your own letter that induced   285
me to the semblance I put on; with the which I doubt not but to
do myself much right, or you much shame. Think of me as you
please. I leave my duty a little unthought of and speak out of my
injury.

The madly used Malvolio.'   290

---

269 h'as] *Rowe;* has F   274 SD *Reads madly*] *Alexander; not in* F   281 SD *To Fabian*] *Rowe; not in* F

repeating the verb stem in 'distract' and 'extract-ing', see 240 n. above. Older editors frequently followed the later Folios and read 'exacting'. In 3.4.14, Olivia acknowledged she was as 'mad' as Malvolio.

266 remembrance memory.

268 holds...end keeps the devil at a distance. ('Belzebub' is F's spelling in its three instances, as opposed to 'Beelzebub'.) B. J. and H. W. Whiting (*Proverbs, Sentences, and Proverbial Phrases*, 1968, s653) date the expression from *c*. 1375. See Tilley s807.

270–1 epistles...gospels Feste plays on 'epistles' (specified as 'epistles of love' at 2.3.131) as (1) letters and (2) New Testament Epistles, and on 'gospels' as (1) the first four books of the New Testament and (2) unquestionable truths, with a glance at the proverb 'All is not gospel that cometh out of his mouth' (Tilley A147).

271 skills not much does not much matter.

271 delivered (1) transferred to the recipient, (2) related. The latter meaning is frequent in

Shakespeare, as in *Err.* 2.2.163–4: 'for even her very words / Didst thou deliver to me on the mart'.

273 delivers speaks (for). Still another meaning of the verb, as when Menenius wishes to tell the fable of the belly and the members, the First Citizen says, 'But and't please you, deliver' (*Cor.* 1.1.94–5).

276 and if.

277 vox voice (Latin). Used here for the tone and volume appropriate to the impersonation.

278 read...wits read according to your true faculties.

279 to read...thus 'to read his *wits right* is to read thus' (Dr Johnson, *Var.* 1785, quoted in Furness). An example of hyperbaton (improper word order) for the sake of the jest.

280 perpend consider. As Schmidt notes, it is a word used only by Pistol, Polonius and the clowns.

286 with the which i.e. with the letter.

288 leave...unthought of i.e. ignore some-what my respect (for) and submission (to you) – decorum proper to a steward.

OLIVIA Did he write this?

FESTE Ay, madam.

ORSINO This savours not much of distraction.

OLIVIA See him delivered, Fabian; bring him hither.

[Exit Fabian]

My lord, so please you, these things further thought on,   295
To think me as well a sister as a wife,
One day shall crown th'alliance on't, so please you,
Here at my house, and at my proper cost.

ORSINO Madam, I am most apt t'embrace your offer.
[To Viola] Your master quits you; and for your service
                    done him,   305... 300
So much against the mettle of your sex,
So far beneath your soft and tender breeding,
And since you called me master for so long,
Here is my hand; you shall from this time be
Your master's mistress.

OLIVIA   Ah, sister, you are she!   305

Enter [FABIAN with] MALVOLIO

ORSINO Is this the madman?

OLIVIA   Ay, my lord, this same.
How now, Malvolio?

MALVOLIO   Madam, you have done me wrong,
Notorious wrong.

OLIVIA   Have I, Malvolio? No.

MALVOLIO Lady, you have. Pray you, peruse that letter.
You must not now deny it is your hand;   310
Write from it, if you can, in hand, or phrase,

---

294 SD *Exit Fabian*] *Capell; not in* F   300 SD *To Viola*] *Rowe; not in* F   305 *Ah*] *Sugg. NS;* A F   305 SD *Fabian with*]
Capell; not in F   306–7 *Ay...Malvolio*] *As Capell; one line in* F

294 delivered released. A fourth sense of the word in this scene.

295–6 so please...wife if it please you, these matters having been further considered, to have as much regard for me as a sister as you would have had as a wife. Orsino, accordingly, addresses Olivia at 361 as 'sweet sister'.

297 One day...on't The same (wedding) day shall perfect (this) joining of relationship; 'one' = 'same', as in 200 above;

297 on't of it. A frequent sense.

298 proper own.

299 apt ready.

300 quits releases.

301 mettle nature.

305 *Ah NS suggests that 'A' (the reading in F) is a common spelling for 'Ah' and refers to the ballad from which Feste sings (quoted in 4.2.58–65 n.). Viola is already Olivia's sister by virtue of the contract with Sebastian (as Ard. points out). The emphasis in the line would thus be on 'she', looking back to Orsino's 'master's mistress'.

308 Notorious wrong See 4.2.73 n.

311 from it differently.

Or say 'tis not your seal, not your invention.
You can say none of this. Well, grant it then,
And tell me, in the modesty of honour,
Why you have given me such clear lights of favour,   315
Bade me come smiling and cross-gartered to you,
To put on yellow stockings, and to frown
Upon Sir Toby, and the lighter people;
And acting this in an obedient hope,
Why have you suffered me to be imprisoned,   320
Kept in a dark house, visited by the priest,
And made the most notorious geck and gull,
That e'er invention played on? Tell me, why?

OLIVIA Alas, Malvolio, this is not my writing,
Though I confess much like the character.   325
But, out of question, 'tis Maria's hand.
And now I do bethink me, it was she
First told me thou wast mad; then cam'st in smiling,
And in such forms which here were presupposed
Upon thee in the letter. Prithee, be content;   330
This practice hath most shrewdly passed upon thee;
But when we know the grounds, and authors of it,
Thou shalt be both the plaintiff and the judge
Of thine own cause.

FABIAN   Good madam, hear me speak,
And let no quarrel, nor no brawl to come,   335
Taint the condition of this present hour,
Which I have wondered at. In hope it shall not,
Most freely I confess, myself and Toby
Set this device against Malvolio here,

312 **invention** device. This sense of the word is used also at 323, and is so specified at 339.
314 **in...honour** in the name of decency and propriety (Ard.).
315 **clear lights** manifest notice.
318 **Sir Toby...people** i.e. your inferiors, specified in Maria's letter, 2.5.124.
319 **an obedient hope** a dutiful expectancy.
321 **the priest** Referring to the impersonating Sir Topas (not to the Priest who was summoned at 131); a curate is an assistant to a parish priest.
322 **geck** dupe. The only other instance in Shakespeare is in *Cym.* 5.4.67–8: 'And to become the geck and scorn / O'th'other's villainy'; according to Onions, the term survives in midland dialect.
323 **played on** sported with.

325 **the character** my handwriting.
326 **out of** beyond.
328 **then cam'st** With the second-person singular, the nominative (here 'thou') is readily understood (Abbott 401).
329 **forms** ways.
329 **presupposed** earlier enjoined. Used only here in Shakespeare.
331 **This...passed** This trick has been most mischievously perpetrated.
335 **nor no brawl to come** nor any squabble in the future. For the use of double negatives, see 3.1.144 n.
336 **condition** (happy) situation.
337 **wondered** marvelled.

Upon some stubborn and uncourteous parts   340
We had conceived against him. Maria writ
The letter, at Sir Toby's great importance,
In recompense whereof he hath married her.
How with a sportful malice it was followed
May rather pluck on laughter than revenge,   345
If that the injuries be justly weighed,
That have on both sides passed.

OLIVIA Alas, poor fool, how have they baffled thee!

FESTE Why, 'Some are born great, some achieve greatness, and some
have greatness thrown upon them.' I was one, sir, in this interlude,   350
one Sir Topas, sir – but that's all one. 'By the Lord, fool, I am not
mad.' But do you remember – 'Madam, why laugh you at such a
barren rascal, and you smile not, he's gagged'? And thus the
whirligig of time brings in his revenges.

MALVOLIO I'll be revenged on the whole pack of you!   [*Exit*] 355

OLIVIA He hath been most notoriously abused.

341 against] F; *in* Rann, *conj.* Tyrwhitt   355 SD *Exit*] Rowe; *not in* F

340–1 **Upon…him** As a consequence of some
rude and uncivil characteristics, and perhaps
actions, we had attributed to him in our minds.
Compare *AWW* 4.5.74–6: 'His Highness hath
promis'd me to do it, and to stop up the displeasure
he hath conceiv'd against your son…' For 'upon'
meaning 'as a consequence', see Abbott 191; rather
oddly, he suggests (244) that there is a confusion in
the speech between 'conceiving enmity' and
'disliking parts', but in explaining the motivation
for their actions, Fabian is also tactfully implying
that *their* conception of Malvolio may not quite
square with the actuality. Some editors, following
Rann, needlessly emend 'against' to 'in' but only
to produce the same interpretation as above.

341–2 **Maria…importance** It was Maria, of
course, who determined 'to gull him into an
ayword' and contrived the means to do so
(2.3.114 ff. and 139 ff.). Fabian is again being
tactful.

342 **importance** importunity.

343 **In recompense…her** As projected at
2.5.150.

344 **sportful malice** merry displeasure (oxymoron); 'malice' is used as in *AYLI* 1.2.277–83,
and again in *Cor.* 2.2.21–3: 'Now, to seem to affect
the malice and displeasure of the people is as bad
as that which he dislikes, to flatter them for their
love.' In other contexts it has a stronger force.

344 **followed** carried out.

345 **pluck on** induce.

348 **fool** victim.

348 **baffled** contemptuously treated. It is the
term Malvolio himself had earlier used in
considering how he would behave towards Sir Toby
(2.5.134).

349–50 '**Some…them**' Here again (and at
351–2 and 352–3) Feste has a chance to
impersonate Malvolio's manner of speaking.

351 **that's all one** no matter. As at 181 above and
again at 384.

352–3 **But do you…gagged** Specifically
recalling Malvolio's putting down of Feste at
1.5.67–72.

354 **whirligig of time** i.e. a 'whirling gig' (as
Mulcaster calls a child's top in *Positions* (1581), ed.
R. H. Quick, 1888, p. 80) which time spins.
Compare *LLL* 5.1.66–7 where Holofernes exaspe-
ratedly says to Moth, 'Thou disputes like an infant;
go whip thy gig.' For Sir Toby's earlier reference
to the 'parish top' which was used by adults, see
1.3.34.

355 **pack** gang (of conspirators). As in *Wiv.*
4.2.117–18: 'O you panderly rascals, there's a knot,
a ging [= gang], a pack, a conspiracy against me.'

356 **notoriously** Given Malvolio's repetition of
the adjective 'notorious' at 308 and 322, and his
earlier use of it in complaining to Feste, Olivia's use
of the term here suggests a more lighthearted mood
than some critics tend to acknowledge. See 4.2.73 n.

ORSINO Pursue him, and entreat him to a peace.
    He hath not told us of the captain yet.

                                        [*Exit Fabian*]

    When that is known, and golden time convents,
    A solemn combination shall be made   360
    Of our dear souls. Meantime, sweet sister,
    We will not part from hence. Cesario, come –
    For so you shall be while you are a man,
    But when in other habits you are seen,
    Orsino's mistress, and his fancy's queen.   365

                            Exeunt [*all but Feste*]

                (*Clown sings*)

    When that I was and-a little tiny boy,
        With hey, ho, the wind and the rain,
    A foolish thing was but a toy,
        For the rain it raineth every day.

    But when I came to man's estate,   370
        With hey, ho, the wind and the rain,
    'Gainst knaves and thieves men shut their gate,
        For the rain it raineth every day.

---

358 SD *Exit Fabian*] Ard.; *not in* F   365 SD.1 *all but Feste*] Dyce subst.; *not in* F

---

358 the captain i.e. who holds Viola's last token – her maiden weeds (239) – and who is imprisoned at Malvolio's suit (259–60).

359 golden time golden = (1) auspicious and (2) precious (as in *Sonnets* 3.12: 'thy golden time'); time = (1) occasion and (2) season. These multiple significances serve to evoke earlier motifs – the transitory nature of youth and beauty, the reliance on time to resolve situations – and also to evoke the antique 'golden world' (*AYLI* 1.1.118–19) of idyllic contentment.

359 convents calls (us).

360 combination union.

365 fancy's love's. As at 1.1.14 and 2.4.31.

365 SD The exiting of all the cast except Feste, whose song is in place of the usual spoken epilogue, parallels the endings, for example, of *MND* and *AYLI* where Puck and Rosalind, respectively, remain alone on stage to ask for the plaudit. *TN* is the only play of Shakespeare that begins and ends in music.

366–85 The surviving music of Feste's song is a 'traditional tune' with a number of related versions; the earliest is in Joseph Vernon's *The New Songs in the Pantomime of the Witches: the Celebrated Epilogue in the Comedy of Twelfth Night....Sung by*

Mr. Vernon at Vaux Hall, composed by *J. Vernon* [1772]. It was also later attributed to [?Henry] Fielding in a version which was printed by William Chappell in *A Collection of National English Airs*, 2 vols., 1840. Sternfeld (*Music in Shakespearean Tragedy*, 1963, pp. 189–91, and *Songs from Shakespeare's Tragedies*, 1964, pp. 22–5) gives transcriptions of both. For details, see Seng, pp. 123–30.

366–9 When that...day For a related stanza, see the Fool's song in *Lear* 3.2.74–7.

366 and-a The same musical adjustment appears (as NS notes) in *Oth.* 2.3.89 (in the ballad of King Stephen) where F hyphenates 'and-a', though in *Lear* (in another stanza of the Fool's song – see previous note) F hyphenates 'and a little-tyne wit'. Compare the line in Silence's song (*2H4* 5.3.48): 'And a merry heart lives long-a', and the rhymes in Autolycus's ballads (*WT* 4.3.124–6, 4.4.317, 320, 323): 'stile-a', 'mile-a', 'dear-a', 'wear-a', 'ware-a' (these also from F).

368 A foolish...toy A childish prank was accepted as something trivial.

372 i.e. in an adult, such pranks were considered proper only to knaves and thieves.

But when I came, alas, to wive,
　　With hey, ho, the wind and the rain,
By swaggering could I never thrive,
　　For the rain it raineth every day.   375

But when I came unto my beds,
　　With hey, ho, the wind and the rain,
With tosspots still 'had drunken heads,   380
　　For the rain it raineth every day.

A great while ago the world begun,
　　With hey, ho, the wind and the rain,
But that's all one, our play is done,
　　And we'll strive to please you every day.   [*Exit*]   385

378, 380 beds...heads] F; *bed...head / Hanmer* 380 'had] *This edn; had* F; *I had / Hanmer; still I had / Collier²* 382 begun] *Rowe; begon* F 383 With hey] F2; *hey* F 385 SD *Exit*] *Rowe;* FINIS. F

---

376 swaggering blustering. Compare Sir Toby's advice to Sir Andrew before the mock duel with Cesario, where he acknowledges that a 'terrible oath, with a swaggering accent sharply twanged off' can better attest to an individual's manliness than an actual fight (3.4.150–2).

376 thrive prosper. The rhyme thrive / wive is commonplace, as with Petruchio in *Shr.* 1.2.55–6: 'And I have thrust myself into this maze, / Happily to wive and thrive as best I may.'

378–80 But when...heads This stanza has been variously interpreted (as well as rejected by some as non-Shakespearean). The first interpretation is Kittredge's: 'beds' means 'being drunk on various occasions'; ''had' (380) means 'I had', with an elision of the pronoun (as with F's 'ha's' for 'he has' at 1.5.122 and F's 'has' at 181 and 269 above). A paraphrase would be: 'But on whatever occasion I fell into bed / ... / Like other topers I was always drunk.' (Compare 'drunken heads' with 'drunken

brain' (*Venus and Adonis* 910).) The second interpretation is suggested by Halliwell who (after Hanmer) emended 'beds/heads' to singular forms and quotes a passage from Overbury's *Characters* (1615) which, like the chronological progression in the song, equates 'bed' with death or old age. Thus if a man dies in his infancy, it is said, he has only broken his fast in this world; if he dies in his youth, he has left us at dinner; but at three score and ten 'it is bedde time' (cited in Furness). Accordingly, a paraphrase would be: 'But at the time I reached three score and ten [the normal span of one's life according to the psalmist, Ps. 90.10] like other topers I was always drunk.'

384–5 But...every day These lines have a parallel in the epilogue to *AWW*, where the title of the play is echoed in the request for the plaudit: 'now the play is done; / All is well ended, if this suit be won, / That you express content'. For the aptness of the phrase 'that's all one', see p. 5 above.

TEXTUAL ANALYSIS

As Charlton Hinman has determined from his bibliographical investigation of the First Folio, the first 21 quires, allocated to the section of the Comedies (from the beginning of quire A to the end of quire X, pp. 1–252, *The Tempest* to the first 23 pages of *All's Well That Ends Well*), were produced in regular alphabetical sequence.[1] Then because of some 'short-lived' trouble, the normal sequence was interrupted: quire X, which included 12 pages of *All's Well*, was not followed by Y and Z but rather by quires a and b in the section allocated to the Histories (pp. 1–24, *King John* and 2 pages of *Richard II*). Then came a return to the Comedies with quires Y and Z (pp. 253–75, the ending of *All's Well*, $1\frac{1}{4}$ pages, and *Twelfth Night*). There was another short delay occasioning another shift to the Histories with quire c (pp. 25–36, 12 pages of *Richard II*) and, finally, a return to the Comedies with the last 3 quires given over to *The Winter's Tale* (Aa–Cc, pp. 277–303). Thus the sequence of printing that was followed in bringing the section of the Comedies to completion was as follows:

A–X, a–b (*King John* and 2 pages of *Richard II*), Y–Z ($1\frac{1}{4}$ pages of *All's Well* and *Twelfth Night*), c (12 pages of *Richard II*), Aa–Cc (*Winter's Tale*).

Twelfth Night occupies signatures Y2–z6, with the verso blank (pp. 255–75, with 265 mispaged as 273). In itself, this blank verso suggests some irregularity in the sequence of printing, since it is the only instance of a blank page coming between plays in the section of the Comedies, though there are two such in the section allocated to the Tragedies with *Timon* and – the originally cancelled – *Troilus and Cressida*, both of which caused difficulties in the sequence of printing, the latter probably because of problems of copyright. Having determined, by several sorts of bibliographical analysis, the order of the printing of the plays in the Folio, Hinman concluded that the copy for both *Twelfth Night* and *The Winter's Tale*, which would complete the section of the Comedies, was not readily available, though, since neither had been printed before, it would not have been in their case a question of copyright, and he concluded that it was probably the result of some 'short-lived' trouble (II, 521). What that short-lived trouble might have been is discussed below.

By tracing the compositor's preferred spellings – *do, go, heere* – Hinman established that it was Compositor B who set all of *Twelfth Night*;[2] he also established that only 3 pages of the text were proofread and that this proofing removed only 3 inked space quads, leaving the text untouched (I, 263–4). Though Compositor B, in fact, set more

---

[1] This survey of the textual history of *Twelfth Night* is based on Hinman's invaluable two-volume study (*The Printing and Proof-reading of the First Folio of Shakespeare*, 1963; the pagination is that of the original numbering in the Folio not of the modern pagination in the Hinman facsimile cited at p. 152, n. 1).

[2] Hinman, I, 422. For other preferred characteristics of Compositor B, see Alan E. Craven, 'Justification of prose and Jaggard Compositor B', *ELN* 3 (1965), 15–17, and T. H. Howard-Hill, 'The compositors of Shakespeare's Folio Comedies', *SB* 26 (1973), 61–106.

than half of the Folio, Hinman characterises him as taking all manner of liberties with the text and exhibiting a careless disregard for the authority of the copy.[1] Such evaluation can, of course, be made most readily when there is an earlier printed exemplar extant for comparison. Since *Twelfth Night* was set from manuscript, there is no certainty as to whether Compositor B did or did not take any undue liberties; and, all editors agree, the text is remarkably free of verbal cruxes though there are some misprints or, perhaps, misreadings, some probable misassignment of speeches, and some missing stage directions.[2] The division into acts and scenes is adequate except perhaps for 3.4.231, where the exiting of Cesario with Fabian clears the stage as if a new (but unmarked) scene was to begin. One peculiarity of the text is the use of Latin to indicate the end of four of its five acts. Though it is the normal practice in the Comedies to have *Finis* at the end of Act 5, a notation of it at the end of the other acts is not.

Act 1 reads *Finis, Actus primus* (the comma saving it from 'gross' grammatical fault, though it is changed to the correct *primi* in F2 +).

Act 2 reads *Finis Actus secundus* (changed to *secundi* in F2 +).

Act 4 reads *Finis Actus Quartus* (changed to *Quarti* in F2 +).

The same ungrammatical *Finis Actus Primus* appears at the end of Act 1 of *Love's Labour's Lost* while a simple *Finis*, apparently standing for the full phrase, appears at the end of Act 1 of *The Two Gentlemen of Verona*. Neither of these plays was set by Compositor B. The text of *Love's Labour's Lost* derives from the first quarto (1598), which like most quartos lacks act and scene division, and it is generally accepted as having derived from Shakespeare's (very) foul papers. In this case the ungrammatical Latin ending *may* have been used to fill up the bottom of the b column in the Folio where otherwise there would have been a good bit of 'white' space. *Two Gentlemen of Verona* is also generally accepted as deriving from foul papers but this time from a transcript of them made by the scribe Ralph Crane, and its use of the Latin form at the end of Act 1, together with the similar instances in *Twelfth Night* at the ends of Acts 1, 2 and 4, cannot be accounted for on the basis of the typographic appearance of the page. E. E. Willoughby, who first pointed out the five instances, concluded, somewhat diffidently, that all of them were provided by the same person, while W. W. Greg concluded that in the case of *Two Gentlemen of Verona* and *Twelfth Night* they were non-editorial and probably in the copy which the compositors used from the start.[3] As pointed out above, *Two Gentlemen* probably derives from a transcript of Shakespeare's foul papers prepared by Ralph Crane. Could the source of copy for *Twelfth Night* also have been a transcript of Shakespeare's foul papers?

This is, in fact, what Robert K. Turner suggested in 1975 in his careful analysis

---

[1] *The First Folio of Shakespeare* (The Norton Facsimile), 1968, pp. xviii–xix.

[2] An anomaly appears at 1.5.138 SD where the name *Violenta* is given in place of Viola; the same name, curiously, is also wrongly substituted in *All's Well That Ends Well* (3.4.0 SD) for Diana. Since the quire in which this appears was also set by Compositor B, Robert K. Turner ('The text of *Twelfth Night*', *SQ* 26 (1975), 130 n.) suggests that on seeing the abbreviation *Vio.* he merely expanded it to the name he had set, a good bit earlier, in *All's Well*.

[3] Willoughby, 'Phrases marking the termination of acts in the First Folio', *MLN* 45 (1930), 463–4, and Greg, *The Editorial Problem in Shakespeare*, 1942, 3rd edn, 1954, pp. 128 n., 141, 145 and n.

of the text (cited at p. 152, n. 2), and his suggestion was endorsed in the Arden edition which appeared in 1975. Up until then the generally accepted view was that the copy for *Twelfth Night* was a prompt copy (or a transcript of it), though, as G. Blakemore Evans observed in 1974 (Riverside edn, p. 440), the evidence for its theatre provenance is comparatively slight. Turner not only presents evidence to counter this prompt-copy theory, but he also presents cogent reasons for acknowledging that the copy-text was a scribal transcription of Shakespeare's foul papers.

Defined as the author's last complete draft before its being transcribed in a fair copy, foul papers exhibit the following characteristics: (1) loose ends, false starts and unresolved confusions in the text; (2) inconsistencies in designating characters in speech headings and in stage directions, particularly exits, which would have to be straightened out in the prompt-book; (3) the appearance of indefinite and permissive stage directions; and (4) a vague number of supernumeraries.[1]

As Turner points out, *Twelfth Night* exhibits a good many of these characteristics. There is the confusion about the rank of Orsino, whether duke or count (see p. 16 above); there are some inconsistencies and loose ends (see pp. 16–17 above); some exits are not provided for (1.5.26, 88, 114, 179, 266; 2.2.38; 2.3.100; 2.4.12; 3.1.78; 3.4.14, 54, 57 (incomplete), 167, 184, 323 (incomplete), 335, 342; 4.1.26, 44; 4.2.3, 57 (incomplete); 5.1.131, 192, 294, 355, 358) just as some entrances are missing or incomplete (1.5.26 SD omits the attendants whom Feste addresses at 32 and 43; 5.1.305 SD (incomplete)). The number of supernumeraries is not specified (*other Lords*, 1.1.0 SD.2; *sailors*, 1.2.0 SD; *Attendants*, 1.4.8 SD; *others*, 2.4.0 SD; *Lords*, 5.1.5 SD; *Attendants*, 5.1.85 SD). Curio is specified as entering with 'LORDS' in Act 5 but has nothing to say or do. Asides are not marked, though this lapse is common in printed dramatic texts. Some of the stage directions, moreover, could as easily be authorial as theatrical, for example '*Enter* Valentine *and* Viola *in man's attire*', 1.4.0 SD; '*Enter* Viola *and* Malvolio *at several doors*', 2.2.0 SD. At 3.1.115, Olivia says, 'The clock upbraids me with the waste of time'; an experienced dramatist, envisioning the scene, might well have inserted the earlier '*Clock strikes*'. Finally, the scant evidence that any oaths or profanities were expurgated (see p. 20 above, n. 1) argues for copy based on foul papers since they, of course, antedated the Act of Abuses (1606).

Given, then, the degree to which the text of *Twelfth Night* exhibits the characteristics of foul papers as well as the characteristics of a scribal copy – for example, the regularisation of Orsino's title in stage directions but not within the text – when could such a copy have been made? It could, of course, have been before the preparation of the prompt copy, but since there was an interruption of the sequence of the printing of the Comedies, Jaggard (the head of the printing-house and a member of the syndicate that undertook to publish the Folio) may have decided that it was preferable to halt production of that section until good copies were available before setting both *Twelfth Night* and *The Winter's Tale* and thus completing the section of the Comedies. It should be recognised that *The Winter's Tale* is generally accepted as having been

[1] See Fredson Bowers, *On Editing Shakespeare and the Elizabethan Dramatists*, 1955, pp. 13–14; W. W. Greg, *The Shakespeare First Folio*, 1955, p. 142; David Bevington, *Complete Works of Shakespeare*, 1980, p. 81.

set from a transcript made by Ralph Crane especially for inclusion in the Folio, the prompt-book having, it seems, been lost.[1] If a transcript of *Twelfth Night* had also been prepared at this time, the 'short-lived' trouble delaying the printing of both plays that Hinman referred to (see p. 151 above) would thus be accounted for by the time required to prepare scribal copies of both plays.

It may be recalled that the first four Comedies in the Folio were also set from transcriptions especially prepared for the press, which led Greg to conclude that at the outset transcription appears to have been the editorial policy for the printing of the Folio (*First Folio*, pp. 217, 336). These four comedies (*Tempest, Two Gentlemen, Merry Wives* and *Measure for Measure*), together with *Winter's Tale*, are generally accepted as set from scribal copies prepared by Ralph Crane. Of the Folio's fourteen comedies, these five plus *As You Like It* and *Twelfth Night* are the only ones which are regularly divided into acts and scenes.[2] Copy for *As You Like It* is also accepted as a transcript but of exactly what is debated: Evans (1974) suggested a transcript of 'some form of Shakespeare's manuscript (perhaps "fair copy")'; Agnes Latham (1975), a transcript of 'good prompt copy' made either when the play was new or later for the Folio; and Richard Knowles (1977), a form of Shakespeare's manuscript but now, specifically, 'foul papers'.[3]

Thus it appears that half of the Comedies, and these characterised (like *Twelfth Night*) by division into acts and scenes, were set from scribal transcriptions. That it was standard practice to employ scribes within printing-houses was, most interestingly, substantiated in 1977 by James Binns. In a survey of about 550 Latin books printed in England between *c*. 1550 and 1640, he noted that it was standard for a printer to employ a scribe to make a fair copy of an author's work. In one of the instances he cites, the printer accounts for compositorial errors in the printed text on two grounds: (1) the scribe's 'hasty copying' of the manuscript and (2) the 'maladroit hands' of the workmen.[4] Although his references are to works in Latin, the practice of printers in Latin and English must have been much the same; such a conclusion would certainly be indicated by one instance Binns cites dating from 1584 where there is a rare reference to printing by formes; the practice of casting off copy for books printed in England, it may be remembered, was first posited in 1948.[5]

Was, then, the scribe responsible for the transcription of *Twelfth Night* a nameless employee of the Jaggard firm or was he Ralph Crane, who, possessing 'one blest Gift,

[1] G. B. Evans, *The Riverside Shakespeare*, 1974, p. 1604, citing the *Office Book* of the Master of the Revels from Malone's *Shakespeare*, 1790, I, Pt. ii, p. 226, since the *Office Book* was also subsequently lost.

[2] *The Taming of the Shrew* is imperfectly divided and the rest of the plays have act division only.

[3] Evans, p. 400; Agnes Latham (ed.), *AYLI*, 1975, p. xi; Richard Knowles (ed.), *AYLI*, 1977, p. 334.

[4] 'STC Latin books: evidence for printing-house practice', *The Library*, 5th ser., 32 (1977), 1–27. Also of great editorial interest are the comments relating to the necessity of correct punctuation for clarity of meaning.

[5] William H. Bond, 'Casting off copy by Elizabethan printers: a theory', *PBSA* 42 (1948), 281–91. A check of *STC* books published by the Jaggard firm up to 1623 (on the basis of Paul G. Morrison, *Index of Printers, Publishers and Booksellers*, 1950) reveals that the firm was in the main oriented to publishing books in English; in 1608, however, it published Robert Glover's *Nobilitas et civilis* and in 1620 a now untraced *Lexico-Graeco-Latinum*.

A ready Writers Pen', is accepted as having transcribed at least five of the Comedies?[1]
Some of the general characteristics of Crane's manuscripts appear in the text of
Twelfth Night: the division into acts and scenes; the heavy use of colons and
semi-colons (see p. 41 above); the use of apostrophes to mark shortened forms (like
ha's), along with a preference for *o'th* (the only form in *Twelfth Night*) over *a'th*, and,
most conspicuously, to mark the elision of *-ed* forms even in prose passages; the heavy
use of parentheses for parenthetical remarks and single words of address; and, lastly,
hyphenated forms.[2]

According to the specialist on Crane's scribal characteristics, T. H. Howard-Hill,
it is his orthography, however, that is the most decisive factor in providing evidence
of his practice.[3] He concludes, in accord with what has long been believed, that Crane
transcribed the first four Comedies and *The Winter's Tale* for the Folio, but he also
concludes that he worked from foul papers, which in the case of *The Winter's Tale*
underwent two transcriptions, once to replace the missing prompt-book (relicensed
on 19 August 1623) and a second time from his own transcription to provide the copy
that was used for setting up the Folio text.[4]

In his attempt to establish the characteristics of Crane's transcripts that might be
reflected in the Folio Comedies, Howard-Hill examined the ones set by Compositor
B, including *Twelfth Night*. After excluding possibly justified spellings in long lines
and those for which there were no alternatives, he considered for this play 47 examples
of what he believed represented B's 'preferred' spellings (*Ralph Crane*, Appendix 4).
These examples were taken from a study by W. S. Kable who based his investigation
on the assumption that B had set all the Pavier quartos,[5] a collection of 10
Shakespearean and non-Shakespearean items published in 1619 by Thomas Pavier
and printed by the Jaggard firm, 5 of which carried false dates. Subsequently Kable's
findings were questioned on two grounds: (1) that B as sole compositor of the Pavier
quartos has not been established and (2) that the study showed statistical error.[6]

For his investigation of *Twelfth Night*, Howard-Hill correlated these 'preferred'
spellings of B (as set forth by Kable) with the 'preferred' spellings of Crane (as
determined by his own studies), along with other possible spellings of these words,
and concluded that Crane did not prepare the copy for *Twelfth Night*. But since the

---

[1] See F. P. Wilson's informative account, 'Ralph Crane, scrivener to the king's players', *The Library*, 4th
  ser., 7 (1926–7), 194–215. The quotation comes from one of Crane's biographical prefaces, cited *ibid.*,
  p. 196.
[2] See Evans's textual note to *The Tempest* (p. 1636) for a fuller listing of Crane's characteristics. He notes
  that the combined appearance in the text of four or five of the seven he lists may be taken as strong
  evidence of Crane's hand in the manuscript copy.
[3] *Ralph Crane and Some Shakespeare First Folio Comedies*, 1972, p. 91.
[4] *Ralph Crane*, pp. 130–1, and 'Knight, Crane and the copy for the Folio *Winter's Tale*', *N&Q* 211
  (1966), 139–40.
[5] 'Compositor B, the Pavier quartos, and copy spellings', *SB* 21 (1968), 131–61, and *The Pavier Quartos
  and the First Folio of Shakespeare* (Shakespeare Studies Monograph Series), 1970.
[6] See Peter W. M. Blayney, '"Compositor B" and the Pavier quartos: problems of identification and their
  implications', *The Library*, 5th ser., 27 (1972), 179–206; the correspondence between Blayney and
  S. W. Reid, *The Library*, 5th ser., 31 (1976), 143–5, 392–4; and also Howard-Hill, *Ralph Crane*, p. 154,
  n. 101.

evidence of B's preferred spellings as established by the Pavier quartos has been challenged – that is, since the 47 control words Howard-Hill uses for *Twelfth Night* may *not*, in fact, represent B's preferences – it follows that the result of his findings is also open to question. Moreover, by noting (thanks to Howard-Hill's Oxford Concordances) the frequency of the 47 spellings Compositor B actually set in *Twelfth Night*, one finds that Crane-spellings (some of which may have concurred with B's preferences) appear more than 50 per cent of the time. Specifically 56 per cent of the total frequency reflects Crane's spellings; if those appearing in *possibly* justified lines are excluded, the percentage rises to 59.[1] Twelve of Crane's 47 preferred spellings (such as *beutie, breif, togeather*) are not represented in the text at all.[2] On the face of it, these frequencies do not seem to eliminate the possibility that he could have been the scribe. Still, until we know more of his preferred spellings, together with those of Compositor B (as Howard-Hill recognises, *Ralph Crane*, p. 99), we shall not know with any degree of certainty whether the transcript of *Twelfth Night* (and perhaps that of other texts in the Folio) was his work or that of an anonymous scribe with similar habits.

Though the identity of the scribe is uncertain, the argument that the copy from which Compositor B set the generally excellent text of *Twelfth Night* was scribal rests on three bases. It rests on the nature of the text, which exhibits characteristics of foul papers as well as characteristics of a scribal copy. It rests on the delay in setting and machining the last two of the Comedies, which resulted in the interruption of an orderly printing sequence for the section allocated to the Comedies. And it rests, finally, on the evidence that printers commonly employed scribes to prepare copies for their compositors, at least in the case of books printed in Latin, and that the Jaggard firm also did so in preparing certain of the Folio Comedies. On these several bases, it seems most likely that the Folio copy for *Twelfth Night* falls into the same category as those other Comedies set from scribal copies – that is, it derives from a transcript, and specifically, in this case, a transcript of Shakespeare's foul papers.

[1] Whether or not a spelling *may* have been affected by the compositor's need to justify is not easily determined, since the point in the line when a compositor adopted a particular spelling may have been before the end of the measure was reached, in what S. W. Reid calls 'anticipatory justification' ('Justification and spelling in Jaggard's Compositor B', *SB* 27 (1974), 91–111). To take an example from Howard-Hill's list: *breefe* appears twice, once in a possibly justified line; *briefe*, with the same number of characters, appears once but this, too, in a possibly justified line; neither of these represents Crane's preference. It should be noted that I have included the plurals for *heart, jest* and *hour* in my frequency count; these plurals do not appear in Howard-Hill's list though *master/s* does.

[2] Though only 47 words are used in the analysis of *Twelfth Night*, Howard-Hill compiled a list of some 2,200 Crane-preferred spellings ranging in date from 1618 to 1632 (*Ralph Crane*, p. 61). Allowance, of course, should be made for changes in habits over the years. In 1631 Crane presented a 'manuscription' of a theological tract ('The Faultie Fauorite') to the Earl of Bridgewater as a New Year's gift; now in the Huntington Library, this shows, for example, that while he invariably used his preferred spelling *deuill* (21 instances), he also, invariably, opted for *heart* (15 instances) though his preferred spelling as given by Howard-Hill is *hart*. Crane's own variability within the manuscript is illustrated by the spelling *powre/full* (7 times) as against *power/full* (18 times) – this in a small manuscript consisting of 52½ pages of 14–15 lines each.

READING LIST

This list includes details of books and articles referred to in the Introduction or Commentary and may serve as a guide to those who wish to undertake further study of the play.

Barton, Anne. '*As You Like It* and *Twelfth Night*: Shakespeare's sense of an ending', in Bradbury and Palmer, *Shakespearian Comedy*, pp. 160–80

Bradbrook, M. C. 'Robert Armin and *Twelfth Night*', in Palmer, *Casebook*, pp. 222–43

Bradbury, Malcolm, and Palmer, D. J. (eds.). *Shakespearian Comedy*, Stratford-upon-Avon Studies 14, 1972 (includes essays on the middle comedies by J. R. Brown, R. A. Foakes, G. L. Evans and A. Barton)

Brown, John Russell. 'Directions for *Twelfth Night*', in Palmer, *Casebook*, pp. 188–203

Shakespeare and his Comedies, 1957

'The presentation of comedy: the first ten plays', in Bradbury and Palmer, *Shakespearian Comedy*, pp. 9–30

Bullough, Geoffrey (ed.). *Narrative and Dramatic Sources of Shakespeare*, 8 vols., 1957–75, II, 269–372

Draper, John. *The 'Twelfth Night' of Shakespeare's Audience*, 1950

Evans, Gareth Lloyd. 'Shakespeare's fools: the shadow and the substance of drama', in Bradbury and Palmer, *Shakespearian Comedy*, pp. 142–59

Foakes, R. A. 'The owl and the cuckoo: voices of maturity in Shakespeare's comedies', in Bradbury and Palmer, *Shakespearian Comedy*, pp. 121–41

Goldsmith, R. H. *Wise Fools in Shakespeare*, 1958 (first published 1955)

Granville-Barker, Harley, and Harrison, G. B. (eds.). *A Companion to Shakespeare Studies*, 1934 (interesting essays on various aspects of the drama and on the period)

Hartwig, Joan. 'Feste's "whirligig" and the comic providence of *Twelfth Night*', *ELH* 40 (1973), 501–13

Hotson, Leslie. *The First Night of 'Twelfth Night'*, 1955

Jenkins, Harold. 'Shakespeare's *Twelfth Night*', Rice Institute Pamphlet 45 (1958–9), 19–42

Lawry, J. S. '*Twelfth Night* and "salt waves fresh in love"', *S.St.* 6 (1970), 89–108

Mares, F. H. 'Viola and other transvestist heroines' (Stratford Papers, 1965–7, ed. B. A. W. Jackson), 1969

Muir, Kenneth. *The Sources of Shakespeare's Plays*, rev. edn, 1978

Palmer, D. J. (ed.). '*Twelfth Night*': *A Casebook*, 1972 (contains eleven useful, previously published accounts of the play)

Rich, Barnaby. *Rich's Farewell to Military Profession*, ed. T. M. Cranfill, 1959

Salgādo, Gāmini. *Eyewitnesses of Shakespeare*, 1975

Salingar, L. G. 'The design of *Twelfth Night*', *SQ* 9 (1958), 117–39

Sprague, A. C., and Trewin, J. C. *Shakespeare's Plays Today*, 1970

Styan, John. *The Shakespeare Revolution*, 1977

Summers, Joseph H. 'The masks of *Twelfth Night*', in Palmer, *Casebook*, pp. 86–97

Trewin, J. C. *Shakespeare on the English Stage, 1900–1964*, 1964

Turner, Robert K. 'The text of *Twelfth Night*', *SQ* 26 (1975), 128–38

Watkins, Ronald. *On Producing Shakespeare*, 1950 (an interesting account of practical matters of dramatic representation)

Williams, Porter, Jr. 'Mistakes in *Twelfth Night* and their resolution', in Palmer, *Casebook*, pp. 170–87